D1765716

KEELE
UNIVERSITY

LIBRARY

Economic and Financial Decisions under Risk

Economic and Financial Decisions under Risk

Louis Eeckhoudt
Catholic University of Mons

Christian Gollier
University of Toulouse

Harris Schlesinger
University of Alabama

Princeton University Press
Princeton and Oxford

Copyright © 2005 by Princeton University Press

Published by Princeton University Press,
41 William Street, Princeton, New Jersey 08540

In the United Kingdom: Princeton University Press,
3 Market Place, Woodstock, Oxfordshire OX20 1SY

Library of Congress Cataloguing-in-Publication Data

Eeckhoudt, Louis
    Economic and financial decisions under risk / Louis Eeckhoudt, Christian Gollier and
    Harris Schlesinger.
        p. cm.
    Includes bibliographical references and index.
    ISBN 0-691-09655-4 (cloth : alk. paper) — ISBN 0-691-12215-6 (pbk : alk. paper)
    1. Risk. 2. Risk assessment. 3. Risk management. 4. Finance—Decision making. 5.
Economics—Decision making. I. Gollier, Christian. II. Schlesinger, Harris. III. Title.

HB615.E44 2005
338.5—dc22   2004058689

British Library Cataloguing-in-Publication Data

A catalogue record for this book is available from the British Library

This book has been composed in Times and typeset by T&T Productions Ltd, London
Printed on acid-free paper ⊗
www.pup.princeton.edu

Printed in the United States of America

10 9 8 7 6 5 4 3 2

Contents

Preface

Risk is an ever-prevalent challenge to both individuals and society. When you dress yourself every morning, do you not ask what the weather will be like today? And after recalling the latest weather forecast, do you not wonder whether or not the forecast for today will be accurate? The weather forecast itself relies heavily on the rules of probability theory, as does the fact that today's weather might not behave as the forecast predicts. How you react to the uncertain weather ahead says something about your so-called "risk preferences." If the forecast calls for a 10% chance of rain, do you carry your umbrella when you walk to a restaurant for lunch? How about with a 50% chance of rain? Obviously the answer will not be the same for each individual.

Likewise, an individual may react differently to different consequences from the same risk. A person who decides she does not need to carry her umbrella with such a small risk of rain may decide nonetheless to stop by the parking lot on the way to the restaurant to put the top up on her new cabriolet automobile. To quote from Peter Bernstein, "The ability to define what may happen in the future and to choose among alternatives lies at the heart of contemporary societies" (Bernstein 1998). An understanding of risk and how to deal with it is an essential part of modern economies. Recognizing risks, quantifying risks, analyzing them, treating them and incorporating risks into our decision-making processes is the focus of this book.

Of course attempting to model human behavior is never easy. People may behave slightly differently from day to day. They also like to experiment in order to learn about their own tastes and preferences. Still, there are many basic principles that hold with much regularity. For the most part, this book models behavior using the expected-utility (EU) model as developed in its modern form by von Neumann and Morgenstern (1948). While this basic approach is generally well accepted, it is not without its detractors. We discuss many of the major criticisms in the last chapter of this book.

It is important when reading this book to keep in mind that we are deriving models that help us to understand behavior towards risk. It is not assumed that people actually solve the mathematical problems that we present here. Indeed, most readers probably have a relative who cannot solve an optimization problem, yet decide every year to purchase an automobile insurance policy.

We also confine ourselves to risks that involve economic and financial decisions. Obviously there are many other risks that one must deal with in everyday life, such as whether or not to take a new medication with potential untoward side effects, or which scientific journal provides the best publication outlet for a newly written research paper.

This book is designed for use in advanced undergraduate and beginning doctoral courses. We cover a broad array of topics in enough detail that the book may be used as a self-contained text. Alternatively, one can use the first two "basics" chapters, together with a selection of later chapters, as a basis for courses in macroeconomics, insurance, portfolio choice and asset pricing. Such courses can easily adapt the book for the intended use, and supplement it with additional readings or projects.

The book starts by introducing the basic concepts of risk and risk aversion that are crucial throughout the rest of the text. Part II of the text applies these basic concepts to a multitude of personal decisions under risk. Part III uses the results about personal decision making to show how markets for risk are organized and how risky assets are priced. Our final part introduces two important points of departure: decision making under imperfect information and alternatives to the expected-utility framework.

Each chapter of the book concludes with a discussion of the relevant literature, together with some suggestions for readers who would like to read more on the topic. We also provide a set of exercises at the end of each chapter.

The only mathematics contained in this book is calculus and simple algebra. We use discrete examples for time and for probabilities throughout the text. Although the mathematics is important, the logic and intuition are more important and this is stressed throughout the book. Many of the concepts that are derived here might not be easy to understand upon a first reading. We urge the readers to take the time to re-read difficult parts of the book and to work on the related problems at the end of each chapter.

The book's three authors have spent collectively more than 60 years working on research projects related to the topics we present here. We each learned many new things while writing this book. And we continue to be curious, as we still have much to learn. We will feel that this book has been a "success" if some of our curiosity transfers to the reader.

Chapter Bibliography

Bernstein, P. L. 1998. *Against the Gods*. Wiley.
von Neumann, J. and O. Morgenstern. 1948. *Theory of games and economic behavior*. Princeton, NJ: Princeton University Press.

Louis Eeckhoudt, Mons (Belgium)
Christian Gollier, Toulouse (France)
Harris Schlesinger, Tuscaloosa, Alabama (USA)

Part I

Decision Theory

1

Risk Aversion

This chapter looks at a basic concept behind modeling individual preferences in the face of risk. As with any social science, we of course are fallible and susceptible to second-guessing in our theories. It is nearly impossible to model many natural human tendencies such as "playing a hunch" or "being superstitious." However, we can develop a systematic way to view choices made under uncertainty. Hopefully, our models can capture the basic human tendencies enough to be useful in understanding market behavior towards risk. In other words, even if we are not correct in predicting behavior under risk for every individual in every circumstance, we can still make general claims about such behavior and can still make market predictions, which after all are based on the "marginal consumer."

To use (vaguely) mathematical language, the understanding of this chapter is a *necessary* but not *sufficient* condition to go further into the analysis. Because of the importance of risk aversion in decision making under uncertainty, it is worthwhile to first take an "historical" perspective about its development and to indicate how economists and decision scientists progressively have elaborated upon the tools and concepts we now use to analyze risky choices. In addition, this "history" has some surprising aspects that are interesting in themselves. To this end, our first section in this chapter broadly covers these retrospective topics. Subsequent sections are more "modern" and they represent an intuitive introduction to the central contribution to our field, that of Pratt (1964).

1.1 An Historical Perspective on Risk Aversion

As it is now widely acknowledged, an important breakthrough in the analysis of decisions under risk was achieved when Daniel Bernoulli, a distinguished Swiss mathematician, wrote in St Petersburg in 1738 a paper in Latin entitled: "*Specimen theoriae novae de mensura sortis*," or "Exposition of a new theory on the measurement of risk." Bernoulli's paper, translated into English in Bernoulli (1954), is essentially nontechnical. Its main purpose is to show that two people facing the same lottery may value it differently because of a difference in their psychology. This idea was quite novel at the time, since famous scientists before Bernoulli (among them

Pascal and Fermat) had argued that the value of a lottery should be equal to its mathematical expectation and hence identical for all people, independent of their risk attitude.

In order to justify his ideas, Bernoulli uses three examples. One of them, the "St Petersburg paradox" is quite famous and it is still debated today in scientific circles. It is described in most recent texts of finance and microeconomics and for this reason we do not discuss it in detail here. Peter tosses a fair coin repetitively until the coin lands head for the first time. Peter agrees to give to Paul 1 ducat if head appears on the first toss, 2 ducats if head appears only on the second toss, 4 ducats if head appears for the first time on the third toss, and so on, in order to double the reward to Paul for each additional toss necessary to see the head for the first time. The question raised by Bernoulli is how much Paul would be ready to pay to Peter to accept to play this game.

Unfortunately, the celebrity of the paradox has overshadowed the other two examples given by Bernoulli that show that, most of the time, the value of a lottery is not equal to its mathematical expectation. One of these two examples, which presents the case of an individual named "Sempronius," wonderfully anticipates the central contributions that would be made to risk theory about 230 years later by Arrow, Pratt and others.

Let us quote Bernoulli:[1]

> Sempronius owns goods at home worth a total of 4000 ducats and in addition possesses 8000 ducats worth of commodities in foreign countries from where they can only be transported by sea. However, our daily experience teaches us that of [two] ships one perishes.

In modern-day language, we would say that Sempronius faces a risk on his wealth. This wealth may represented by a lottery $\tilde{x}$, which takes on a value of 4000 ducats with probability $\frac{1}{2}$ (if his ship is sunk), or 12 000 ducats with probability $\frac{1}{2}$. We will denote such a lottery $\tilde{x}$ as being distributed as $(4000, \frac{1}{2}; 12\,000, \frac{1}{2})$. Its mathematical expectation is given by:

$$E\tilde{x} \equiv \tfrac{1}{2}4000 + \tfrac{1}{2}12\,000 = 8000 \text{ ducats.}$$

Now Sempronius has an ingenious idea. Instead of "trusting all his 8000 ducats of goods to one ship," he now "trusts equal portions of these commodities to two ships." Assuming that the ships follow independent but equally dangerous routes, Sempronius now faces a more diversified lottery $\tilde{y}$ distributed as

$$(4000, \tfrac{1}{4}; 8000, \tfrac{1}{2}; 12\,000, \tfrac{1}{4}).$$

---

[1] We altered Bernoulli's probabilities to simplify the computations. In particular, Bernoulli's original example had one ship in ten perish.

Indeed, if both ships perish, he would end up with his sure wealth of 4000 ducats. Because the two risks are independent, the probability of these joint events equals the product of the individual events, i.e. $(\frac{1}{2})^2 = \frac{1}{4}$. Similarly, both ships will succeed with probability $\frac{1}{4}$, in which case his final wealth amounts to 12 000 ducats. Finally, there is the possibility that only one ship succeeds in downloading the commodities safely, in which case only half of the profit is obtained. The final wealth of Sempronius would then just amount to 8000 ducats. The probability of this event is $\frac{1}{2}$ because it is the complement of the other two events which have each a probability of $\frac{1}{4}$.

Since common wisdom suggests that diversification is a good idea, we would expect that the value attached to $\tilde{y}$ exceeds that attributed to $\tilde{x}$. However, if we compute the expected profit, we obtain that

$$E\tilde{y} = \tfrac{1}{4}4000 + \tfrac{1}{2}8000 + \tfrac{1}{4}12\,000 = 8000 \text{ ducats,}$$

before the event

the same value as for $E\tilde{x}$! If Sempronius would measure his well-being *ex ante* by his expected future wealth, he should be indifferent about whether to diversify or not. In Bernoulli's example, we obtain the same expected future wealth for both lotteries, even though most people would find $\tilde{y}$ more attractive than $\tilde{x}$. Hence, according to Bernoulli and to modern risk theory, the mathematical expectation of a lottery is not an adequate measure of its value. Bernoulli suggests a way to express the fact that most people prefer $\tilde{y}$ to $\tilde{x}$: a lottery should be valued according to the "expected utility" that it provides. Instead of computing the expectation of the monetary outcomes, we should use the expectation of the utility of the wealth. Notice that most human beings do not extract utility from wealth. Rather, they extract utility from consuming goods that can be purchased with this wealth. The main insight of Bernoulli is to suggest that there is a nonlinear relationship between wealth and the utility of consuming this wealth.

refer to past event

What ultimately matters for the decision maker *ex post* is how much satisfaction he or she can achieve with the monetary outcome, rather than the monetary outcome itself. Of course, there must be a relationship between the monetary outcome and the degree of satisfaction. This relationship is characterized by a utility function u, which for every wealth level x tells us the level of "satisfaction" or "utility" $u(x)$ attained by the agent with this wealth. Of course, this level of satisfaction derives from the goods and services that the decision maker can purchase with a wealth level x. While the outcomes themselves are "objective," their utility is "subjective" and specific to each decision maker, depending upon his or her tastes and preferences. Although the function u transforms the objective result x into a perception $u(x)$ by the individual, this transformation is assumed to exhibit some basic properties of rational behavior. For example, a higher level of x (more wealth) should induce a higher level of utility: the function should be increasing in x. Even for someone who is very altruistic, a higher x will allow them to be more philanthropic. Readers familiar with indirect utility functions from microeconomics (essentially utility over budget sets, rather than over bundles of goods and services) can think of $u(x)$ as essentially an indirect utility of wealth, where we assume that prices for goods and services are fixed. In other words, we may think of $u(x)$ as the highest achievable level of utility from bundles of goods that are affordable when our income is x.

Bernoulli argues that if the utility u is not only increasing but also concave in the outcome x, then the lottery $\tilde{y}$ will have a higher value than the lottery $\tilde{x}$, in accordance with intuition. A twice-differentiable function u is concave if and only if its second derivative is negative, i.e. if the marginal utility $u'(x)$ is decreasing in x.[2] In order to illustrate this point, let us consider a specific example of a utility function, such as $u(x) = \sqrt{x}$, which is an increasing and concave function of x. Using these preferences in Sempronius's problem, we can determine the expectation of $u(x)$:

$$Eu(\tilde{x}) = \tfrac{1}{2}\sqrt{4000} + \tfrac{1}{2}\sqrt{12\,000} = 86.4$$

$$Eu(\tilde{y}) = \tfrac{1}{4}\sqrt{4000} + \tfrac{1}{2}\sqrt{8000} + \tfrac{1}{4}\sqrt{12\,000} = 87.9.$$

Because lottery $\tilde{y}$ generates a larger expected utility than lottery $\tilde{x}$, the former is preferred by Sempronius. The reader can try using concave utility functions other than the square-root function to obtain the same type of result. In the next section, we formalize this result.

Notice that the concavity of the relationship between wealth x and satisfaction/utility u is quite a natural assumption. It simply implies that the marginal utility of wealth is decreasing with wealth: one values a one-ducat increase in wealth more when one is poorer than when one is richer. Observe that, in Bernoulli's example, diversification generates a mean-preserving transfer of wealth from the extreme events to the mean. Transferring some probability weight from $x = 4000$ to $x = 8000$ increases expected utility. Each probability unit transferred yields an increase in expected utility equaling $u(8000) - u(4000)$. On the contrary, transferring some probability weight from $x = 12\,000$ to $x = 8000$ reduces expected utility. Each probability unit transferred yields a reduction in expected utility equaling $u(12\,000) - u(8000)$. But the concavity of u implies that

$$u(8000) - u(4000) > u(12\,000) - u(8000), \tag{1.1}$$

i.e. that the positive effect of these combined transfers must dominate the negative effect. This is why all investors with a concave utility would support Sempronius's strategy to diversify risks.

---

[2] For simplicity, we maintain the assumption that u is twice differentiable throughout the book. However, a function need not be differentiable to be concave. More generally, a function u is concave if and only if $\lambda u(a) + (1 - \lambda)u(b)$ is smaller than $u(\lambda a + (1 - \lambda)b)$ for all (a, b) in the domain of u and all scalars λ in $[0, 1]$. A function must, however, be continuous to be concave.

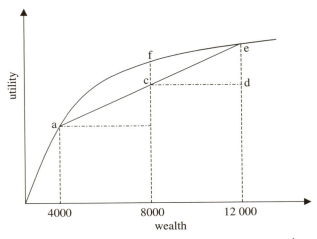

Figure 1.1. Measuring the expecting utility of final wealth $(4000, \frac{1}{2}; 12000, \frac{1}{2})$.

1.2 Definition and Characterization of Risk Aversion

We assume that the decision maker lives for only one period, which implies that he immediately uses all his final wealth to purchase and to consume goods and services. Later in this book, we will disentangle wealth and consumption by allowing the agent to live for more than one period. Final wealth comes from initial wealth w plus the outcome of any risk borne during the period.

Definition 1.1. An agent is risk-averse if, at any wealth level w, he or she dislikes every lottery with an expected payoff of zero: $\forall w$, $\forall \tilde{z}$ with $E\tilde{z} = 0$, $Eu(w + \tilde{z}) \leqslant u(w)$.

Observe that any lottery $\tilde{z}$ with a non-zero expected payoff can be decomposed into its expected payoff $E\tilde{z}$ and a zero-mean lottery $\tilde{z} - E\tilde{z}$. Thus, from our definition, a risk-averse agent always prefers receiving the expected outcome of a lottery with certainty, rather than the lottery itself. For an expected-utility maximizer with a utility function u, this implies that, for any lottery $\tilde{z}$ and for any initial wealth w,

$$Eu(w + \tilde{z}) \leqslant u(w + E\tilde{z}). \tag{1.2}$$

If we consider the simple example from Sempronius's problem, with only one ship the initial wealth w equals 4000, and the profit $\tilde{z}$ takes the value 8000 or 0 with equal probabilities. Because our intuition is that Sempronius must be risk averse, it must follow that

$$\tfrac{1}{2}u(12\,000) + \tfrac{1}{2}u(4000) \leqslant u(8000). \tag{1.3}$$

If Sempronius could find an insurance company that would offer full insurance at an actuarially fair price of $E\tilde{z} = 4000$ ducats, Sempronius would be better off by purchasing the insurance policy. We can check whether inequality (1.3) is verified in Figure 1.1. The right-hand side of the inequality is represented by point 'f' on the utility curve u. The left-hand side of the inequality is represented by the middle point on the arc 'ae', i.e. by point 'c'. This can immediately be checked by observing that the two triangles 'abc'and 'cde'are equivalent, since they have the same base and the same angles. We observe that 'f' is above 'c': *ex ante*, the welfare derived from lottery $\tilde{z}$ is smaller than the welfare obtained if one were to receive its expected payoff $E\tilde{z}$ with certainty. In short, Sempronius is risk-averse. From this figure, we see that this is true whenever the utility function is concave. The intuition of the result is very simple: if marginal utility is decreasing, then the potential loss of 4000 reduces utility more than the increase in utility generated by the potential gain of 4000. Seen *ex ante*, the expected utility is reduced by these equally weighted potential outcomes.

It is noteworthy that Equations (1.1) and (1.3) are exactly the same. The preference for diversification is intrinsically equivalent to risk aversion, at least under the Bernoullian expected-utility model.

Using exactly the opposite argument, it can easily be shown that, if u is convex, the inequality in (1.2) will be reversed. Therefore, the decision maker prefers the lottery to its mathematical expectation and he reveals in this way his inclination for taking risk. Such individual behavior will be referred to as risk loving. Finally, if u is linear, then the welfare Eu is linear in the expected payoff of lotteries. Indeed, if $u(x) = a + bx$ for all x, then we have

$$Eu(w + \tilde{z}) = E[a + b(w + \tilde{z})] = a + b(w + E\tilde{z}) = u(w + E\tilde{z}),$$

which implies that the decision maker ranks lotteries according to their expected outcome. The behavior of this individual is called risk-neutral.

In the next proposition, we formally prove that inequality (1.2) holds for any lottery $\tilde{z}$ and any initial wealth w if and only if u is concave.

Proposition 1.2. *A decision maker with utility function u is risk-averse, i.e. inequality (1.2) holds for all w and $\tilde{z}$, if and only if u is concave.*

Proof. The proof of sufficiency is based on a second-order Taylor expansion of $u(w + z)$ around $w + E\tilde{z}$. For any z, this yields

$$u(w + z) = u(w + E\tilde{z}) + (z - E\tilde{z})u'(w + E\tilde{z}) + \tfrac{1}{2}(z - E\tilde{z})^2 u''(\xi(z))$$

for some $\xi(z)$ in between z and $E\tilde{z}$. Because this must be true for all z, it follows that the expectation of $u(w + \tilde{z})$ is equal to

$$Eu(w + \tilde{z}) = u(w + E\tilde{z}) + u'(w + E\tilde{z})E(\tilde{z} - E\tilde{z}) + \tfrac{1}{2}E[(\tilde{z} - E\tilde{z})^2 u''(\xi(\tilde{z}))].$$

Observe now that the second term of the right-hand side above is zero, since $E(\tilde{z} - E\tilde{z}) = E\tilde{z} - E\tilde{z} = 0$. In addition, if u'' is uniformly negative, then the third term takes the expectation of a random variable $(\tilde{z} - E\tilde{z})^2 u''(\xi(\tilde{z}))$ that is always negative, as it is the product of a squared scalar and negative u''. Hence, the sum of these three terms is less than $u(w + E\tilde{z})$. This proves sufficiency.

Necessity is proven by contradiction. Suppose that u is not concave. Then, there must exist some w and some $\delta > 0$ for which $u''(x)$ is positive in the interval $[w - \delta, w + \delta]$. Now take a small zero-mean risk $\tilde{\varepsilon}$ such that the support of final wealth $w + \tilde{\varepsilon}$ is entirely contained in $(w - \delta, w + \delta)$. Using the same Taylor expansion as above yields

$$Eu(w + \tilde{\varepsilon}) = u(w) + \tfrac{1}{2}E[\tilde{\varepsilon}^2 u''(\xi(\tilde{\varepsilon}))].$$

Because $\xi(\tilde{\varepsilon})$ has a support that is contained in $[w - \delta, w + \delta]$ where u is locally convex, $u''(\xi(\tilde{\varepsilon}))$ is positive for all realizations of $\tilde{\varepsilon}$. Consequently, it follows that $E[\tilde{\varepsilon}^2 u''(\xi(\tilde{\varepsilon}))]$ is positive, and $Eu(w + \tilde{\varepsilon})$ is larger than $u(w)$. Thus, accepting the zero-mean lottery $\tilde{\varepsilon}$ raises welfare and the decision maker is not risk-averse. This is a contradiction. ☐

The above proposition is in fact nothing more than a rewriting of the famous Jensen inequality. Consider any real-valued function ϕ. Jensen's inequality states that $E\phi(\tilde{y})$ is smaller than $\phi(E\tilde{y})$ for any random variable $\tilde{y}$ if and only if ϕ is a concave function. It builds a bridge between two alternative definitions of the concavity of u: the negativity of u'' and the property that any arc linking two points on curve u must lie below this curve. Figure 1.1 illustrates this point. It is intuitive that decreasing marginal utility ($u'' < 0$) means risk aversion. In a certain world, decreasing marginal utility means that an increase in wealth by 100 dollars has a positive effect on utility that is smaller than the effect of a reduction in wealth by 100 dollars. Then, in an uncertain world, introducing the risk to gain or to lose 100 dollars with equal probability will have a negative net impact on expected utility. In expectation, the benefit of the prospect of gaining 100 dollars is overweighted by the cost of the prospect of losing 100 dollars with the same probability. Over the last two decades, many prominent researchers in the field have challenged the idea that risk aversion comes only from decreasing marginal utility. Some even challenged the idea itself, that there should be any link between the two.[3]

1.3 Risk Premium and Certainty Equivalent

A risk-averse agent is an agent who dislikes zero-mean risks. The qualifier "zero-mean" is very important. A risk-averse agent may like risky lotteries if the expected

---

[3]This question will be discussed in the last chapter of this book. Yaari (1987) provides a model that is dual to expected utility, where agents may be risk-averse in spite of the fact that their utility is linear in wealth.

payoffs that they yield are large enough. Risk-averse investors may want to purchase risky assets if their expected returns exceed the risk-free rate. Risk-averse agents may dislike purchasing insurance if it is too costly to acquire. In order to determine the optimal trade-off between the expected gain and the degree of risk, it is useful to quantify the effect of risk on welfare. This is particularly useful when the agent subrogates the risky decision to others, as is the case when we consider public safety policy or portfolio management by pension funds, for example. It is important to quantify the degree of risk aversion in order to help people to know themselves better, and to help them to make better decisions in the face of uncertainty. Most of this book is about precisely this problem. Clearly, people have different attitudes towards risks. Some are ready to spend more money than others to get rid of a specific risk. One way to measure the degree of risk aversion of an agent is to ask her how much she is ready to pay to get rid of a *zero-mean* risk $\tilde{z}$. The answer to this question will be referred to as the risk premium Π associated with that risk. For an agent with utility function u and initial wealth w, the risk premium must satisfy the following condition:

$$Eu(w + \tilde{z}) = u(w - \Pi). \tag{1.4}$$

The agent ends up with the same welfare either by accepting the risk or by paying the risk premium Π. When risk $\tilde{z}$ has an expectation that differs from zero, we usually use the concept of the certainty equivalent. The certainty equivalent e of risk $\tilde{z}$ is the sure increase in wealth that has the same effect on welfare as having to bear risk $\tilde{z}$, i.e.

$$Eu(w + \tilde{z}) = u(w + e). \tag{1.5}$$

When $\tilde{z}$ has a zero mean, comparing (1.4) and (1.5) implies that the certainty equivalent e of $\tilde{z}$ is equal to minus its its risk premium Π.

A direct consequence of Proposition 1.2 is that the risk premium Π is nonnegative when u is concave, i.e. when she is risk-averse. In Figure 1.2, we measure Π for the risk $(-4000, \frac{1}{2}; 4000, \frac{1}{2})$ for initial wealth $w = 8000$. Notice first that the risk premium is zero when u is linear, and it is nonpositive when u is convex.

One very convenient property of the risk premium is that it is measured in the same units as wealth, e.g. we can measure Sempronius's risk premium in ducats. Although the measure of satisfaction or utility is hard to compare between different individuals—what would it mean to say Sempronius was "happier" than Alexander?—the risk premium is not. We can easily determine whether Sempronius or Alexander is more affected by risk $\tilde{z}$ by comparing their two risk premia.

The risk premium is a complex function of the distribution of $\tilde{z}$, of initial wealth w and of the utility function u. We can estimate the amount that the agent is ready to pay for the elimination of this zero-mean risk by considering small risks. Assume

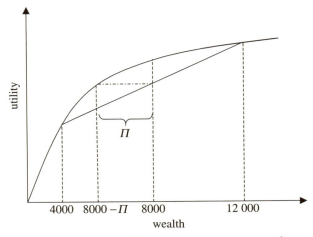

Figure 1.2. Measuring the risk premium P of risk $(-4000, \frac{1}{2}; 4000, \frac{1}{2})$ when initial wealth is $w = 8000$.

that $E\tilde{z} = 0$. Using a second-order and a first-order Taylor approximation for the left-hand side and the right-hand side of equation (1.4), respectively, we obtain that

$$u(w - \Pi) \simeq u(w) - \Pi u'(w)$$

and

$$\begin{aligned} Eu(w + \tilde{z}) &\simeq E[u(w) + zu'(w) + \tfrac{1}{2}\tilde{z}^2 u''(z)] \\ &= u(w) + u'(w)E\tilde{z} + \tfrac{1}{2}u''(w)E\tilde{z}^2 \\ &= u(w) + \tfrac{1}{2}\sigma^2 u''(w), \end{aligned}$$

where $E\tilde{z} = 0$ and $\sigma^2 = E\tilde{z}^2$ is the variance of the outcome of the lottery. Replacing these two approximations in equation (1.4) yields

$$\Pi \simeq \tfrac{1}{2}\sigma^2 A(w), \tag{1.6}$$

where the function A is defined as

$$A(w) = \frac{-u''(w)}{u'(w)}. \tag{1.7}$$

Under risk aversion, function A is positive. It would be zero or negative respectively for a risk-neutral or risk-loving agent. $A(\cdot)$ is hereafter referred to as the degree of absolute risk aversion of the agent. From (1.6), we see that the risk premium associated with risk $\tilde{\varepsilon}$ for an agent with wealth w is approximately equal to one-half the product of the variance of $\tilde{z}$ and the degree of absolute risk aversion of the agent evaluated at w. Equation (1.6) is known as the Arrow–Pratt approximation, as it was developed independently by Arrow (1963) and Pratt (1964).

The cost of risk, as measured by the risk premium, is approximately proportional to the variance of its payoffs. Thus, the variance might appear to be a good measure of the degree of riskiness of a lottery. This observation induced many authors to use a mean–variance decision criterion for modeling behavior under risk. In a mean–variance model, we assume that individual risk attitudes depend only upon the mean and the variance of the underlying risks. However, the validity of these models is dependent on the degree of accuracy of the approximation in (1.6), which can be considered accurate only when the risk is small or in very special cases. In such cases, the mean–variance approach for decisions under risk, which has historically played a very important role in the development of the theory of finance, can be seen as a special case of the expected-utility theory. In most cases however, the risk premium associated with any (large) risk will also depend upon the other moments of the distribution of the risk, not just its mean and variance. For example, it seems intuitive that whether or not $\tilde{x}$ is symmetrically distributed about its mean matters for determining the risk premium. The degree of skewness (i.e. third moment) might very well affect the desirability of a risk. Hence, two risks with the same mean and variance, but one with a distribution that is skewed to the right and the other with a distribution that is skewed to the left, should not be expected to necessarily have the same risk premium. A similar argument can be made about the kurtosis (fourth moment), which is linked to the probability mass in the tails of the distribution.

At this stage, it is worth noting that, at least for small risks, the risk premium increases with the size of the risk proportionately to the square of this size. To see this, let us assume that $\tilde{z} = k\tilde{\varepsilon}$, with $E\tilde{\varepsilon} = 0$. Parameter k can be interpreted as the size of the risk. When k tends to zero, the risk becomes very small. Of course, the risk premium is a function of the size of the risk. We may expect that this function $\Pi(k)$ is increasing in k. We are interested in describing the functional form linking the risk premium Π to the size k of the risk. Because the variance of $\tilde{z}$ equals k^2 times the variance of $\tilde{\varepsilon}$,[4] we obtain that

$$\Pi(k) \simeq \tfrac{1}{2}k^2\sigma_{\tilde{\varepsilon}}^2 A(w),$$

i.e. the risk premium is approximately proportional to the square of the size of the risk. From this observation, we can observe directly that, not only does $\Pi(k)$ approach zero as k approaches zero, but also $\Pi'(0) = 0$. This is an important property of expected-utility theory. At the margin, accepting a small zero-mean risk has *no* effect on the welfare of risk-averse agents! We say that risk aversion is a

---

[4]The general formula is

$$\mathrm{var}(a\tilde{x} + b\tilde{y}) = a^2\,\mathrm{var}(\tilde{x}) + b^2\,\mathrm{var}(\tilde{y}) + 2ab\,\mathrm{cov}(\tilde{x}, \tilde{y}).$$

second-order phenomenon.[5] "In the small," we—the expected-utility maximizers—
are all risk neutral.

Proposition 1.3. *If the utility function is differentiable, the risk premium tends to
zero as the square of the size of the risk.*

Proof. In the following, we prove formally that $\Pi'(0) = 0$, as suggested by the
Arrow–Pratt approximation in our comments above. The relationship between Π and
k can be obtained by fully differentiating the equation $Eu(w + k\tilde{\varepsilon}) = u(w - \Pi(k))$
with respect to k. This yields

$$\Pi'(k) = \frac{-E\tilde{\varepsilon}u'(w + k\tilde{\varepsilon})}{u'(w - \Pi(k))}. \tag{1.8}$$

We directly infer that $\Pi'(0) = 0$, since by assumption $E\tilde{\varepsilon} = 0$. □

1.4   Degree of Risk Aversion

Let us consider the following simple decision problem. An agent is offered a take-
it-or-leave-it offer to accept lottery $\tilde{z}$ with mean μ and variance σ^2. Of course, the
optimal decision is to accept the lottery if

$$Eu(w + \tilde{z}) \geqslant u(w), \tag{1.9}$$

or, equivalently, if the certainty equivalent e of $\tilde{z}$ is positive. In the following, we
examine how this decision is affected by a change in the utility function.

Notice at this stage that an increasing linear transformation of u has no effect on the
decision maker's choice, and on certainty equivalents. Indeed, consider a function
$v(\cdot)$ such that $v(x) = a + bu(x)$ for all x, for some pair of scalars a and b, where
$b > 0$. Then, obviously $Ev(w + \tilde{z}) \geqslant v(w)$ yields exactly the same restrictions on
the distribution of $\tilde{z}$ as condition (1.9). The same analysis can be done on equation
(1.5) defining certainty equivalents. The neutrality of certainty equivalents to linear
transformations of the utility function can be verified in the case of small risks by
using the Arrow–Pratt approximation. If $v \equiv a + bu$, it is obvious that

$$A(x) = \frac{-v''(x)}{v'(x)} = \frac{-bu''(x)}{bu'(x)} = \frac{-u''(x)}{u'(x)}$$

for all x. Thus, by (1.6), risk premia for small risks are not affected by the linear
transformation. Because the certainty equivalent equals the mean payoff of the risk
minus the risk premium, the same neutrality property holds for certainty equivalents.

---

[5]This property in general models, not restricted to expected utility, is called "second-order risk
aversion." Within the expected-utility model, this property relies on the assumption that the utility function
is differentiable.

Limiting the analysis to small risks, we see from this analysis that agents with a larger absolute risk aversion $A(w)$ will be more reluctant to accept small risks. The minimum expected payoff that makes the risk acceptable for them will be larger. This is why we say that A is a measure of the degree of risk aversion of the decision maker. From a more technical viewpoint, $A = -u''/u'$ is a measure of the degree of concavity of the utility function. It measures the speed at which marginal utility is decreasing.

We are now interested in extending these observations to any risk, not only small risks. We consider the following definition for comparative risk aversion.

Definition 1.4. Suppose that agents u and v have the same wealth w, which is arbitrary. An agent v is more risk-averse than another agent u with the same initial wealth if any risk that is undesirable for agent u is also undesirable for agent v. In other words, the risk premium of any risk is larger for agent v than for agent u.

This must be true independently of the common initial wealth level w of the two agents. If this definition were restricted to small risks, we know from the above analysis that this would be equivalent to requiring that

$$A_v(w) = \frac{-v''(w)}{v'(w)} \geqslant \frac{-u''(w)}{u'(w)} = A_u(w),$$

for all w. If limited to small risks, v is more risk-averse than u if function A_v is uniformly larger than A_u. We say in this case that v is more concave than u in the sense of Arrow–Pratt. It is important to observe that this is equivalent to the condition that v is a *concave* transformation of u, i.e. that there exists an increasing and concave function ϕ such that $v(w) = \phi(u(w))$ for all w. Indeed, we have that $v'(w) = \phi'(u(w))u'(w)$ and

$$v''(w) = \phi''(u(w))(u'(w))^2 + \phi'(u(w))u''(w),$$

which implies that

$$A_v(w) = A_u(w) + \frac{-\phi''(u(w))u'(w)}{\phi'(u(w))}.$$

Thus, A_v is uniformly larger than A_u if and only if ϕ is concave. This is equivalent to requiring that A_v be uniformly larger than A_u or that v be a concave transformation of u. It yields that agent v values small risks less than agent u. Do we need to impose more restrictions to guarantee that agent v values any risk less than agent u, i.e. that v is more risk-averse than u? The following proposition, which is due to Pratt (1964), indicates that no additional restriction is required.

Proposition 1.5. *The following three conditions are equivalent.*

(a) *Agent v is more risk-averse than agent u, i.e. the risk premium of any risk is larger for agent v than for agent u.*

(b) *For all w, $A_v(w) \geqslant A_u(w)$.*

(c) *Function v is a concave transformation of function u : $\exists \phi(\cdot)$ with $\phi' > 0$ and $\phi'' \leqslant 0$ such that $v(w) = \phi(u(w))$ for all w.*

Proof. We have already shown that (b) and (c) are equivalent. That (a) implies (b) follows directly from the Arrow–Pratt approximation. We now prove that (c) implies (a). Consider any lottery $\tilde{z}$. Let Π_u and Π_v denote the risk premium for zero-mean lottery $\tilde{z}$ of agent u and agent v, respectively. By definition, we have that

$$v(w - \Pi_v) = Ev(w + \tilde{z}) = E\phi(u(w + \tilde{z})).$$

Define random variable $\tilde{y}$ as $\tilde{y} = u(w + \tilde{z})$. Because ϕ is concave, $E\phi(\tilde{y})$ is smaller than $\phi(E\tilde{y})$ by Jensen's inequality. It thus follows that

$$v(w - \Pi_v) \leqslant \phi(Eu(w + \tilde{z})) = \phi(u(w - \Pi_u)) = v(w - \Pi_u).$$

Because v is increasing, this implies that Π_v is larger than Π_u. $\qquad\square$

In the case of small risks, the only thing that we need to know to determine whether a risk is desirable is the degree of concavity of u locally at the current wealth level w. For larger risks, the proposition above shows that we need to know much more to take a decision. Namely, we need to know the degree of concavity of u at all wealth levels. The degree of concavity must be increased at all wealth levels to guarantee that a change in u makes the decision maker more reluctant to accept risks. If v is locally more concave at some wealth levels and is less concave at other wealth levels, the comparative analysis is intrinsically ambiguous.

To illustrate the proposition, let us go back to the example of Sempronius's single ship yielding outcome $\tilde{z} = (0, \frac{1}{2}; 8000, \frac{1}{2})$, with a initial wealth $w_0 = 4000$ ducats. If Sempronius's utility function is $u(w) = \sqrt{w}$, his certainty equivalent of $\tilde{z}$ equals $e_u = 3464.1$, since

$$\tfrac{1}{2}\sqrt{4000} + \tfrac{1}{2}\sqrt{12\,000} = 86.395 = \sqrt{7464.1}$$

Alternatively, suppose that Sempronius's utility function is $v(w) = \ln(w)$, which is also increasing and concave. It is easy to check that v is more concave than u in the sense of Arrow–Pratt. Indeed, these functions yield

$$A_v(w) = \frac{1}{w} \geqslant \frac{1}{2w} = A_u(w)$$

for all w. From the above proposition, this change in utility should reduce the certainty equivalent of any risk. In the case of $w_0 = 4000$ and $\tilde{z} \sim (0, \frac{1}{2}; 8000, \frac{1}{2})$, the certainty equivalent of $\tilde{z}$ under v equals $e_v = 2928.5$, since

$$\tfrac{1}{2}\ln(4000) + \tfrac{1}{2}\ln(12\,000) = 8.8434 = \ln(6928.5).$$

Thus, e_v is smaller than e_u. Notice that the risk premium $\Pi_v = 1071.5$ under v is approximately twice the risk premium $\Pi_u = 535.9$. This was predicted by the Arrow–Pratt approximation, since A_v is equal to $2A_u$.

1.5 Decreasing Absolute Risk Aversion and Prudence

We have seen that risk aversion is driven by the fact that one's marginal utility is decreasing with wealth. In this section, we examine another question related to increasing wealth. Namely, we are interested in determining how the risk premium for a given zero-mean risk $\tilde{z}$ is affected by a change in initial wealth w. Arrow argued that intuition implies that wealthier people are generally less willing to pay for the elimination of fixed risk. A lottery to gain or lose 100 with equal probability is potentially life-threatening for an agent with initial wealth $w = 101$, whereas it is essentially trivial for an agent with wealth $w = 1\,000\,000$. The former should be ready to pay more than the latter for the elimination of risk. We can check that this property holds for the square-root utility function, with $\Pi = 43.4$ when $w = 101$ and $\Pi = 0.0025$ when $w = 1\,000\,000$. If wealth is measured in euros, the individual would be willing to pay over 43 euros to avoid the risk when wealth is $w = 101$, whereas the same individual would not even pay one euro cent to get rid of this risk when wealth is one million euros! In the following, we characterize the set of utility functions that have this property.

The risk premium $\Pi = \pi(w)$ as a function of initial wealth w can be evaluated by solving

$$Eu(w + \tilde{z}) = u(w - \pi(w)) \tag{1.10}$$

for all w. Fully differentiating (1.10) with respect to w yields

$$Eu'(w + \tilde{z}) = (1 - \pi'(w))u'(w - \pi),$$

or, equivalently,

$$\pi'(w) = \frac{u'(w - \pi) - Eu'(w + \tilde{z})}{u'(w - \pi)}. \tag{1.11}$$

Thus, the risk premium is decreasing with wealth if and only if

$$Ev(w + \tilde{z}) \leqslant v(w - \pi(w)), \tag{1.12}$$

where function $v \equiv -u'$ is defined as minus the derivative of function u. Because the function v is increasing, we can also interpret it as *another* utility function. Condition (1.12) then just states that the risk premium of agent v is larger than the risk premium π of agent u. From Proposition 1.5, this is true if and only if v is more concave than u in the sense of Arrow–Pratt, that is, if $-u'$ is a concave transformation of u. For this utility v, the measure of absolute risk aversion is $A_v = A_{-u'} = -u'''/u''$. This measure has several uses, which will be made clearer later in this book. For this reason, without justifying the terminology at this stage, we will define $P(w) = -u'''(w)/u''(w)$ as the degree of absolute prudence of the agent with utility u. It follows from (1.12) that $-u'$ is more concave than u if and only if

$$P(w) \geqslant A(w)$$

for all w. We conclude that condition $P \geqslant A$ uniformly is necessary and sufficient to guarantee that an increase in wealth reduces risk premia. Because

$$A'(w) = A(w)[A(w) - P(w)],$$

condition $P \geqslant A$ is equivalent to the condition $A' \leqslant 0$. We obtain the following proposition.

Proposition 1.6. *The risk premium associated to any risk $\tilde{z}$ is decreasing in wealth if and only if absolute risk aversion is decreasing; or equivalently if and only if prudence is uniformly larger than absolute risk aversion.*

Observe that the utility function $u(w) = \sqrt{w}$ satisfies this condition. Indeed, we have $A_u(w) = \frac{1}{2}w^{-1}$, which is decreasing. This can alternatively checked by observing that $v(w) = -\frac{1}{2}w^{-1/2}$ and $A_v(w) = P_u(w) = 1.5w^{-1}$, which is uniformly larger than $A_u(w)$. Notice that Decreasing Absolute Risk Aversion (DARA) requires that the third derivative of the utility function be positive. Otherwise, prudence would be negative, which would imply that $P < A$: a condition that implies that absolute risk aversion would be increasing in wealth. Thus, DARA, a very intuitive condition, requires the necessary (but not sufficient) condition that u''' be positive, or that marginal utility be convex.

1.6 Relative Risk Aversion

Absolute risk aversion is the rate of decay for marginal utility. More particularly, absolute risk aversion measures the rate at which marginal utility decreases when wealth is increased *by one euro*.[6] If the monetary unit were the dollar, absolute risk aversion would be a different number. In other words, the index of absolute risk aversion is not unit free, as it is measured per euro (per dollar, or per yen).

Economists often prefer unit-free measurements of sensitivity. To this end, define the index of *relative* risk aversion R as the rate at which marginal utility decreases

---

[6]In general, the *growth rate* for a function $f(x)$ is defined as

$$\frac{\mathrm{d}f(x)}{\mathrm{d}x} \cdot \frac{1}{f(x)}.$$

Since marginal utility $u'(x)$ declines in wealth, its growth rate is negative. The absolute value of this negative growth rate, which is the measure of absolute risk aversion, is called the *decay rate*.

when wealth is increased *by one percent*. In terms of standard economic theory, this measure is simply the wealth-elasticity of marginal utility. It can be computed as

$$R(w) = -\frac{\mathrm{d}u'(w)/u'(w)}{\mathrm{d}w/w} = \frac{-wu''(w)}{u'(w)} = wA(w). \qquad (1.13)$$

Note that the measure of relative risk aversion is simply the product of wealth and absolute risk aversion.

The (absolute) risk premium and the index of absolute risk aversion are linked by the Arrow–Pratt approximation and by Propositions 1.5 and 1.6. We can develop analogous kinds of results for relative risk aversion. Suppose that your initial wealth w is invested in a portfolio whose return $\tilde{z}$ over the period is uncertain. Let us assume that $E\tilde{z} = 0$. Which share of your initial wealth are you ready to pay to get rid of this proportional risk? The solution to this problem is referred to as the relative risk premium $\hat{\Pi}$. This measure also is a unit-free measure, unlike the absolute risk premium, which is measured in euros. It is defined implicitly via the following equation:

$$Eu(w(1 + \tilde{z})) = u(w(1 - \hat{\Pi})). \qquad (1.14)$$

Obviously, the relative risk premium and the absolute risk premium are equal if we normalize initial wealth to unity. More generally, the relative risk premium for proportional risk $\tilde{z}$ equals the absolute risk premium for absolute risk $w\tilde{z}$, divided by initial wealth w: $\hat{\Pi}(\tilde{z}) = \Pi(w\tilde{z})/w$. From this observation, we obtain the fact that, if agent v is more risk-averse than agent u with the same initial wealth, then agent v will be ready to pay a larger share of his wealth than agent u to insure against a given proportional risk $\tilde{z}$. Moreover, if σ^2 denotes the variance of $\tilde{z}$, then the variance of $w\tilde{z}$ equals $w^2\sigma^2$. Using the Arrow–Pratt approximation thus yields

$$\hat{\Pi}(\tilde{z}) = \frac{\Pi(w\tilde{z})}{w} \simeq \frac{\frac{1}{2}w^2\sigma^2 A(w)}{w} = \frac{1}{2}\sigma^2 R(w). \qquad (1.15)$$

The relative risk premium is approximately equal to half of the variance of the proportional risk times the index of relative risk aversion. This can be used to establish a range for acceptable degrees of risk aversion. Suppose that one's wealth is subject to a risk of a gain or loss of 20% with equal probability. What is the range that one would find reasonable for the share of wealth Π that one would be ready to pay to get rid of this zero-mean risk? From our various experiments in class, we found that most people would be ready to pay between 2% and 8% of their wealth. Because risk $\tilde{z}$ in this experiment has a variance of $0.5(0.2)^2 + 0.5(-0.2)^2 = 0.04$, using approximation (1.15) yields a range for relative risk aversion between 1 and 4. This information will be useful later in this book.

There is no definitive argument for or against decreasing relative risk aversion. Arrow originally conjectured that relative risk aversion is likely to be constant, or perhaps increasing, although he stated that the intuition was not as clear as was the intuition for decreasing absolute risk aversion. Since then, numerous empirical studies have offered conflicting results. We might also try to examine this question by introspection. If your wealth would increase, would you want to devote a larger or a smaller share of your wealth to get rid of a given zero-mean proportional risk? For example, what would you pay to avoid the risk of gaining or losing 20% of your wealth, each with an equal probability? If the share is decreasing with wealth, you have decreasing relative risk aversion. There are two contradictory effects here that need to be considered. On the one hand, under the intuitive DARA assumption, becoming wealthier also means becoming less risk-averse. This effect tends to reduce Π. But, on the other hand, becoming wealthier also means facing a larger absolute risk $w\tilde{z}$. This effect tends to raise Π. There is no clear intuition as to whether the first effect or the second effect will dominate. For example, many of the classic models in macroeconomics are based on relative risk aversion being constant over all wealth levels, which is implicitly assuming that our two effects exactly cancel each other out. Of course, there also is no *a priori* reason to believe that the dominant effect will not change over various wealth levels. For instance, some recent empirical evidence indicates a possible "U-shape" for relative risk aversion, with R decreasing at low wealth levels, then leveling off somewhat before increasing at higher wealth levels.

1.7 Some Classical Utility Functions

As already noted above, expected-utility (EU) theory has many proponents and many detractors. In Chapter 13, we examine some generalizations of the EU criterion that satisfy those who find expected utility too restrictive. But researchers in both economics and finance have long considered—and most of them still do—EU theory as an acceptable paradigm for decision making under uncertainty. Indeed, EU theory has a long and prominent place in the development of decision making under uncertainty. Even detractors of the theory use EU as a standard by which to compare alternative theories. Moreover, many of the models in which EU theory has been applied can be modified, often yielding better results.

Whereas the current trend is to generalize the EU model, researchers often *restrict* EU criterion by considering a specific subset of utility functions. This is done to obtain tractable solutions to many problems. It is important to note the implications that derive from the choice of a particular utility function. Some results in the literature may be robust enough to apply for all risk-averse preferences, while others might be restricted to applying only for a narrow class of preferences. In this section, we examine several particular types of utility functions that are often encountered in the economics and the finance literature. Remember that utility is unique only up to a linear transformation.

Historically, much of the theory of finance was developed during the 1960s by considering the subset of utility functions that are quadratic of the form

$$u(w) = aw - \tfrac{1}{2}w^2, \quad \text{for } w \leqslant a.$$

Note that the domain of wealth on which u is defined comes from the necessary requirement that u be nondecreasing, which is true only if w is smaller than a. This set of functions is useful because the EU generated by any distribution of final wealth is a function of only the first two moments of this distribution:

$$Eu(\tilde{w}) = aE\tilde{w} - \tfrac{1}{2}E\tilde{w}^2.$$

Therefore, in this case, the EU theory simplifies to a mean–variance approach to decision making under uncertainty. However, as already discussed, it is very hard to believe that preferences among different lotteries be determined only by the mean and variance of these lotteries.

Above wealth level a, marginal utility becomes negative. Since quadratic utility is decreasing in wealth for $w > a$, many people might feel this is not appropriate as a utility function. However, it is important to remember that we are trying to model human behavior with mathematical models. For example, if the quadratic utility function models your behavior quite well with $a = 100$ million euros, is it really a problem that this function declines for higher wealth levels? The point is that the quadratic utility might work well for more realistic wealth levels, and if it does, we should not be overly concerned about its properties at unrealistically high wealth levels. However, the quadratic utility function has another property that is more problematic. Namely, the quadratic utility functions exhibit increasing absolute risk aversion:

$$A(w) = \frac{1}{a - w} \Rightarrow A'(w) = \frac{1}{(a - w)^2} > 0.$$

For this reason, quadratic utility functions are not as in fashion anymore.

A second set of classical utility functions is the set of so-called constant-absolute-risk-aversion (CARA) utility functions, which are exponential functions characterized by

$$u(w) = -\frac{\exp(-aw)}{a},$$

where a is some positive scalar. The domain of these functions is the real line. The distinguishing feature of these utility functions is that they exhibit constant absolute risk aversion, with $A(w) = a$ for all w. It can be shown that the Arrow–Pratt approximation is exact when u is exponential and $\tilde{w}$ is normally distributed with mean μ and variance σ^2. Indeed, we can take expectations to see that

$$Eu(\tilde{w})$$

$$= \frac{-1}{\sigma a \sqrt{2\pi}} \int \exp(-aw) \exp\left(-\frac{(w-\mu)^2}{2\sigma^2}\right) dw$$

$$= -\frac{1}{a} \exp(-a(\mu - \tfrac{1}{2}a\sigma^2)) \left[\frac{1}{\sigma\sqrt{2\pi}} \int \exp\left(-\frac{(w-(\mu-\tfrac{1}{2}a\sigma^2))^2}{2\sigma^2}\right) dw\right]$$

$$= -\frac{1}{a} \exp(-a(\mu - \tfrac{1}{2}a\sigma^2)) = u(\mu - \tfrac{1}{2}a\sigma^2). \tag{1.16}$$

The third equality comes from the fact that the bracketed term is the integral of the density of the normal distribution $N(\mu - \tfrac{1}{2}a\sigma^2, \sigma)$, which must be equal to unity. Thus, the risk premium is indeed equal to $\tfrac{1}{2}\sigma^2 A(w)$. In this very specific case, we obtain that the Arrow–Pratt approximation is exact. The fact that risk aversion is constant is often useful in analyzing choices among several alternatives. As we will see later, this assumption eliminates the income effect when dealing with decisions to be made about a risk whose size is invariant to changes in wealth. However, this is often also the main criticism of the CARA utility, since absolute risk aversion is constant rather than decreasing.

Finally, one set of preferences that has been by far the most used in the literature is the set of power utility functions. Researchers in finance and in macroeconomics are so accustomed to this restriction that many of them do not even mention it anymore when they present their results. Suppose that

$$u(w) = \frac{w^{1-\gamma}}{1-\gamma} \quad \text{for } w > 0.$$

The scalar γ is chosen so that $\gamma > 0$, $\gamma \neq 1$. It is easy to show that γ equals the degree of relative risk aversion, since $A(w) = \gamma/w$ and $R(w) = \gamma$ for all w. Thus, this set exhibits decreasing absolute risk aversion and constant relative risk aversion, which are two reasonable assumptions. For this reason, these utility functions are called the constant-relative-risk-aversion (CRRA) class of preferences. Notice that our definition does not allow for $\gamma = 1$. However, it is straightforward to show that function $u(w) = \ln(w)$ satisfies the property that $R(w) = 1$ for all w. Thus, the set of all CRRA utility functions is completely defined by[7]

$$u(w) = \begin{cases} \dfrac{w^{1-\gamma}}{1-\gamma} & \text{for } \gamma \geqslant 0, \ \gamma \neq 1, \\ \ln(w) & \text{for } \gamma = 1. \end{cases} \tag{1.17}$$

---

[7]We can also show that $u(w) = \ln(w)$ as a limiting case of the power utility function. To this end, rewrite the power utility function, using a linear transformation, as

$$u(w) = \frac{1}{1-\gamma}(w^{1-\gamma} - 1).$$

As we will see later in this book, this class of utility functions eliminates any income effects when making decisions about risks whose size is proportional to one's level of wealth. For example, the relative risk premium $\hat{\Pi}$ defined by equation (1.14) is independent of wealth w in this case. The assumption that relative risk aversion is constant enormously simplifies many of the problems often encountered in macroeconomics and finance.

1.8 Bibliographical References, Extensions and Exercises

The contribution by Pratt (1964) basically opened and closed the field covered in this chapter. It is, however, fair to mention that the measure of absolute risk aversion has been discovered independently by Arrow (1963) and de Finetti (1952). The paper by de Finetti was written in Italian and even today is not given the attention it deserves. The paper by Pratt is by far the most advanced in defining the notions of an increase in risk aversion and of decreasing absolute risk aversion. The orders of risk aversion are introduced by Segal and Spivak (1990).

Ross (1981) challenged the idea that $A = -u''/u'$ is a good measure of the degree of risk aversion of an agent. Kihlstrom, Romer and Williams (1981) and Nachman (1982) showed that if initial wealth is uncertain, it is not true that an agent v, who is more risk-averse than another agent u in the sense of Arrow–Pratt, will be ready to pay more to get rid of another risk. Ross (1981) characterized the conditions on u and v that imply that $\Pi_v \geqslant \Pi_u$ even when initial wealth is uncertain and potentially correlated with the risk under scrutiny. These conditions are of course stronger than $A_v \geqslant A_u$.

There is much contradictory empirical evidence on the shape of relative risk aversion as a function of wealth. Many authors have empirically estimated R, assuming that we have CRRA. Fewer authors have examined whether R might be increasing or decreasing in wealth. A good summary of many of these results appears in Ait-Sahalia and Lo (2000).

Chapter Bibliography

Ait-Sahalia, Y. and A. W. Lo. 2000. Nonparametric risk management and implied risk aversion. *Journal of Econometrics* 94:9–51.

Arrow, K. J. 1963. Liquidity preference. Lecture VI in *Lecture Notes for Economics 285, The Economics of Uncertainty*, pp. 33-53, undated, Stanford University.

———. 1965. *Yrjo Jahnsson lecture notes*, Helsinki. (Reprinted in Arrow 1971).

———. 1971. *Essays in the theory of risk bearing*. Chicago: Markham Publishing Co.

Taking the limit as $\gamma \to 1$ and applying L'Hôpital's rule, we obtain

$$\lim_{\gamma \to 1} u(w) = \lim_{\gamma \to 1} \frac{-(w^{1-\gamma})\ln(w)}{-1} = \ln(w).$$

Bernoulli, D. 1954. Exposition of a new theory on the measurement of risk. (English Transl. by Louise Sommer.) *Econometrica* 22: 23–36.

Bernstein, P. L. 1998. *Against the Gods*. Wiley.

de Finetti, B. 1952. Sulla preferibilita. *Giornale Degli Economisti E Annali Di Economia* 11:685–709.

Kihlstrom, R., D. Romer, and S. Williams. 1981. Risk aversion with random initial wealth. *Econometrica* 49:911–920.

Nachman, D. C. 1982. Preservation of 'more risk averse' under expectations. *Journal of Economic Theory* 28:361–368.

Pratt, J. 1964. Risk aversion in the small and in the large. *Econometrica* 32:122–136.

Ross, S. A. 1981. Some stronger measures of risk aversion in the small and in the large with applications. *Econometrica* 3:621–638.

Segal, U. and A. Spivak. 1990. First order versus second order risk aversion. *Journal of Economic Theory* 51:111–125.

Yaari, M. E. 1987. The dual theory of choice under risk. *Econometrica* 55:95–115.

Exercises

(1.1) An individual has the following utility function:

$$u(w) = w^{1/2}.$$

Her initial wealth is 10 and she faces the lottery $\tilde{X} : (-6, \frac{1}{2}; +6, \frac{1}{2})$.

(a) Compute the exact value of the certainty equivalent and of the risk premium.

(b) Apply Pratt's formula to obtain an approximation of the risk premium.

(c) Show that with such a utility function absolute risk aversion is decreasing in wealth while relative risk aversion is constant.

(d) If the utility function becomes

$$v(w) = w^{1/4},$$

answer again part (a). Are you surprised by the changes in the certainty equivalent and in the risk premium? Relate this change to the notion of 'more risk averse' (i.e. express $v(w)$ as a concave transformation of $u(w)$).

(e) If the risk becomes $\tilde{Y} : (-3, \frac{1}{2}; +3, \frac{1}{2})$, compute the new risk premium as approximated by Pratt's formula. Why is the approximated risk premium four times smaller than the risk premium for $\tilde{X}$?

(1.2) As in the previous exercise, consider an initial wealth of 10 and the lottery $\tilde{X}$. Assume now that the utility is:

$$u = \begin{cases} w & \text{for } w \leqslant 10, \\ \frac{1}{2}w + 5 & \text{for } w \geqslant 10. \end{cases} \tag{1.18}$$

(a) Draw the utility function. Is it globally concave?

(b) Compute the certainty equivalent and the risk premium attached to $\tilde{X}$.

(c) Can you apply the Arrow–Pratt approximation? Why?

(d) Consider now the lottery $\tilde{Y}$ defined in exercise 1.1. Compute the risk premium attached to $\tilde{Y}$. Is it smaller than for $\tilde{X}$? Why?

(e) Answer (b) and (d) above if the individual has an initial wealth of 20. How do the risk premia for $\tilde{X}$ and $\tilde{Y}$ compare?

(1.3) Let $u = w^2$ for $w \geqslant 0$.

(a) Compute the exact risk premium if initial wealth is 4 and if a decision maker faces the lottery $(-2, \frac{1}{2}; +2, \frac{1}{2})$. Explain why the risk premium is negative.

(b) If the utility function becomes $v = w^4$, what happens to the risk premium? Show that v is a convex transformation of u.

(1.4) Let $u = \ln w$.

(a) Does this utility function exhibit the DARA property?

(b) Compute $-u'''/u''$ and compare it with $-u''/u'$.

(e) Prove that $-u'(w)$ is a concave transformation of $u(w)$ (hint: use Pratt's theorem).

(1.5) Consider the family of exponential utility functions

$$u = \frac{1 - \exp(-aw)}{a}.$$

(a) Show that a is the degree of absolute risk aversion.

(b) Show that u becomes linear in w when a tends to zero (hint: use L'Hôpital's rule).

(c) Consider lottery $\tilde{x}$ with positive and negative payoffs. Determine the value of $Eu(\tilde{x})$ when a tends to infinity.

2
The Measures of Risk

In Chapter 1, we defined the concept of risk aversion by considering the effect of the introduction of a zero-mean risk on welfare. That is, we assumed that the initial environment of the consumer was risk free. Our only conclusion from risk aversion was that the individual preferred no risk to a zero-mean risk. But what about choices among different zero-mean risks? For example, recall from the previous chapter that we might interpret Sempronius's situation as facing the risk $(-4000, \frac{1}{2}; 4000, \frac{1}{2})$ with initial wealth $w = 8000$. The alternative, using two separate ships, can be thought of as facing the risk $(-4000, \frac{1}{4}; 0, \frac{1}{2}; +4000, \frac{1}{4})$ from the same initial wealth. We argued that the second alternative seemed more valuable, in some sense. In this chapter, we will examine this question more closely and consider the comparison of such competing risks.

If one could know the utility function of the agent, ranking lotteries would be easy. For example, let us compare two different wealth prospects (i.e. two distributions of final wealth) $\tilde{w}_1$ and $\tilde{w}_2$. The first is preferred to the second by an agent with utility function u if $Eu(\tilde{w}_1) \geqslant Eu(\tilde{w}_2)$. This preference order, which is specific to a single utility function u, is complete in the sense that, for any pair $(\tilde{w}_1, \tilde{w}_2)$, $\tilde{w}_1$ is preferred to $\tilde{w}_2$, or $\tilde{w}_2$ is preferred to $\tilde{w}_1$, or we are indifferent to both wealth prospects. In this chapter, we consider several relatively weak restrictions on preferences; for example, that "agents are risk-averse" or that "agents are prudent." We want to find restrictions on the change in risk from $\tilde{w}_1$ to $\tilde{w}_2$ that are unanimously disliked by the group of agents under scrutiny. In that case, we say that $\tilde{w}_1$ dominates $\tilde{w}_2$ for this class of utility functions. As soon as the class is not limited to a single utility function, these preference orders are incomplete in the sense that it is not true that, for any pair of lotteries, one must necessarily dominate the other. Some people in the group may prefer the first, whereas other members in the group may prefer the second. Imposing unanimity in the group is a very strong constraint on the change in risk. Considering a larger group makes the constraint of unanimity stronger. On the other hand, if among our group we do find unanimity that $\tilde{w}_1$ dominates $\tilde{w}_2$, it allows us to choose $\tilde{w}_1$ over $\tilde{w}_2$ when these are our only two options.

The theory of stochastic dominance looks at certain statistical properties of the distributions of $\tilde{w}_1$ and $\tilde{w}_2$, which allow us to infer unanimous agreement for certain classes of preferences. This is important not only for our understanding of individual behavior, but also for decision making designed to benefit a group, such as a corporate manager making decisions on behalf of the company's shareholders. In this book, we will consider basically three stochastic orders. In Section 2.1, we first consider the most natural set of utility functions from what we have seen in Chapter 1. We consider in that section the set of all risk-averse agents. It generates the concept of an increase in risk that was first examined by Rothschild and Stiglitz (1970). In Section 2.2, we focus on the set of prudent agents, which yields the concept of an increase in downside risk introduced by Menezes, Geiss and Tressler (1980). Finally, in Section 2.3, we assume only that agents have an increasing utility function. The corresponding stochastic order is called "first-order stochastic dominance."

2.1 Increases in Risk

In this section, we characterize the changes in risk that make all risk-averse agents worse off. We focus the analysis on changes in risk which preserve the expected outcome, i.e. mean-preserving changes in risk. These changes are called "increases in risk." There are at least three equivalent ways to define them.

2.1.1 Adding Noise

Consider the binary lottery faced by Sempronius using a single ship. This may be written as $\tilde{w}_1 \sim (4000, \frac{1}{2}; 12\,000, \frac{1}{2})$. In the low wealth state, the ship is lost, whereas in the high wealth state, the ship succeeds in bringing the spices safely to the harbor. Let us assume that the ship contains 8000 pounds of spices, which will be sold at a unit price of one ducat. This environment generates a distribution $\tilde{w}_1$ for Sempronius's final wealth.

Suppose alternatively that the price at which the spices will be sold at the harbor is unknown at the time that the ship leaves the East Indies. More precisely, let us suppose that the unit price will be either 0.5 ducats or 1.5 ducats with equal probabilities. In this alternative environment, the final wealth is still 4000 in the case of the ship being sunk. But, conditional on the ship's arriving safely in Europe, Sempronius's final wealth will be either 8000 or 16 000 with equal probabilities, or $12\,000 + \tilde{\varepsilon}$, with $\tilde{\varepsilon} \sim (-4000, \frac{1}{2}, 4000, \frac{1}{2})$. Because $E\tilde{\varepsilon} = 0$, the price uncertainty adds a zero-mean noise to Sempronius's final wealth, conditional upon the no-loss state. *Ex ante*, the agent faces an uncertain wealth distributed as $\tilde{w}_2 \sim (4000, \frac{1}{2}; 12\,000 + \tilde{\varepsilon}, \frac{1}{2})$. This situation describes what is called a compound lottery, i.e. a lottery for which some of the outcomes are themselves lotteries.

Intuition suggests that Sempronius should dislike this additional uncertainty. The reader can check that this is indeed the case. For example, if Sempronius's utility

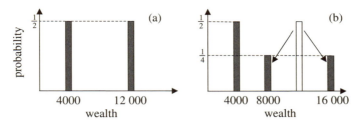

Figure 2.1. Transfer of probability mass to describe an increase in risk.

function is a square root, we have that

$$Eu(\tilde{w}_1) = \tfrac{1}{2}\sqrt{4000} + \tfrac{1}{2}\sqrt{12\,000} = 86.395,$$

whereas

$$Eu(\tilde{w}_2) = \tfrac{1}{2}\sqrt{4000} + \tfrac{1}{2}\left[\tfrac{1}{2}\sqrt{8000} + \tfrac{1}{2}\sqrt{16\,000}\right] = 85.606 < 86.395.$$

The same qualitative result would hold if Sempronius would have another concave utility function. In fact, adding a zero-mean noise conditional upon some specific state always reduces the EU of risk-averse agents, as we now show.

To keep the presentation relatively simple, suppose that $\tilde{w}_1$ can take n different possible values $\omega_1, \omega_2, \ldots, \omega_n$. Let p_s denote the probability that $\tilde{w}_1$ takes value ω_s. Suppose that the alternative wealth distribution $\tilde{w}_2$ be obtained by compounding $\tilde{w}_1$ with zero-mean noises $\tilde{\varepsilon}_s$ for the different outcomes ω_s of $\tilde{w}_1$. This means that each outcome ω_s of $\tilde{w}_1$ is replaced by $\omega_s + \tilde{\varepsilon}_s$ with $E\tilde{\varepsilon}_s = 0$:

$$\tilde{w}_2 = \tilde{w}_1 + \tilde{\varepsilon} \quad \text{with } E[\tilde{\varepsilon} \mid \tilde{w}_1 = \omega_s] = E[\tilde{\varepsilon}_s] = 0.$$

The price uncertainty presented above is an example of this technique of adding noises to each possible outcome of the initial distribution of wealth.

With this notation, it is easy to show that any such alternative lottery $\tilde{w}_2$ makes all risk-averse agents worse off. Because $E\tilde{\varepsilon}_s$ is zero, risk aversion implies that $Eu(\omega_s + \tilde{\varepsilon}_s) \leqslant u(\omega_s)$. It follows that

$$Eu(\tilde{w}_2) = \sum_{s=1}^{n} p_s Eu(\omega_s + \tilde{\varepsilon}_s) \leqslant \sum_{s=1}^{n} p_s u(\omega_s) = Eu(\tilde{w}_1).$$

All risk-averse agents dislike adding zero-mean noises to the possible outcomes of their wealth.

2.1.2 Mean-Preserving Spreads in Probability

The existence of price uncertainty in the situation faced by Sempronius can alternatively be seen as transferring probability masses. In Figure 2.1(a), we represent the probability distribution in the absence of price uncertainty. Figure 2.1(b) describes the probability distribution when the price uncertainty is taken into account. We see that adding noise $\tilde{\varepsilon} \sim (-4000, \frac{1}{2}, 4000, \frac{1}{2})$ is equivalent to transfering half of the $\frac{1}{2}$-probability mass at 12 000 to 8000, and the remaining of the probability mass at 12 000 to 16 000. By doing this, we do not modify the center of gravity of the probability distribution, i.e. we preserve the mean. In short, we construct what is called a "mean-preserving spread" of the probability distribution.

Let $f_i(w)$ denote the probability mass of $\tilde{w}_i$ at w. In the case of a continuous distribution, $f_i(\cdot)$ is the probability density of $\tilde{w}_i$. The following definition formalizes the concept of a mean-preserving spread, which is an operation consisting of the partial removal of probability mass from some interval I in order to transfer it outside this interval.

Definition 2.1. $\tilde{w}_2$ is a mean-preserving spread (MPS) of $\tilde{w}_1$ if

1. $E\tilde{w}_2 = E\tilde{w}_1$, and
2. there exists an interval I such that $f_2(w) \leqslant f_1(w)$ for all w in I, and $f_2(w) \geqslant f_1(w)$ for all w outside I.

Adding noise or constructing a sequence of MPS's are obviously two equivalent ways to increase risk. In some circumstances, it is easier to use one representation than the other. For example, let us compare distribution $\tilde{w}_1 \sim (4000, \frac{1}{2}; 12\,000, \frac{1}{2})$ to distribution $\tilde{w}_2 \sim (2000, \frac{1}{2}; 14\,000, \frac{1}{2})$. Obviously, the two distributions have the same mean, and the second is obtained by transferring some probability mass from interval $I = [4000, 12\,000]$ outside I. Thus, $\tilde{w}_2$ is an increase in risk of $\tilde{w}_1$. It must be the case that $\tilde{w}_2$ is obtained from $\tilde{w}_1$ by adding some noise $\tilde{\varepsilon}_1$ to outcome 4000 and another noise $\tilde{\varepsilon}_2$ to outcome 12 000 of $\tilde{w}_1$. The reader may easily verify that indeed defining

$$\tilde{\varepsilon}_1 \sim (-2000, \tfrac{5}{6}; 10\,000, \tfrac{1}{6}) \quad \text{and} \quad \tilde{\varepsilon}_2 \sim (2000, \tfrac{5}{6}; -10\,000, \tfrac{1}{6})$$

does the job.

It is often useful to translate the definition of a mean-preserving spread into a condition on the *cumulative* distribution functions of $\tilde{w}_1$ and $\tilde{w}_2$. Let $F_i(w)$ denote the probability that $\tilde{w}_i$ be no greater than w. That is, define

$$F_i(w) = \sum_{s \mid \omega_s \leqslant w} f_i(s)$$

in the discrete case, and

$$F_i(w) = \int^{w} f_i(s) \, \mathrm{d}s$$

in the continuous case. In the latter case, the density function f_i is simply the derivative of F_i. To keep the level of technicality at a minimum, let us assume that

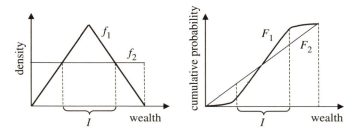

Figure 2.2. Example of a mean-preserving spread for a continuous distribution.

all possible final wealth levels are in the interval $(a, b]$. Suppose that $\tilde{w}_2$ is an MPS of $\tilde{w}_1$. Integrating by parts, preservation of the mean implies that

$$\int_a^b [F_2(s) - F_1(s)]\,ds = -\int_a^b s[f_2(s) - f_1(s)]\,ds = E\tilde{w}_2 - E\tilde{w}_1 = 0.$$

The fact that the expectation is preserved means that the area between F_1 and F_2 (counted as positive when F_2 is above F_1 and counted as negative otherwise) must sum up to zero. Also, by definition of an MPS, the derivative of F_2 is smaller (resp. larger) than the derivative of F_1 within the interval I (resp. outside I). Thus, F_2 must be larger than F_1 to the left of some threshold $\hat{w}$ and F_2 must be smaller than F_1 to its right. We illustrate this property in Figure 2.2 in the continuous case, and in Figure 2.3 in the discrete case considered in the previous paragraph.

This so-called "single-crossing" property of MPS implies in particular that

$$S(w) = \int_a^w [F_2(s) - F_1(s)]\,ds \geqslant 0 \tag{2.1}$$

for all w, with an equality when w equals b. This integral condition is examined in more detail in the next section.

2.1.3 The Integral Condition and Risk-Averse Preferences

We now examine the problem of characterizing changes in risk that reduce the EU of all risk-averse agents. By integrating by parts, we obtain

$$Eu(\tilde{w}_i) = \int_a^b u(\omega) f_i(\omega)\,d\omega = u(\omega) F_i(\omega)|_{\omega=a}^{\omega=b} - \int_a^b u'(\omega) F_i(\omega)\,d\omega,$$

or, equivalently, that

$$Eu(\tilde{w}_i) = u(b) - \int_a^b u'(\omega) F_i(\omega)\,d\omega.$$

It follows that

$$Eu(\tilde{w}_2) - Eu(\tilde{w}_1) = \int_a^b u'(\omega)[F_1(\omega) - F_2(\omega)]\,d\omega. \tag{2.2}$$

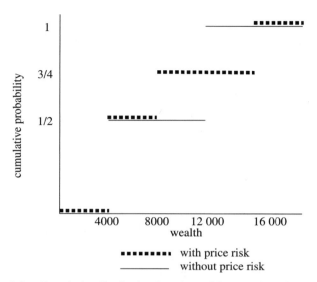

Figure 2.3.   Cumulative distribution functions of Sempronius's final wealth
with one ship, and with or without price uncertainty.

The difference in EU in transforming $\tilde{w}_1$ into $\tilde{w}_2$ is equal to the areas between F_1
and F_2 ("+" if F_1 is above F_2, and "−" otherwise) weighted by the marginal value
of wealth. Integrating by parts once again yields

$$Eu(\tilde{w}_2) - Eu(\tilde{w}_1) = -u'(\omega)S(\omega)|_{\omega=a}^{\omega=b} + \int_a^b u''(\omega)S(\omega)\,d\omega,$$

where function S is defined by equation (2.1) and is such that $S'(w) = F_2(w) - F_1(w)$. Because we focused the analysis on changes in risk that preserve the mean,
we have that $S(a) = S(b) = 0$. The above equation thus simplifies to

$$Eu(\tilde{w}_2) - Eu(\tilde{w}_1) = \int_a^b u''(\omega)S(\omega)\,d\omega. \tag{2.3}$$

Equation (2.3) implies that all risk-averse agents dislike mean-preserving increases
in risk, that is changes in risk for which the condition $S(w) \geqslant 0$ is satisfied for all w.
This condition would indeed imply that the integrand in (2.3) is uniformly negative.
Its integral in $[a, b]$ should therefore be negative. The condition that $S(w) \geqslant 0$ for all
w is also necessary to guarantee that every risk averter would unanimously prefer
$\tilde{w}_1$ over $\tilde{w}_2$. Indeed, suppose by contradiction that S is positive in some interval
$J \subseteq [a, b]$. Let us consider the concave utility function u that is linear outside J,
and which is strictly concave in J. Then, from equation (2.3), agent u increases her
EU by transforming $\tilde{w}_1$ into $\tilde{w}_2$. The integrand $u''S$ is zero for w outside J and is
positive for w in J.

To sum up, the condition that $S(w) = \int^w (F_2(s) - F_1(s))\,\mathrm{d}s$ be nonnegative is both a necessary and a sufficient condition for mean-preserving changes in risk to reduce the EU of all risk-averse agents. It was examined by Rothschild and Stiglitz (1970). Notice from equation (2.2) that the condition $S(w) \geqslant 0$ implies that agents with the concave utility functions $u_w(x) = \min(x, w) \ \forall w \in [a, b]$ all prefer risk $\tilde{w}_1$ to risk $\tilde{w}_2$. We hope that this observation makes this integral condition less artificial.

There is a clear link between the integral condition $S \geqslant 0$ and the notion of a mean-preserving spread. It has been partly derived at the end of the previous section, where we have shown that a mean-preserving spread *implies* that S is nonnegative. Rothschild and Stiglitz (1970) have shown that the integral condition is *equivalent to* a sequence of mean-preserving spreads. In fact, they have proved the following proposition, showing how several interpretations of a mean-preserving increase in risk are all the same.

Proposition 2.2. *Consider two random variables $\tilde{w}_1$ and $\tilde{w}_2$ with the same mean. The following four conditions are equivalent.*

(a) *All risk-averse agents prefer $\tilde{w}_1$ to $\tilde{w}_2$: $Eu(\tilde{w}_2) \leqslant Eu(\tilde{w}_1)$ for all concave functions u.*

(b) *$\tilde{w}_2$ is obtained from $\tilde{w}_1$ by adding zero-mean noise terms to the possible outcomes of $\tilde{w}_1$:*

$$\tilde{w}_2 \overset{d}{=} \tilde{w}_1 + \tilde{\varepsilon},$$

with $E[\tilde{\varepsilon} \mid \tilde{w}_1 = \omega] = 0$ for all ω, where "$\overset{d}{=}$" means "equal in distribution."

(c) *$\tilde{w}_2$ is obtained from $\tilde{w}_1$ by a sequence of mean-preserving spreads.*

(d) *$S(w) \equiv \int^w (F_2(w) - F_1(w))\,\mathrm{d}w \geqslant 0$ for all w.*

Any one of these four equivalent conditions may define what we call an increase in risk from $\tilde{w}_1$ to $\tilde{w}_2$. Correspondingly, a change from $\tilde{w}_2$ to $\tilde{w}_1$ is labeled a reduction in risk.

2.1.4 *Preference for Diversification*

In Chapter 1, we have shown that Sempronius prefers to transfer the spices from the colonies by two ships rather than by only one. By doing so, he diversifies the risk. Let us now formalize this example by defining the random variable $\tilde{x}_i$ which takes value 0 if ship i is sunk (probability $\frac{1}{2}$), and which takes value 1 otherwise. In short, $\tilde{x}_i$ is distributed as $(0, \frac{1}{2}; 1, \frac{1}{2})$. By assumption, the risks faced by the two ships are independent. If Sempronius puts his 8000 pounds of spice in ship 1, his final wealth would equal

$$\tilde{w}_2 = w + 8000\tilde{x}_1.$$

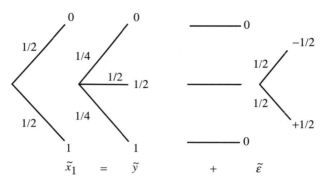

Figure 2.4. Diversification and reduction of risk.

We assume here that the price of spice is risk free and normalized to unity. If he splits the goods in two equal parts to be brought to London in ships 1 and 2, his final wealth equals

$$\tilde{w}_1 = w + 8000\left(\frac{\tilde{x}_1 + \tilde{x}_2}{2}\right) = w + 8000\tilde{y},$$

where $\tilde{y} = \frac{1}{2}(\tilde{x}_1 + \tilde{x}_2)$ can be interpreted as the rate of success. The rate of success is distributed as $(0, \frac{1}{4}; \frac{1}{2}, \frac{1}{2}; 1, \frac{1}{4})$. It is easy to check that $\tilde{x}_1$ can be obtained from $\tilde{y}$ by adding the noise $\tilde{\varepsilon} \sim (-\frac{1}{2}, \frac{1}{2}; +\frac{1}{2}, \frac{1}{2})$ conditional upon $\tilde{y} = \frac{1}{2}$, as seen in Figure 2.4. It then follows from Proposition 2.2 that, independent of the utility function of Sempronius, he must prefer two ships to one ship as soon as this function is concave. Diversifying the transfer of spice to two ships is a way to diversify the risk faced by Sempronius. Not "putting all the eggs in one basket" is a rational behavior for risk-averse agents.

More generally, one can verify that, if $\tilde{x}_1$ and $\tilde{x}_2$ are two independent and identically distributed (i.i.d.) random variables, then $\tilde{y} = \frac{1}{2}(\tilde{x}_1 + \tilde{x}_2)$ is a reduction of risk with respect to $\tilde{x}_1$. We have that

$$\tilde{x}_1 = \tilde{y} + \tilde{\varepsilon} \quad \text{with } \tilde{\varepsilon} = \frac{\tilde{x}_1 - \tilde{x}_2}{2}$$

and

$$E[\tilde{\varepsilon} \mid \tilde{y} = y] = E\left[\frac{\tilde{x}_1 - \tilde{x}_2}{2} \,\middle|\, \frac{\tilde{x}_1 + \tilde{x}_2}{2} = y\right]$$
$$= E\left[\tilde{x}_1 \,\middle|\, \frac{\tilde{x}_1 - \tilde{x}_2}{2}\right] - E\left[\tilde{x}_2 \,\middle|\, \frac{\tilde{x}_1 - \tilde{x}_2}{2}\right],$$

which must be equal to zero by symmetry. Thus, $\tilde{x}_1$ is riskier than $\tilde{y}$. In other words, diversification is a risk-reduction device in the sense of Rothschild and Stiglitz. All risk-averse agents should diversify their risks when possible. This guideline does not rely on any preference restrictions other than risk aversion.

2.1.5 And the Variance?

The risk premium is the amount of money that the agent is ready to pay to eliminate the (zero-mean) risk. Facing the risk $\tilde{w}_i$ or receiving its certainty equivalent $E\tilde{w}_i - \Pi_i$ generates the same EU. Consider two risky wealth prospects $\tilde{w}_1$ and $\tilde{w}_2$ with equal means. It is clear that $\tilde{w}_1$ is preferred to $\tilde{w}_2$ if and only if Π_2 is larger than Π_1. Proposition 2.2 states the conditions on $\tilde{w}_1$ and $\tilde{w}_2$ that guarantee that Π_2 is larger than Π_1. Notice that, for small risks, we can use the Arrow–Pratt approximation

$$\Pi_i \simeq \tfrac{1}{2}\sigma_i^2 A$$

to claim that $\tilde{w}_1$ is preferred to $\tilde{w}_2$ if and only if the variance of $\tilde{w}_2$ is larger than the variance of $\tilde{w}_1 : \sigma_2^2 \geqslant \sigma_1^2$. Should not it also be the case that this holds for larger risks as well? That is to say, could we not add another equivalent statement (e) to Proposition 2.2 that would be written as follows:

(e) *the variance of $\tilde{w}_2$ is larger than the variance of $\tilde{w}_1$?*

The answer is definitely no! In general, statistical moments of orders higher than 2 will matter when comparing two random variables. By limiting the development of Taylor of the utility function to the second order, the Arrow–Pratt approximation is of no value for larger risks. The only exception is when the utility function is quadratic. A correct statement would then be that all risk-averse agents *with a quadratic utility function* prefer $\tilde{w}_1$ to $\tilde{w}_2$ if and only if the variance of the second is larger than the variance of the first.[1]

However, it is easy to check that an increase in variance is a necessary, but not sufficient, condition for an increase in risk. Indeed, it is a necessary condition for those agents with a quadratic concave utility function to dislike this change in risk. Thus, it is a necessary for *all* agents with a concave function to dislike it.

It is noteworthy that the necessary condition for an increase in the variance can be can be written as

$$\sigma_2^2 - \sigma_1^2 = \int_a^b w^2(f_2(w) - f_1(w))\,\mathrm{d}w$$

$$= 2\int_a^b S(w)\,\mathrm{d}w \geqslant 0.$$

This equation is a direct consequence of equation (2.3) applied for $u(w) = w^2$. We see that the increase in variance just means that the integral of function S must be nonnegative. The Rothschild–Stiglitz increase in risk is a much stronger requirement that S be uniformly nonnegative.

---

[1] Another strategy is to limit the set of random variables to those that can be parametrized by their mean and variance only, as the set of normal distributions.

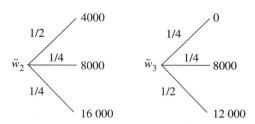

Figure 2.5.   Increase in downside risk.

2.2   Aversion to Downside Risk

In this short section, we explore another set of changes in risk which are referred to as increases in downside risk. These changes have the property that they preserve both the mean and the variance of final wealth. To illustrate, consider again the distribution of final wealth $\tilde{w}_2 \sim (4000, \frac{1}{2}; 12\,000 + \tilde{\varepsilon}, \frac{1}{2})$, with $\tilde{\varepsilon} \sim (-4000, \frac{1}{2}, 4000, \frac{1}{2})$. Sempronius faces the price risk $\tilde{\varepsilon}$ in addition to the risk of losing his single ship. Observe that this is a situation where the additional zero-mean risk $\tilde{\varepsilon}$ is borne only in the good state, i.e. when the ship arrives safely at the harbor of London. Consider an alternative situation where this zero-mean risk would be borne in the bad state. It would thus yield a final wealth distributed as $\tilde{w}_3 \sim (4000 + \tilde{\varepsilon}, \frac{1}{2}; 12\,000, \frac{1}{2})$. Which of these two distributions of final wealth do you think Sempronius would prefer? To assist you in your choice, we represent these two distribution in Figure 2.5.

Observe that the means are the same: $E\tilde{w}_2 = E\tilde{w}_3 = 8000$. The variance is also unchanged by the change in distribution: $\sigma_2^2 = \sigma_3^2 = 24 \times 10^6$. In fact, the reader can check that function S alternates in sign in the interval of final wealth levels $[0, 16\,000]$. Thus, this cannot be an increase in risk. Hence, by Proposition 2.2, some risk-averse agents will like this change, whereas others will dislike it. However, experiments have shown that most people in the real world prefer $\tilde{w}_2$ to $\tilde{w}_3$. That is to say, they prefer to bear a zero-mean risk in the wealthier state. In other words, they dislike transferring a zero-mean risk from a richer to a poorer state. In this case, we say that they are averse to downside risk.

We are interested in determining a condition on the utility function that guarantees that an agent is averse to downside risk. Suppose that the agent is initially facing a risk that is characterized by $\tilde{w} \sim (z_1, 1/n; z_2, 1/n; \ldots; z_n, 1/n)$. We assume for simplicity that these n states have the same probability of occurrence. Consider an additional risk $\tilde{\varepsilon}$ with a zero mean. The EU of final wealth depends upon the state i to which this additional risk is imposed. We denote

$$V^i = \frac{1}{n} Eu(z_i + \tilde{\varepsilon}) + \sum_{j \neq i} \frac{1}{n} u(z_j)$$

for the EU when $\tilde{\varepsilon}$ is borne in state i. Observe that

$$n(V^i - V_j) = [Eu(z_i + \tilde{\varepsilon}) - u(z_i)] - [Eu(z_j + \tilde{\varepsilon}) - u(z_j)]$$
$$= \int_{z_j}^{z_i} [Eu'(\omega + \tilde{\varepsilon}) - u'(\omega)] \, d\omega.$$

Although intuition suggests the empirical observation that $V^i > V_j$ when $z_i > z_j$, we see from the above equation that this is true if and only if

$$Eu'(\omega + \tilde{\varepsilon}) \geqslant u'(\omega)$$

for all ω. Because $\tilde{\varepsilon}$ is constrained only to have a zero mean, this condition is satisfied if and only if $u'(\cdot)$ is itself convex, i.e. if the agent is prudent. This is a direct application of Jensen's inequality. We thus obtain the following result.

Proposition 2.3. *An agent dislikes any increase in downside risk if and only if he is prudent.*

Prudence and aversion to downside risk are two equivalent concepts.

2.3   First-Degree Stochastic Dominance

Up to now, we have focused the analysis to changes in risk that preserve the mean. This is a strong requirement. For example, two portfolios with different proportions invested in stocks typically have different expected returns. Or, purchasing more insurance typically induces a reduction in expected wealth, since the insurance premium likely contains a loading. More generally, most decision making under uncertainty yields a trade-off between risk and (expected) return. In this section, we explore an important stochastic order named "First-degree Stochastic Dominance" (FSD), in which changes in mean are required.

There is often a discrepancy in the common use of the wording of "an increase in risk" between economists and the rest of the world. In common language, one often says that the risk is increased when the probability of an accident is increased. However, taken to the extreme this would imply that someone who always has an accident with the highest possible loss is the most "risky," whereas in a technical sense, there is no risk at all involved here: the lowest wealth value is realized with certainty! Of course, if the probability of an accident is increased, the expected final wealth of the risk bearer is reduced, which implies that this change in risk cannot be an increase in risk in the sense of Rothschild and Stiglitz. Economists say that the risk undergoes a dominated shift in the sense of FSD. More generally, any change in risk that is generated by a transfer of probability mass from high wealth states to low wealth states is said to be FSD-deteriorating. Such transfers of probability obviously raise $F(w)$, the probability that final wealth be no greater than than w, for all w.

Definition 2.4. $\tilde{w}_2$ is dominated by $\tilde{w}_1$ in the sense of the first-degree stochastic dominance order if $F_2(w) \geqslant F_1(w)$ for all w.

It is obvious that all consumers in the real world dislike FSD-dominated shifts in the distribution of final wealth. Rewriting condition (2.2) as

$$Eu(\tilde{w}_2) - Eu(\tilde{w}_1) = - \int_a^b u'(\omega)[F_2(\omega) - F_1(\omega)]\,d\omega, \qquad (2.4)$$

we see that $Eu(\tilde{w}_2)$ is smaller than $Eu(\tilde{w}_1)$ if $\tilde{w}_2$ is dominated by $\tilde{w}_1$ in the sense of FSD and if u' is positive. These two conditions indeed imply that the integrand of the above equation is always positive. Suppose that the only restriction that we impose on the utility function is that it be nondecreasing: more wealth is preferred to less. This means that we allow for both risk aversion and risk-loving behavior. Then, equation (2.4) tells us that $F_2 - F_1$ nonnegative is a necessary and sufficient condition for $Eu(\tilde{w}_2)$ to be smaller than $Eu(\tilde{w}_1)$. To prove this suppose by contradiction that $F_2 - F_1$ is negative in the neighborhood of some ω_0. Then, consider the nondecreasing utility function that is flat everywhere except in this neighborhood of ω_0. For this specific utility function, the integrand of (2.4) is zero everywhere except in the neighborhood of ω_0, where it is negative. Thus, the integral is negative, and this agent prefers $\tilde{w}_2$ to $\tilde{w}_1$, a contradiction. We have thus just proven the equivalence of (a) and (b) in the following proposition. The equivalence of (c) has been shown by several authors.

Proposition 2.5. *The following conditions are equivalent.*

(a) *All agents with a nondecreasing utility function prefer $\tilde{w}_1$ to $\tilde{w}_2$: $Eu(\tilde{w}_2) \leqslant Eu(\tilde{w}_1)$ for all nondecreasing functions u.*

(b) *$\tilde{w}_2$ is dominated by $\tilde{w}_1$ in the sense of FSD: $\tilde{w}_2$ is obtained from $\tilde{w}_1$ by a transfer of probability mass from the high wealth states to lower wealth states, or $F_2(\omega) \geqslant F_1(\omega)$ for all ω.*

(c) *$\tilde{w}_1$ is obtained from $\tilde{w}_2$ by adding nonnegative noise terms to the possible outcomes of $\tilde{w}_2$: $\tilde{w}_1 \overset{d}{=} \tilde{w}_2 + \tilde{\varepsilon}$, where $\tilde{\varepsilon} \geqslant 0$ with probability one.*

Without surprise, this type of change in risk, where the probability of lower wealth states is increased, is disliked by a very wide set of agents.

Of course, we can combine various changes in risk. For example, combining any FSD-dominated shift in distribution with any increase in risk yields what is called a (SSD) shift in distribution. Obviously, SSD shifts are disliked by the set of agents with a nondecreasing and concave utility function. Combining any SSD shift with any increase in downside risk yields a Third-degree Stochastically Dominated (TSD) shift in distribution. They are disliked by all prudent agents with a nondecreasing and concave utility function.

Of these three stochastic dominance orders, FSD is the most demanding one. For many applications however, it is considered to be too broad to yield unambiguous comparative static results. In the principal–agent literature, for example, one usually uses the more restrictive concept of the Monotone Likelihood Ratio (MLR) order. We say that $\tilde{w}_2$ is dominated by $\tilde{w}_1$ in the sense of MLR if $f_2(\omega)/f_1(\omega)$ is nonincreasing in ω. One can check that MLR is a special case of FSD.

2.4 Bibliographical References, Extensions and Exercises

The origin of the concepts developed in the literature on stochastic dominance can be found in an old book by famous mathematicians Hardy, Littlewood and Polya (1934). Its revival in the late 1960s is due to Hadar and Russell (1969) and Hanoch and Levy (1969) for the concepts of first-degree and second-degree stochastic dominance, while Rothschild and Stiglitz (1970) discussed mean-preserving increases in risk, a special case of SSD. Whitmore (1971) and Menezes, Geiss and Tressler (1980) were interested in third-degree stochastic dominance. The proof that diversification is liked by all risk-averse agents can be found in Samuelson (1967) and Rothschild and Stiglitz (1971).

Chapter Bibliography

Geiss, C., C. Menezes, and J. Tressler. 1980. Increasing downside risk. *American Economic Review* 70(5):921–931.

Hadar, J. and W. R. Russell. 1969. Rules for ordering uncertain prospects. *American Economic Review* 59:25–34.

Hanoch, G. and H. Levy. 1969. Efficiency analysis of choices involving risk. *Review of Economic Studies* 36:335–346.

Hardy, G. H., J. E. Littlewood and G. Polya. 1934. *Inequalities.* (Reprinted in 1997 by Cambridge University Press.)

Rothschild, M. and J. Stiglitz. 1970. Increasing risk. I. A definition. *Journal of Economic Theory* 2:225–243.

———. 1971. Increasing risk. II. Its economic consequences. *Journal of Economic Theory* 3:66–84.

Samuelson, P. A. 1967. General proof that diversification pays. *Journal of Financial and Quantitative Analysis.* 2(2):1–13.

Whitmore, G. A. 1970. Third-degree stochastic dominance. *American Economic Review* 60:457–459.

Exercises

(2.1) Consider the following two random variables: $\tilde{X}$ has a (continuous) uniform density on $[-1, +1]$, while $\tilde{Y}$ is a discrete random variable defined by $(-1, \frac{1}{2}; +1, \frac{1}{2})$.

    (a) Do $\tilde{X}$ and $\tilde{Y}$ have the same mean?

    (b) Compute their variances.

    (c) Draw their cumulative distributions.

    (d) Which random variable is riskier? Apply the 'integral condition' and also ask yourself which random variable has more weight in the center.

    (e) Find the distributions of the 'white noise' that must be added to the less risky lottery to obtain the riskier one.

(2.2) Let $\tilde{X}$ be a binomial random variable with $n = 2$ and $p = \frac{1}{2}$, while $\tilde{Y}$ is also binomial but with $n = 3$ and $p = \frac{1}{3}$.

    (a) Draw their cumulative distribution functions. Is $\tilde{Y}$ riskier than $\tilde{X}$ in the sense of Rothschild and Stiglitz?

    (b) Compute σ^2 for $\tilde{X}$ and $\tilde{Y}$. (You should of course obtain that $\sigma_{\tilde{Y}}^2$ exceeds $\sigma_{\tilde{X}}^2$.)

(2.3) Besides a certain wealth of 100, Ms. A owns one house, the value of which is 80. The probability of full loss (due to fire) for this house is equal to 0.10 for a given time period and Ms. A has no access to an insurance market. In the absence of fire, the value of the house remains equal to its initial value. Mr. B has the same initial wealth but owns two houses valued at 40 for each. The probability of full loss for each house is 0.10 and the fires are assumed to be independent random variables (e.g. because one house is in Toulouse (France) and the other one in Mons (Belgium)).

    (a) Draw the cumulative distribution functions of final wealth for Ms. A and Mr. B and compute the expected final wealth for each of them.

    (b) Show that Ms. A has a riskier portfolio of houses.

    (c) Select three (or more) concave utility functions and compute the expected utility for Ms. A and Mr. B. If you do not make mistakes, then the expected utility of Mr. B must be systematically higher than that of Ms. A for each utility curve you have selected.

(2.4) Consider lottery $\tilde{X}$ distributed as $(-10, \frac{1}{3}; 0, \frac{1}{3}; +10, \frac{1}{3})$ and a 'white noise' $\tilde{\varepsilon}$ distributed as $(-5, \frac{1}{2}; +5, \frac{1}{2})$. First generate lottery $\tilde{Y}$ by attaching the white noise to the worst outcome of $\tilde{X}$ (i.e. -10) and then generate lottery $\tilde{Z}$ by attaching the white noise instead to the best outcome of $\tilde{X}$ (i.e. $+10$).

(a) Compute $E(\tilde{Y})$, $E(\tilde{Z})$, $\mathrm{var}(\tilde{Y})$, $\mathrm{var}(\tilde{Z})$.

(b) Draw the cumulative distributions of $\tilde{Y}$ and $\tilde{Z}$. Can you say that one is riskier than the other? Why or why not?

(c) If a decision maker has a quadratic utility such as $u(w) = w - 0.01w^2$, compute $E[u(\tilde{Y})]$ and $E[u(\tilde{Z})]$. Are you surprised by the fact that $E[u(\tilde{Y})] = E[u(\tilde{Z})]$?

(d) Choose a utility function such that $u''' > 0$ and then show that

$$E[u(\tilde{Y})] < E[u(\tilde{Z})].$$

(2.5) A corporation must decide between two mutually exclusive projects. Both projects require an initial outlay of 100 million euro, and they generate cash flows that are independent of the growth of the economy. Project A has an equal probability of four gross payoffs: 80 million euro, 100 million euro, 120 million euro or 140 million euro. Project B has a 50:50 chance of paying either 90 million euro or 130 million euro. Assuming that shareholders are all risk averse, show that they unanimously prefer Project B to Project A.

Part II

Risk Management

3

Insurance Decisions

Insurance occurs when one party agrees to pay an indemnity to another party in case of the occurrence of a prespecified random event generating a loss for the initial risk-bearer. The most common example is an insurance policy, where the insurer is compensated by being paid a fixed premium by the policyholder. But many other contracts involve some form of insurance. For example, in share-cropping contracts, a landlord agrees to reduce the rent for his land in case of a low crop yield. In cost-plus contracts, a buyer agrees to pay a higher price if the producer incurs an unexpected increase in cost. In the case of income taxes, the state partially insures the losses of taxpayers by reducing the tax payment when incomes are low.

The shifting of risk is of considerable importance for the functioning of our modern economies.[1] Insurance allows for disentangling investment decisions from risk-taking decisions. Without it, we would certainly not have experienced the historical economic growth of the last century. Ford, Solvay, Rockefeller and others would not have taken the investment risks that they actually took without the possibility of sharing the risk with shareholders and insurers. Similarly, many consumers may not purchase new expensive cars or houses if they do not have a possibility of insuring them. Without an acceptable social net, young people would not engage in profitable but very risky investments in their human capital or in risky professional activities where their talents would most likely be recognized.

By pooling the risks of many policyholders, the insurer can take advantage of the Law of Large Numbers. So long as there is not much correlation between the insured risks of different policyholders, the insurer can diversify its risk. It is often convenient to think of the insurer as risk neutral: only the level of expected profits is what matters to the insurer. Indeed, the insurer might be thought of as a type of intermediary who collects and disperses funds amongst the policyholders. So in some sense, it is essentially the policyholders who are insuring one another. This concept is often referred to as the mutuality principle.

---

[1] Apparently, it was important in ancient economies as well. For example, ancient Chinese, Babylonian, Greek and Roman cultures had various types of insurance and risk-sharing arrangements. See Outreville (1997).

Insurance is a particular example of a type of risk-transfer strategy known as hedging. Hedging strategies typically involve entering into contracts whose payoffs are negatively related to one's overall wealth or to one component of that wealth. Thus, for example, if wealth falls, the value of the contract rises, partially offsetting the loss in wealth. For instance, one might enter into contracts in the futures market to hedge against exchange-rate risk, when part of one's income is in a foreign currency. Or one might use an option contract on the Standard and Poor (S&P) 500 Index to protect a pension fund against a precipitous fall in the value of stocks. Such options and futures contracts are typically based on financial-market data. Moreover, they contain various standardized attributes which make them fairly "liquid" assets, i.e. which allow them to be readily bought and sold in the market place. However, these hedging instruments typically entail another type of risk called a basis risk, which is a risk that the payoff does not offset losses exactly. For example, the value of one's pension fund is not likely to be perfectly correlated with the S&P 500 Index, and hence index options will be an imperfect hedge.

Unlike these contracts, insurance is based on the level of one's own individual loss rather than some index. Since there is no financial market for this unique loss, insurance contracts are not easily tradeable in secondary markets, and transaction costs are high. Even if a policyholder needed more insurance for her home, it would not help her to buy your homeowners' insurance policy, since your policy will only pay when you have a loss, rather than when the policyholder has a loss. Thus, there is no secondary market for insurance contracts. In other words, compared to options and futures contracts, insurance is a rather "illiquid" asset. At the same time, insurance is a perfect hedge—the insurance indemnity is based on the occurrence of a prespecified loss. Insurance contracts do not contain the basis risk, which is prevalent in options and futures contacts.[2]

There is an added value to the policyholder from insurance because policyholders are risk-averse, that is they dislike risk on their wealth. Consider an individual facing a random loss $\tilde{x}$ to her wealth, where $\tilde{x} \geqslant 0$. An insurance contract stipulates a premium to be paid by the policyholder, P, and an indemnity schedule, $I(x)$, which indicates the amount to be paid by the insurer for a loss of size x. There is full coverage if the insurer reimburses the policyholder for the full value of any loss, so that $I(\cdot)$ is the identity function, $I(x) = x$. The actuarial value of the contract is the expected indemnity $EI(\tilde{x})$, which is the expected gross payoff from the insurance contract. The insurance premium is said to be actuarially fair (or often just "fair") if it is equal to the actuarial value of the contract, i.e. $P = EI(\tilde{x})$.

---

[2]At least, there is no basis risk in theory. In reality, the exact value of a loss is often not perfectly observable, or else subject to some debate. Likewise, insurance companies might not have sufficient funds to pay all of their liabilities. These possibilities would introduce a type of basis risk, but are ignored here in modeling a theory of insurance contracts.

Table 3.1. Sempronius's EU as a function of his insurance coverage I.

I	P	EU
0	0	86.395
1000	550	86.856
2000	1100	87.202
3000	1650	87.439
4000	2200	87.576
5000	2750	87.617
6000	3300	87.564
7000	3850	87.418
8000	4400	87.178

When the premium is fair, the expected net payoff on the insurance contract is zero. The purchase of a full insurance contract at an actuarially fair premium has the effect of replacing a random loss $\tilde{x}$ by its expectation $P = E\tilde{x}$. The private value of such a contract is equal to the value of the Arrow–Pratt risk premium attached to the risk $\tilde{x}$ by the policyholder. Indeed, if we let Π denote this Arrow–Pratt risk premium, then the maximum premium the individual would be willing to pay for a full-coverage insurance policy is $P = E\tilde{x} + \Pi$. This maximum premium increases with the policyholder's degree of risk aversion and with the riskiness of the loss. In other words, buying full insurance at a fair price would provide the policy owner with a surplus value of Π, compared with the case of having no insurance.

When insurance prices are actuarially fair, the insurance decision is simple for risk-averse agents: full insurance is optimal, as we show below. But insurance contracts typically entail transaction costs in the real world. In many lines of casualty insurance, for example, transaction costs may be as much as 30% of the premium. When we add these costs into the picture, the optimal insurance decision is less obvious, since risk-averse policyholders must compare the marginal cost of more insurance to its marginal benefit, coming from the risk reduction of the contract. In other words, there is a trade-off between risk and expected final wealth. This chapter is mainly devoted to the analysis of this trade-off.

3.1 Optimal Insurance: an Illustration

In this section, we examine the insurance problem faced by Sempronius when he has only one ship. He has an initial wealth of 4000 ducats that would be increased by 8000 ducats only if his ship arrives safely. Both the insurers and Sempronius evaluate the probability of this event to be equal to $\frac{1}{2}$. The insurers, who can diversify Sempronius's risk among a large set of shareholders, are assumed to be risk neutral. They offer a menu of insurance policies. A specific policy is fully described first by

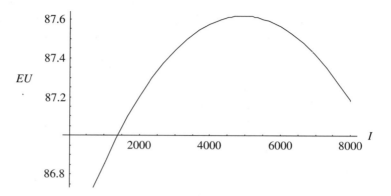

Figure 3.1. Sempronius's expected utility as a function of his insurance coverage.

the indemnity I that is paid to Sempronius if his ship is sunk, and second, by the insurance premium P. In expectation, insurers will have to pay $I/2$ to Sempronius as an indemnity. $I/2$ is called the actuarial value of the policy. In addition to the indemnity, insurers bear various costs that have been evaluated to represent 10% of the actuarial value of the policy. Because insurance markets are competitive, an equilibrium condition is that the expected profits be zero. This yields the following insurance tariff:

$$P(I) = (I/2) + 0.1(I/2) = 0.55I.$$

This implies that Sempronius's expected wealth is decreasing with his insurance coverage:

$$\text{expected wealth} = 8000 - 0.05I.$$

Sempronius must decide which insurance policy to purchase. Suppose that Sempronius has a square-root utility function $u(z) = \sqrt{z}$. In Table 3.1 and in Figure 3.1, we compute Sempronius's EU as a function of the indemnity I. It equals

$$EU = \tfrac{1}{2}\sqrt{4000 + I - P(I)} + \tfrac{1}{2}\sqrt{12\,000 - P(I)}.$$

We see that purchasing some insurance increases Sempronius's EU. The positive effect of reducing risk dominates the negative effect of reducing expected wealth. However, a closer look at these data shows that some insurance coverages are better than others. When I is small, a marginal increase in the insurance coverage has a net positive effect on Sempronius's EU. But when I is large, the opposite happens. The EU is concave in I. Its representation in Figure 3.1 is hump-shaped, with a maximum at $I^* = 4929.29$ ducats.

It is important to understand why EU is not a monotonic function of the insurance coverage. We stressed in Chapter 1 that the cost of risk is approximately proportional to the square of the size of risk. If Sempronius purchases an insurance policy

$(I, P(I))$, the variance of final wealth equals $(4000 - I/2)^2$. Using the Arrow–Pratt approximation, the cost of the uninsured risk is porportional to this variance. It implies that the marginal benefit of insurance, which is to marginally reduce the size of the uninsured risk, decreases linearly as insurance coverage increases. The marginal benefit is in fact approximately proportional to the derivative of the variance with respect to I, i.e. it is approximately proportional to $4000 - I/2$. When Sempronius is almost fully insured, i.e. when I is close to 8000, raising the coverage to full insurance has no benefit. Risk aversion is a second-order effect.

The cost of insurance equals the sure reduction of wealth corresponding to the deadweight transaction cost. It equals $\frac{1}{2}\lambda I = 0.05I$. The marginal cost of insurance is therefore a constant independent of the level of coverage I. Combining these observations explains why EU is hump-shaped with respect to the level of coverage, as shown in Figure 3.1.

3.2 Optimal Coinsurance

Consider a risk-averse agent with initial wealth w_0 bearing a risk of loss $\tilde{x}$. Contrary to the illustration presented in the previous section, $\tilde{x}$ need not to be a binary random variable. Suppose that, for each euro of indemnity paid by the insurance policy, the insurer incurs a cost λ of deadweight transaction costs, including implicit costs. Obviously, more complex cost structures are also possible. Adding these transaction costs to the expected costs of the indemnity itself, the premium for insurance indemnity schedule $I(\cdot)$ must be equal to $P = (1 + \lambda)EI(\tilde{x})$. The level λ is often referred to as the loading factor, or the loading for profit and expenses. Thus, if expenses amount to 10 cents for each euro of indemnity, the competitive insurer will add 10% to the actuarial value of an insurance policy, in order to cover these expenses.

When the loss variable $\tilde{x}$ is not binary, covering the risk can take many different forms characterized by function $I(\cdot)$. One that applies in many cases and is the easiest to work with from a modeling standpoint is a so-called coinsurance policy. That is, suppose that for a fixed premium the insurer agrees to reimburse the individual for a fixed fraction, β, of the loss. Thus $I(x) = \beta x$ for all x. The level β is called the coinsurance rate, while $1 - \beta$ is called the retention rate, since the policyholder retains this fraction of the loss. Quite often, β may be restricted, such as requiring $0 \leqslant \beta \leqslant 1$, though this need not be the case.

The coinsurance rate β is chosen *a priori* by the policyholder, given the following insurance pricing rule:

$$P(\beta) = (1 + \lambda)EI(\tilde{x}) = \beta P_0, \tag{3.1}$$

where $P_0 = (1 + \lambda) E\tilde{x}$ is the full insurance premium. The random final wealth of the policyholder with loss $\tilde{x}$ and coinsurance rate β equals

$$\tilde{y} \equiv y(\tilde{x}, \beta) \equiv w_0 - \beta P_0 - (1 - \beta)\tilde{x}. \tag{3.2}$$

Note that when $\beta = 1$, we have full insurance coverage, and final wealth is non-random, $y(\tilde{x}, \beta) = w_0 - P_0$. On the other hand, when $\beta = 0$ we have the case where no coverage is purchased. The decision problem of the policyholder is to select an optimal coinsurance rate β^*.

Given this decision problem, the policyholder selects the coinsurance rate which maximizes the EU of her final wealth:

$$\max_{\beta} H(\beta) \equiv Eu(\tilde{y}) = Eu(w_0 - \beta P_0 - (1 - \beta)\tilde{x}). \tag{3.3}$$

Differentiating the objective function H twice with respect to β yields

$$H'(\beta) = \frac{\partial Eu(\tilde{y})}{\partial \beta} = E[(\tilde{x} - P_0)u'(\tilde{y})] \tag{3.4}$$

and

$$H''(\beta) = \frac{\partial^2 Eu(\tilde{y})}{\partial \beta^2} = E[(\tilde{x} - P_0)^2 u''(\tilde{y})]. \tag{3.5}$$

Observe that H'' is the expectation of the product of $(\tilde{x} - P_0)^2$, which is always positive, and $u''(\tilde{y})$, which is always negative, by risk aversion. Thus, H'' is the expectation of something which is negative with probability 1. It is therefore negative. This means that the EU of the policyholder is a concave function of the coinsurance rate. As for Sempronius's insurance problem, the EU is hump-shaped with respect to the level of insurance that is measured here by β. It follows that the first-order condition

$$H'(\beta^*) = E[(\tilde{x} - P_0)u'(\tilde{y})] = 0 \tag{3.6}$$

is both necessary and sufficient for the maximization program (3.3). The fact that (3.5) is negative for all β and not just for β^* turns out to be important in our comparative static analyses below.

We can obtain some important insights by examining the sign of $\partial Eu(\tilde{y})/\partial \beta$ evaluated at $\beta = 1$:

$$H'(1) = E[(\tilde{x} - P_0)u'(w_0 - P_0)] = -\lambda u'(w_0 - P_0)E\tilde{x}. \tag{3.7}$$

This implies two important results. First, suppose that there are no transaction costs in the insurance process: $\lambda = 0$. In such a situation, $H'(1) = 0$ and the first-order condition (3.6) is satisfied with $\beta^* = 1$. In other words, when there is no insurance loading, the optimal contract is full insurance. This result is hardly surprising. When

$\lambda = 0$, (3.1) and (3.2) together imply that $E\tilde{y} = Ey(\tilde{x}, \beta)$ is constant for all values of β. In other words, expected final wealth is not affected by our insurance choice. Therefore, a risk averter will prefer this expected wealth level with no risk at all, which is achievable by purchasing full insurance.

Suppose alternatively that there are nonzero transaction costs to the insurance process, $\lambda > 0$. This implies, from (3.7), that $H'(1)$ is negative. This means that reducing the rate of coverage from 100% to a marginally smaller rate raises the policyholder's EU. Since H'' is negative, so that $H(\beta)$ is strictly concave, it follows that the β^* at which H' vanishes must be less than one. In other words, $\beta^* < 1$ and it is optimal for the policyholder to retain some of the risk. These results are summarized in the following proposition, which is sometimes known as Mossin's Theorem.

Proposition 3.1 (Mossin's Theorem). *Full insurance* ($\beta^* = 1$) *is optimal at an actuarially fair price,* $\lambda = 0$, *while partial coverage* ($\beta^* < 1$) *is optimal if the premium includes a positive loading,* $\lambda > 0$.

When λ is positive, one might believe that full insurance could still be optimal if the degree of risk aversion of the policyholder is sufficiently high. However, this intuition is not correct, as shown in the above proposition. The reason is that risk aversion is a second-order phenomenon, as reflected in the Arrow–Pratt approximation of the risk premium. For a very small level of risk, individual behavior towards risk approaches risk neutrality. By retaining some of the risk, $(1 - \beta) > 0$, the policyholder will save on transaction costs, thereby increasing her expected final wealth, which of course is beneficial if someone is risk neutral. When β tends to unity, this first-order effect must dominate the second-order effect of increasing the retained risk. Thus, full insurance will not be optimal.[3]

At the other extreme, when $\lambda > 0$ it may turn out to be the case that β^* is very small. If we restrict $\beta \geqslant 0$, then the first-order condition (3.6) might not hold for any value of β in our restricted range. In this case, we might find $H'(0) \leqslant 0$. Since $H(\beta)$ is strictly concave, we thus obtain a corner solution of no insurance, $\beta^* = 0$.

To illustrate this more clearly, let us examine the sign of $\partial Eu(\tilde{y})/\partial\beta$ evaluated at $\beta = 0$:

$$H'(0) = E[(\tilde{x} - P_0)u'(w_0 - \tilde{x})] = -\lambda E\tilde{x}Eu'(w_0 - \tilde{x}) + \text{cov}(\tilde{x}, u'(w_0 - \tilde{x})). \quad (3.8)$$

The covariance term is clearly positive, since u is concave due to risk aversion. The term $E\tilde{x}Eu'(w_0 - \tilde{x})$ is also positive. Since the loading factor λ only appears once, in a multiplicative fashion, in the right-hand side of (3.8), we see that $H'(0) > 0$ for

---

[3]This behavior results not just in EU models with differentiable utility functions, but in any model exhibiting what is known as risk aversion of order 2, as defined by Segal and Spivak (1990).

$\lambda = 0$. Also, $H'(0)$ is linearly decreasing in λ and will be negative for all $\lambda > \lambda^*$, where

$$\lambda^* = \frac{\text{cov}(\tilde{x}, u'(w_0 - \tilde{x}))}{E\tilde{x}Eu'(w_0 - \tilde{x})}.$$

Thus, we see that whenever insurance is too expensive, in particular whenever $\lambda \geqslant \lambda^*$, no coverage will be optimal.

If we do not make the restriction that insurance be nonnegative, $\beta \geqslant 0$, then we would have $\beta^* < 0$ whenever $\lambda > \lambda^*$. Such contracts typically are not available in the insurance market, but are interesting to consider nonetheless. When the premium loading λ is excessively high, $\lambda > \lambda^*$, the policy owner would rather take a bet that her loss will occur than purchase insurance. She is willing to take on added risk (rather than insuring) in order to increase her expected final wealth. In a sense, the individual has what is known in the finance jargon as a "short position" in her insurance policy.[4] Of course, if we do impose the restriction that $\beta \geqslant 0$, then the optimal coverage level will be $\beta = 0$, which follows from the concavity of $H(\beta)$ and the condition that $H'(0) < 0$.

In some cases, one can link transaction costs to undiversifiable risks. Obviously, many natural, environmental or technological risks are in the class of large risks that are difficult to eliminate by using the mutuality principle. We may question the insurer's risk-neutrality for these risks. Insurance companies will not provide fair insurance premia for them. Indeed, shareholders will not be able to diversify the risk associated with the dividends paid by the insurance companies that cover these large risks. Shareholders will ask for a risk premium, which will increase the cost of funds for these companies. This cost will be passed on to policyholders through a larger premium rate for the component of individual risk that is systematic. This larger premium in turn will provide an incentive for the policyholders to retain a larger part of their individual risks. In short, the fact that the risk is systematic induces insurance premia to contain a positive loading that has an effect equivalent to a transaction cost. In many instances, this effect can be so large as to preclude a market for insurance, or at least hinder it. For example, after the events of 11 September, 2001, many businesses had insurance policies canceled or else found premium increases too high to afford insurance. Also, insurance for many natural disasters requires a high level of coinsurance in order to obtain any coverage at all.

---

[4]In the market for life insurance, fairly new products known as viaticals and life settlements are essentially short positions in insurance policies. These contracts, which typically are designed for the terminally ill, pay the policyholder a lump sum of money now (akin to receiving an insurance premium), in return for a promise by the policyholder to pay a fixed sum of money upon his or her death. Of course, this payment is financed via the death-benefit proceeds of an existing life insurance policy.

3.3 Comparative Statics in the Coinsurance Problem

We examine the effect of a change in various parameters of the problem on the optimal coinsurance rate β^*. One natural question is about the effect of an increase in risk aversion on insurance demand. Intuition suggests that if agent 1 is more risk-averse than agent 2, agent 1 should have a larger insurance demand than agent 2. This intuition is correct, as stated in the following proposition.

Proposition 3.2. *Consider two utility functions u_1 and u_2 that are increasing and concave, and suppose that u_1 is more risk averse than u_2 in the sense of Arrow and Pratt. Then, the optimal coinsurance rate β^* is higher for u_1 than for u_2 : $\beta_1^* \geqslant \beta_2^*$.*

Proof. If $\lambda = 0$, then $\beta_1^* = \beta_2^* = 1$ by Proposition 3.1, and hence we are done. Suppose that $\lambda > 0$ and let β_1^* be optimal for u_1. Define $y_0 = w - P_0$ and note that $y_0 = w - (1 - \beta_1^*)x - \beta_1^* P_0$ evaluated at $x = P_0$. Without loss of generality, suppose that $u_1'(y_0) = u_2'(y_0)$. Because u_1 is more concave than u_2 in the sense of Arrow and Pratt, it must be the case that $u_1'(y) \geqslant u_2'(y)$ for all y smaller than y_0 (i.e. for all $x > P_0$), and $u_1'(y) \leqslant u_2'(y)$ for all y larger than y_0 (i.e. for all $x < P_0$). This implies that

$$(x - P_0)u_2'(w_0 - (1 - \beta_1^*)x - \beta_1^* P_0)$$
$$\leqslant (x - P_0)u_1'(w_0 - (1 - \beta_1^*)x - \beta_1^* P_0) \quad \text{for all } x.$$

It follows that

$$H_2'(\beta_1^*) = E[(\tilde{x} - P_0)u_2'(w_0 - (1 - \beta_1^*)\tilde{x} - \beta_1^* P_0)]$$
$$\leqslant E[(\tilde{x} - P_0)u_1'(w_0 - (1 - \beta_1^*)\tilde{x} - \beta_1^* P_0)] = 0.$$

The last equality follows from the first-order condition for the optimality of β_1^*. Hence, since H is concave, it follows that $\beta_2^* \leqslant \beta_1^*$. This concludes the proof. $\square$

If an increase in risk aversion raises the demand for insurance, it is natural that an increase in initial wealth w_0 reduces the demand for insurance if absolute risk aversion is decreasing (DARA). This is shown in the following result.

Proposition 3.3. *An increase in initial wealth will*

(i) *decrease the optimal rate of coinsurance β^* if u exhibits decreasing absolute risk aversion;*

(ii) *increase the optimal rate of coinsurance β^* if u exhibits increasing absolute risk aversion;*

(iii) *cause no change in the optimal rate of coinsurance β^* if u exhibits constant absolute risk aversion.*

Proof. We show here the proof for the first case, decreasing absolute risk aversion. The proofs for the other two cases are similar. Let β^* be optimal for $w = w_0$. Now consider

$$\frac{\partial H'(\beta)}{\partial w} = E[(\tilde{x} - P_0)u''(\tilde{y})]. \tag{3.9}$$

Since H is strictly concave in β, we only need to show that (3.9) is negative when evaluated at β^*. This will imply that the coinsurance level β^* is too high as wealth increases from w_0. To see why this is indeed the case, recall that DARA implies that $-u'$ has the properties of a risk-averse utility function and is more risk-averse than u. Now, note that

$$\frac{\partial E[-u'(\tilde{y})]}{\partial \beta} = -E[(\tilde{x} - P_0)u''(\tilde{y})],$$

which equals the right-hand side of (3.9) in absolute value, but is opposite in sign. By the previous proposition, we know that the level of coinsurance for $-u'$ is higher than the level for u. This implies that $-E[(\tilde{x} - P_0)u''(\tilde{y})] > 0$ when evaluated at $\beta = \beta^*$. In turn, it follows that (3.9) is negative at $\beta = \beta^*$. This concludes the proof.   □

We need to state a couple of caveats here. First, we need to point out that utility need not satisfy any of the conditions (i)–(iii) above. That is, preferences might exhibit decreasing risk aversion at some wealth levels and increasing risk aversion at others. Also, since decreasing absolute risk aversion is a fairly common assumption, it is often said that insurance is an "inferior good," since demand decreases with wealth. However, it is important here to stress the *ceteris paribus* assumption that the increase in initial wealth does not modify the size of the risk borne by the policyholder. In the real world, wealthier consumers typically purchase bigger houses and more valuable cars. This tends to increase their optimal insurance budget in spite of the fact that their demand for insurance per unit of risk is decreasing. This can explain why the insurance sector has largely benefitted from the economic growth since the industrial revolution. This is not contradictory to the above proposition.

Having examined the effect of changes in wealth on the demand for insurance, we can now easily look at how an increase in the price of insurance coverage affects demand. In particular, the following proposition examines the effects of an increase in the loading factor.

Proposition 3.4. *An increase in the premium loading factor $\lambda \geqslant 0$ will cause the optimal rate of coinsurance β^* to*

   (i) *decrease if u exhibits constant or increasing absolute risk aversion;*

   (ii) *possibly increase and possibly decrease if u exhibits decreasing absolute risk aversion.*

Proof. Differentiate $H'(\beta)$ with respect to (w.r.t.) λ to obtain

$$\frac{\partial H'(\beta)}{\partial \lambda} = -E\tilde{x}Eu'(\tilde{y}) - \beta E\tilde{x}E[(\tilde{x} - P_0)u''(\tilde{y})]. \tag{3.10}$$

The first term on the right-hand side of (3.10) is a negative substitution effect. When insurance becomes more expensive, we substitute away from insurance and towards other goods. However, a higher loading factor also induces a wealth effect, which is captured by the second term. Indeed, note that we may use the previous proposition to rewrite this term as

$$-\beta E\tilde{x}E[(\tilde{x} - P_0)u''(\tilde{y})] = -\beta E\tilde{x}\frac{\partial H'(\beta)}{\partial w}.$$

Clearly (3.10) will be negative whenever the second term is negative or zero, which occurs when u exhibits increasing and constant absolute risk aversion, respectively. However, if u exhibits decreasing absolute risk aversion, then the wealth effect is positive: because the increase in λ makes the consumer "poorer," the individual behaves in a more risk aversion fashion and demands more insurance. Thus, the total effect on insurance demand depends on the relative magnitudes of the income and substitution effects. $\square$

Note that, under the fairly common assumption of DARA, insurance might well be a Giffen good, that is a good whose demand increases when price rises.[5]

Since an increase in risk aversion leads to an increased demand for insurance, it might seem natural to assume that an increase in the riskiness of the loss also should cause policyholders to increase their demand for insurance. However, this statement is not true in general. We know from Rothschild and Stiglitz that an increase in the riskiness of the loss $\tilde{x}$ would cause the EU to fall, so that the policy owner will be worse off. But this does not mean that more insurance will necessarily be purchased. Notice first that a mean-preserving risk increase of the loss $\tilde{x}$ has no effect on the insurance premium βP_0, since it is by assumption based on the expected loss $E\tilde{x}$.

From Rothschild and Stiglitz (1970), we know that a mean-preserving increase in the riskiness of $\tilde{x}$ will always lead to a decrease in $E\phi(\tilde{x})$ if and only if $\phi(x)$ is a concave function. Define

$$\phi(x) \equiv (x - P_0)u'(w_0 - \beta P_0 - (1 - \beta)x).$$

From (3.6) it follows that an increase in the riskiness of $\tilde{x}$ will always lead to a decrease in β^* if and only if $\phi(x)$ as defined above is concave. However, it is straightforward to show that this need not be the case. The fact that an increase in risk does not always lead to a higher demand for insurance was first discussed

---

[5]Conditions that are both necessary and sufficient for insurance not to be a Giffen good are given by Brys, Dionne and Eeckhoudt (1989).

by Rothschild and Stiglitz (1971). The surprising result is that an increase in the risk of loss makes all risk-averse policyholders worse off, but some of them may well reduce their demand for insurance as a reaction to this change. Several authors have restricted the set of acceptable increases in risk or the set of acceptable utility functions in order to get an unambiguous effect.[6]

3.4   The Optimality of Deductible Insurance

There are various ways for policyholders to retain a share of the risk. One of the most common is to accept a straight deductible, in which the indemnity is either zero if the loss is less than a prespecified deductible level, or the loss minus the deductible level otherwise. Alternatively, the insurance contract can contain a coinsurance rule in which case the indemnity is a prespecified percentage of the loss, as we examined in the previous section. Other contractual forms of the indemnity also can be considered, such as upper limits on indemnities and so-called disappearing deductibles. For example, in the area of liability insurance, losses might not be bounded in size. Thus, we find upper-limit policies—policies in which the insurer pays full insurance but with a cap on the maximum indemnity—to be quite common in this line of insurance. Moreover, there is no reason to assume that the above mentioned types of contractual forms are mutually exclusive. For instance, in the area of health insurance, we might find contracts that contain a deductible for each claim, a level of coinsurance above the deductible, and an upper limit that puts a cap on the aggregate indemnity.

Under a reasonable set of conditions, the optimal insurance contract always takes the form of a straight deductible. Any non-deductible insurance contract is dominated by a straight deductible contract with the same actuarial value. Deductibles provide the best compromise between the willingness to cover the risk and the limitation of the insurance deadweight cost. This result is due to Arrow (1971).

To understand more exactly why deductible policies are preferred, consider a model where the risk of loss $\tilde{x}$ may take a finite number of possible values

$$\{x_1, \ldots, x_n\}.$$

The uncertainty is represented by a vector of probabilities $(p_1, \ldots, p_n)$, where

$$p_i = \Pr[\tilde{x} = x_i] > 0 \quad \text{and} \quad \sum_i p_i = 1.$$

Without losing generality, assume that $x_1 < x_2 < \cdots < x_n$. A contract is characterized by a premium P and indemnity schedule $I(\cdot)$. This means that, for each loss x_i, the insurance contract stipulates the indemnity $I(x_i)$ to be paid by the insurer in

---

[6]A review of much of this literature can be found in Eeckhoudt and Gollier (2000).

such a circumstance. As before, we assume that the insurance premium is to be paid *ex ante* by the policyholder and is proportional to the actuarial value of the policy: $P = (1 + \lambda)EI(\tilde{x})$. The final wealth y of the policyholder, after purchasing policy (P, I) is

$$y(x) = w_0 - P - x + I(x), \tag{3.11}$$

if loss x occurs.

Finally, one generally assumes that insurance markets are constrained to provide policies with nondecreasing and nonnegative indemnity schedules, $I(x) \geqslant 0$ for all x. In other words, *ex post* contributions from the policyholder are prohibited. There is a technical justification for imposing this constraint. Indeed, the condition $\lambda > 0$ is not realistic when the indemnity is negative. In this case, the *ex post* contribution of the policyholder would *reduce* transaction costs!

Proposition 3.5. *Suppose a risk-averse policyholder selects an insurance contract* $(P, I(\cdot))$ *with* $P = (1 + \lambda)EI(\tilde{x})$ *and with* $I(x)$ *nondecreasing and* $I(x) \geqslant 0$ *for all* x. *Then the optimal contract contains a straight deductible* D; *that is* $I(x) = \max(0, x - D)$.

Proof. Suppose we have a deductible policy $(P, I(\cdot))$, so that $I(x_i) = 0$ for $x_i \leqslant D$ and $I(x_i) = x_i - D$ for $x_i > D$. We will show that any other indemnity schedule must cause wealth to be riskier in the sense of Rothschild and Stiglitz (1970), and hence must be less preferred by the policyholder. Consider an alternative insurance contract $(P, \hat{I}(\cdot))$ with the same premium P. By our pricing assumption, we know that $E\hat{I}(\tilde{x}) = P/(1 + \lambda)$, which is constant for a fixed P. Thus, if we increase the indemnity for one loss level, we must decrease it for others in order to preserve the mean indemnity.

Consider an increase in the indemnity for some loss level x_j by some amount $\varepsilon_j > 0$, so that $\hat{I}(x_j) = I(x_j) + \varepsilon_j$. First note that, since the indemnity must be nonnegative, $\hat{I}(x_i)$ cannot be reduced for any loss $x_i \leqslant D$. We thus must decrease the indemnity for one or more loss levels $x_i > D$ by amounts ε_i, where $p_j \varepsilon_j = \sum p_i \varepsilon_i$. This leads to the following changes in final wealth.

At x_j: $\hat{y}(x_j) = y(x_j) + \varepsilon_j$, with $y(x_j) = w_0 - P - z_j$, $z_j = \min(x_j, D)$.
At each x_i: $\hat{y}(x_i) = y(x_i) - \varepsilon_i$, with $y(x_i) = w_0 - P - D \leqslant y(x_j)$.

The new indemnity schedule $\hat{I}$ yields a reduction in wealth in states i, where wealth is small, and it yields an increase in wealth where it is large. Thus, it amounts to a mean-preserving increase in risk. It follows that any indemnity schedule $\hat{I}(\cdot)$ will be dominated by the deductible schedule $I(\cdot)$ with the same premium. Since we can make this argument for any level of the insurance premium P, this concludes the proof. $\qquad\square$

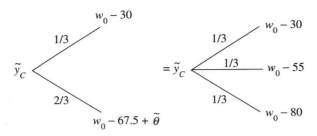

Figure 3.2. A deductible policy dominates coinsurance.

The idea of the proof is intuitive. One way to modify a deductible policy without changing the insurance budget of the policyholder is to reduce the indemnity when the loss exceeds the deductible in order to increase it when the loss is smaller than the deductible. This change reduces final wealth at low wealth levels, and it raises it at larger wealth levels. This yields a mean-preserving spread in final wealth. Notice that this result is proven on the basis that policyholders dislike mean-preserving spreads of final wealth. Therefore, this proposition does not rely on EU per se. Any model in which risk-averse agents dislike mean-preserving spreads will lead to the same conclusion, that deductibles are optimal, even if we do not invoke the EU hypothesis as a basis for decision making.

To illustrate this result and the way it was proven, let us consider the case of a loss $\tilde{x}$, which takes on the values 0, 50 and 100, each with equal probabilities. Assuming $\lambda = 0.2$, a contract with a pure coinsurance rate of 50%, i.e. with $I(x) = x/2$, can be purchased for a premium $P = 30$. Alternatively, a contract with a straight deductible $D = 37.5$ also would have a premium equal to $P = 30$. Final wealth under the deductible policy is given by the lottery $\tilde{y}_D \equiv (w_0 - 30, \frac{1}{3}; w_0 - 67.5, \frac{2}{3})$. Now define $\tilde{\theta} = (+12.5, \frac{1}{2}; -12.5, \frac{1}{2})$. Note that $E\tilde{\theta} = 0$. Final wealth under the coinsurance policy can be written as

$$\tilde{y}_C \equiv (w_0 - 30, \tfrac{1}{3}; w_0 - 67.5 + \tilde{\theta}, \tfrac{2}{3}) = (w_0 - 30, \tfrac{1}{3}; w_0 - 55, \tfrac{1}{3}; w_0 - 80).$$

The final wealth distribution is illustrated in Figure 3.2. Observe how the wealth distribution under coinsurance in Figure 3.2 shows how $\tilde{y}_C$ can be obtained by adding the noise term $\tilde{\theta}$ to the lowest realization of random wealth for the deductible policy, $y_D \equiv w_0 - 67.5$. Since this noise has a zero mean, the wealth distribution under coinsurance in Figure 3.2 is more risky in the sense of Rothschild and Stiglitz. We conclude that a contract with a 50% coinsurance rate will never be purchased, as it is dominated by a contract with a straight deductible for the same premium.

The intuition of the proposition also follows directly from its proof. A straight deductible insurance policy efficiently concentrates the effort of indemnification on only the largest losses. Any other insurance contract will compensate more for lower loss levels, while necessarily reducing the indemnity for some of the larger losses.

The optimality of a straight deductible underscores the relevance of insurance for large risks. Small risks, i.e. risks whose largest potential loss is less than the optimal deductible should not be insured. The same principle applies to buying insurance for differing types of losses when they are covered under different insurance policies. A parent is very willing to purchase life insurance against the important risk of a premature death. A homeowner is willing to purchase insurance for his or her house, which might be their most valuable physical asset. The owner of a new car is likely desirous of insurance to protect against damages, whereas the owner of an old car with much wear and tear might decide that insurance is simply not worth the cost.

3.5 Bibliographical References, Extensions and Exercises

The coinsurance problem was first examined by Mossin (1968). There have been many papers about the effect of a change in the distribution of a risk on its optimal exposure. Rothschild and Stiglitz (1971) were the first to observe that an increase in risk does not necessarily reduce the optimal demand for it by risk-averse agents. Gollier (1995) derived a necessary and sufficient condition on the change in the distribution of a risk to guarantee that all risk-averse consumers reduce their exposure to this risk. Milgrom (1981), Landsberger and Meilijson (1990) and Ormiston and Schlee (1993) showed that all shifts in distribution that satisfy the Monotone Likelihood Ratio (MLR) order have this property. Eeckhoudt and Gollier (1995) and Athey (2002) extended this result to the Monotone Probability Ratio (MPR) order. A change in distribution satisfies the MLR (resp. MPR) order if the ratio of the densities (resp. cumulative probabilities) is monotone with the realization of the random variable. Meyer and Ormiston (1985) found that all strong increases in risk (SIR) also generate this result. An SIR is a mean-preserving spread in which all of the probability mass that is moved is transferred *outside* the initial support of the distribution.

The important result on the optimality of deductibles by Arrow (1971) has been followed by many others. Raviv (1979), Huberman, Mayers and Smith (1983) and Spaeter and Roger (1997), for example, provided alternative proofs to the result and extended it to include more general insurance pricing. Zilcha and Chew (1990), Karni (1992), Machina (1995) and Gollier and Schlesinger (1996) provided various proofs that do not use any specific decision criterion. They just rely on the assumption that policyholders dislike mean-preserving spreads in the distribution of final wealth. Gollier (1987) relaxed the constraint that the indemnity must be nonnegative in all states of nature.

In this chapter, we assumed that the distribution of the loss is exogenous and common knowledge, and that losses are observable by the two parties. In many instances, the risk is affected by some preventive actions of the policyholder. If the insurer cannot observe these actions, they face the moral hazard problem. When the distribution of the loss is not common knowledge, the insurer faces the adverse selection problem. When the loss incurred by the policyholder is observable by the insurer only at a cost, they face the problem of insurance fraud (*ex post* moral hazard) and audit. The economics of moral hazard, adverse selection and audit are now central elements of the economic theory, but they were initially examined in the 1970s in the insurance paradigm. A primer to this literature can be found in Salanié (1997). An introduction to it will be provided in the last part of this book.

Chapter Bibliography

Arrow, K. J. 1971. *Essays in the theory of risk bearing*. Chicago: Markham Publishing Co.

Athey, S. 2002. Monotone comparative statics under uncertainty. *Quarterly Journal of Economics* 117:187–223.

Briys, E., G. Dionne, and L. Eeckhoudt. 1989. More on insurance as a Giffen good. *Journal of Risk and Uncertainty* 2:415–420.

Eeckhoudt, L. and C. Gollier. 1995. Demand for risky assets and the monotone probability ratio order. *Journal of Risk and Uncertainty* 11:113–122.

———. 2000. The effects of changes in risk on risk taking: a survey. In *Handbook of insurance*, ed. G. Dionne. Dordrecht: Kluwer Academic.

Gollier, C. 1987. The design of optimal insurance without the nonnegativity constraint on claims. *Journal of Risk and Insurance* 54:312–324.

———. 1995. The comparative statics of changes in risk revisited. *Journal of Economic Theory* 66:522–536.

Gollier, C. and H. Schlesinger. 1995. Second-best insurance contract design in an incomplete market. *Scandinavian Journal of Economics* 97:123–135.

———. 1996. Arrow's theorem on the optimality of deductibles: a stochastic dominance approach. *Economic Theory* 7:359–363.

Huberman, G., D. Mayers, and C. W. Smith. 1983. Optimal insurance policy indemnity schedules. *The Bell Journal of Economics* 14:415–426.

Karni, E. 1992. Optimal insurance: a nonexpected utility analysis. In *Contributions to insurance economics*, ed. G. Dionne. Dordrecht: Kluwer Academic.

Landsberger, M. and I. Meilijson. 1990. Demand for risky financial assets: a portfolio analysis. *Journal of Economic Theory* 50:204–213.

Machina, M. 1995. Non-expected utility and the robustness of the classical insurance paradigm. In *Non-expected utility and risk management*, ed. C. Gollier and M. Machina. Dordrecht: Kluwer Academic. (Reprinted from *The Geneva Papers on Risk and Insurance Theory* 20:9–50.

Meyer, J. and M. Ormiston. 1985. Strong increases in risk and their comparative statics. *International Economic Review* 26:425–437.

Milgrom, P. 1981. Good news and bad news: representation theorems and applications. *Bell Journal of Economics* 12:380–391.

Mossin, J. 1968. Aspects of rational insurance purchasing. *Journal of Political Economy* 76:533–568.

Outreville, J. F. 1997. *Theory and practice of insurance*. Dordrecht: Kluwer Academic.

Ormiston, M. and E. Schlee. 1993. Comparative statics under uncertainty for a class of economic agents. *Journal of Economic Theory* 61:412–422.

Raviv, A. 1979. The design of an optimal insurance policy. *American Economic Review* 69:84–96.

Rothschild, M. and J. Stiglitz. 1971. Increasing risk. II. Its economic consequences. *Journal of Economic Theory* 3:66–84.

Salanié, B. 1997. *The economics of contracts: a primer.* Cambridge, MA: MIT Press.

Segal, U. and A. Spivak. 1990. First order versus second order risk aversion. *Journal of Economic Theory* 51:111–125.

Spaeter, S. and P. Roger. 1997. The design of optimal insurance contracts: a topological approach. *The Geneva Papers on Risk and Insurance Theory* 22:5–20.

Zilcha, I. and S. H. Chew. 1990. Invariance of the efficient sets when the expected utility hypothesis is relaxed. *Journal of Economic Behaviour and Organizations* 13:125–131.

Exercises

(3.1) Sempronius has a logarithmic utility function. He owns an asset the value of which is 12 ducats. This asset is subject to a potential loss of 8 ducats with probability $\frac{1}{4}$.

    (a) Which insurance premium should Sempronius pay if he selects $\beta = 1$ and if the loading is equal to 0.2?

    (b) What is the optimal value of β?

    (c) Compute Sempronius's expected utility at the optimal value of β and compare it with his expected utility when $\beta = 0$ or when $\beta = 1$.

    (d) What happens to β^*

        (i) when initial wealth becomes 16 ducats while the characteristics of the potential loss are unchanged? Relate your result to Proposition 3.3(i).

        (ii) when the loading falls to zero? Relate your result to Proposition 3.1.

    (e) Caïus has the same utility function as Sempronius but his assets are worth 24 ducats and they are subject to a potential loss of 16 with probability $\frac{1}{4}$. Show that the optimal value of β for Caïus is equal to that of Sempronius. Relate your result to a property of the relative risk aversion coefficient when u is logarithmic. (Hint: alternatively you may show that for any β, the expected utility of Caïus is equal to $\ln 2 +$ the expected utility of Sempronius.)

(3.2) An individual owns assets of value $W_0 = 10$, which may suffer a random loss $(\tilde{x})$ described by a discrete random variable:

x	$p(x)$
0	0.7
4	0.1
8	0.1
10	0.1

    (a) Compute the premium associated to full insurance (assume the loading is zero everywhere in this exercise).

    (b) What is the actuarially fair premium when a deductible $D = 3$ is selected? What happens to the premium when $D = 6$? Why does the premium not fall by 50%?

(c) For each deductible compute the coinsurance rate β that yields the same premium.

(d) Draw the cumulative distribution of final wealth first if $D = 6$ and then if the policy is characterized by the coinsurance rate β that yields the same premium as $D = 6$. By reference to the integral condition, show that the policy with a coinsurance rate induces a riskier distribution of final wealth. Relate your result to Proposition 3.5.

(3.3) A wealth of 10 is subjected to a random loss that has a uniform density on $[0, 10]$.

(a) Compute the premium corresponding to a deductible $D = 4$ (assume $\lambda = 0$).

(b) Which coinsurance rate will induce the same premium?

(c) Consider now a policy with a ceiling C so that:

$$I(x) = \begin{cases} x & \text{if } x \leqslant C, \\ C & \text{if } x \geqslant C. \end{cases}$$

Which value of C yields the same premium as before?

(d) By drawing cumulative distributions of final wealth show that a risk averter will prefer the deductible to the coinsurance policy and that he will prefer the coinsurance to the ceiling. Explain the intuition of your result.

(3.4) A firm owns two buildings which have the same value ($W_0 = 40$ for each building) and which are subjected to a risk of full loss with identical probability $\frac{1}{4}$. Because these buildings are located far away from each other the risks are independent.

The risk manager has a budget of 8 to spend on insurance premia in order to cover the risks.

(a) If he covers the first building at a coinsurance rate $\beta_1 = 0.6$, which coinsurance rate will he obtain for building 2?

(b) What is the coinsurance rate identical for each building (i.e. $\beta = \beta_1 = \beta_2$) that yields the same premium?

(c) Show that—whatever the total budget available—a risk averter should always select $\beta_1 = \beta_2$. As usual, the proof is done by drawing the cumulative distributions of final wealth. This result illustrates the intuitive idea that one should "never gamble with one's insurance budget."

(3.5) Consider again the data of the previous exercise and first express the premium and the distribution of final wealth when the risk manager selects a deductible of 20 for each building (assume the loading is zero to simplify the computation).

Now, his insurer suggests an "umbrella policy" where, for the same premium, you receive a coverage with a deductible of 22.85 on the aggregate loss.

   (a) Check that indeed this umbrella policy induces an actuarially fair premium of 10.

   (b) Again by drawing the cumulative distribution function of final wealth, show that—as compared to the separate deductibles—the umbrella policy reduces the risk without changing the expected final wealth.

4

Static Portfolio Choices

Financial markets are central to the functioning of our decentralized economies. Participants in these markets are risk-averse agents who are willing to take a risk only if they receive appropriate rewards for it. Owning risky assets is compensated by higher expected returns on one's portfolio. Risk-averse households must determine their best trade-off between risk and expected return. A simple version of this problem is examined in the first section of this chapter. Organizing the economy in order to induce risk-averse people to accept the purchase of risky assets is a vital condition for economic growth. Indeed, industrial investments, which must eventually be borne by the population, are risky. Without these investments there would be no growth. Financial markets can be viewed as an institution that transfers entrepreneurial risks to consumers.

The decision problems of investors are in fact much more complex than just determining the best compromise between risk and performance. Investors face a myriad of possible investment opportunities. Selecting the composition of their portfolio requires comparing risks that are potentially correlated. Diversification is a key word in this environment, as we will see in the second section.

In this chapter, we focus on investors who consume their entire wealth at the end of the current period. By doing so, we isolate the investment problem from another of its essential characteristics in real life, namely time. Portfolio management has an intrinsic dynamic nature that will be examined in Chapter 7.

4.1 The One-Risky–One-Risk-Free-Asset Model

4.1.1 Description of the Model

Consider an agent who has a sure wealth w_0 that he can invest in one risk-free asset and in one risky asset. For ease of exposition, we can refer to the risk-free asset as a government bond, whereas the risky asset is a stock, or a portfolio of stocks. The risk-free return of the bond over the period is r. The return of the stock over the period is a random variable $\tilde{x}$. The problem of the agent is to determine the optimal composition $(w_0 - \alpha, \alpha)$ of his portfolio, where $w_0 - \alpha$ is invested in bonds and α is invested in stocks. The value of the portfolio at the end of the period may be written as

$$(w_0 - \alpha)(1 + r) + \alpha(1 + \tilde{x}) = w_0(1 + r) + \alpha(\tilde{x} - r) = w + \alpha\tilde{y}, \qquad (4.1)$$

where $w = w_0(1 + r)$ is future wealth obtained with the risk-free strategy and $\tilde{y} = \tilde{x} - r$ is the so-called "excess return" on the risky asset. We assume in this chapter that the agent consumes all his wealth $w + \alpha\tilde{y}$ at the end of the period. The utility function u, which is assumed to be differentiable, increasing and concave, links the level of consumption at the end of the period to the utility attained by the consumer. We do not consider here the existence of any short-sale constraints, i.e. we allow α to be larger than w or less than zero. The problem of the investor is thus to choose α in order to maximize EU:

$$\alpha^* \in \arg\max_\alpha Eu(w + \alpha\tilde{y}). \qquad (4.2)$$

This problem is formally equivalent to the program (3.3) describing the coinsurance problem of the previous chapter. To see this, define

$$w \equiv w' - P_0, \qquad \alpha \equiv (1 - \beta)P_0, \qquad \tilde{y} \equiv (P_0 - \tilde{x})/P_0$$

in (4.2), where P_0 is the premium for full coverage, β the coinsurance level and $\tilde{x}$ here denotes the loss. Consequently,

$$Eu(w + \alpha\tilde{y}) = Eu[(w' - P_0) + (1 - \beta)P_0((P_0 - \tilde{x})/P_0)] = Eu(w' - \beta P_0 - (1 - \beta)\tilde{x})$$

Thus, we can interpret $\alpha = 0$ as starting at full insurance coverage, which is equivalent to having a 100% risk-free portfolio, i.e. to having all of our wealth invested in bonds in the portfolio problem. By increasing α (i.e. decreasing the coinsurance level β) the consumer accepts some of the risk in exchange for a higher expected final wealth. Here $\tilde{y} \equiv (P_0 - \tilde{x})/P_0$ can be interpreted as the return on coinsuring. In other words, retaining some share of a risk of loss is similar to purchasing a risky asset. In both cases, the problem is to determine the optimal exposure to an exogenous risk. In both cases, risk-averse agents are willing to accept a positive exposure to the risk because of the positive expected net payoff of doing so.

By way of this formal link between the portfolio problem and the insurance problem, we directly obtain the following results from the previous chapter.

Proposition 4.1. *Consider problem (4.2), where $\tilde{y}$ is the excess return of the risky asset over the risk-free rate, and α^* is the optimal dollar investment in the risky asset. The optimal investment in the risky asset is positive if and only if the expected excess return is positive: $\alpha^* = 0$ if $E\tilde{y} = 0$ and $\alpha^* E\tilde{y} > 0$ otherwise. Moreover, when the expected excess return is positive,*

   (i) *α^* is reduced when the risk aversion of the investor is increased in the sense of Arrow and Pratt;*

  (ii) *α^* is increasing in wealth if absolute risk aversion is decreasing.*

Because risk aversion is second order in the EU model, the demand for the risky asset is positive as soon as the expected excess return, also known as the "equity premium," is positive. Thus, this model does not on its own explain why a large proportion of the population does not hold any stock. This "participation puzzle" has various explanations. For example, investing in real-world markets involves some degree of knowledge about how these markets work. Consumers with a low optimal α^* might consider the cost of obtaining such knowledge to be too high.

The two comparative static properties of this standard portfolio problem are very intuitive. More-risk-averse people hold less risky portfolios, and wealthier people have a larger demand for stocks, under decreasing absolute risk aversion. All existing empirical studies on households' portfolios obtain this positive relationship between stock holdings and wealth, thereby offering an additional argument in favor of DARA.

A special case that plays an important role in the theory of finance is when the utility function exhibits constant relative risk aversion. Let us assume accordingly that

$$u(c) = \frac{1}{1-\gamma} c^{1-\gamma} \quad \text{for all } c,$$

where γ is the degree of relative risk aversion. Under this specification, the first-order condition to program (4.2) can be written as

$$E[\tilde{y}u'(w + \alpha^*\tilde{y})] = E[\tilde{y}(w + \alpha^*\tilde{y})^{-\gamma}] = 0. \tag{4.3}$$

Obviously, the solution to this equation is such that $\alpha^* = kw$, where k is a positive constant such that $E\tilde{y}(1 + k\tilde{y})^{-\gamma} = 0$. We conclude that under constant relative risk aversion, the optimal dollar amount invested in the risky asset is proportional to wealth. Or, in other words, it is optimal for CRRA investors to invest a fixed share of their wealth in stocks.

Proposition 4.2. *Under constant relative risk aversion, the demand for stocks is proportional to wealth:* $\alpha^*(w) = kw$.

For more general utility functions, determining the optimal demand may be more difficult. It can be useful to derive an approximate solution to this problem. Using a first-order Taylor approximation to $u'(w + \alpha^*y)$ around w, we can approximate the first-order condition $E\tilde{y}u'(w + \alpha^*\tilde{y}) = 0$ as

$$E\tilde{y}[u'(w) + \alpha^*\tilde{y}u''(w)] \simeq 0.$$

We thus obtain an approximation for the proportion of wealth invested in stocks:

$$\frac{\alpha^*}{w} \simeq \frac{\mu_{\tilde{y}}}{\sigma_{\tilde{y}}^2} \frac{1}{R(w)}, \tag{4.4}$$

where $R(w) = -wu''(w)/u'(w)$ is the degree of relative risk aversion evaluated at w, and $\mu_{\tilde{y}}$ and $\sigma_{\tilde{y}}^2$ are respectively the mean and the variance of the excess stocks return. Approximation (4.4) best fits the exact solution when $\sigma_{\tilde{y}}^2$ is small with respect to $\mu_{\tilde{y}}$; but it can be proven that it is exact when absolute risk aversion is constant and returns are normally distributed. To sum up, the optimal share of wealth invested in stocks is roughly proportional to the equity premium $\mu_{\tilde{y}}$, and inversely proportional to the variance of stock returns and to relative risk aversion.

4.1.2　The Equity Premium and the Demand for Stocks

We can use approximation (4.4) to get an idea of how much of the investor's wealth should be invested in stocks. Historical data on asset returns are available from several sources. Shiller (1989) and Kocherlakota (1996) provide statistics on asset returns for the US over the period from 1889 to 1978. The average real return to S&P 500, a representative portfolio of US stocks, was 7% per year over this period, whereas the average short-term real risk-free rate has been $r = 1\%$. The observed equity premium was thus equal to $\mu_{\tilde{y}} = 6\%$ over the century. The standard deviation of the excess return was approximately equal to $\sigma_{\tilde{y}} = 16\%$.

Using reasonable degrees of relative risk aversion, we obtain unrealistically high shares of total wealth invested in stocks. For example, if $R = 2$, approximation (4.4) yields a share equaling 117%. This means that this investor should borrow 17% of his wealth at the risk-free rate to invest this loan together with his entire wealth in the stock market! An investor with an unrealistically high relative risk aversion of 10 should still invest 23% of his wealth in stocks. This surprising result is related to the so-called "equity premium puzzle" that will be discussed in more details later.

4.2　The Effect of Background Risk

One way to explain the surprisingly large demand for stocks in the theoretical model is to recognize that there are other sources of risk on final wealth than the riskiness of assets returns. Consider, for example, labor income. For obvious reasons, wages are usually not fully insurable. To capture the effects of these types of risks, we can introduce a zero-mean background risk $\tilde{\varepsilon}$ to initial wealth w. This yields the following modified portfolio decision problem:

$$\alpha^{**} \in \arg\max_{\alpha} Eu(w + \tilde{\varepsilon} + \alpha\tilde{y}). \tag{4.5}$$

We want to compare α^{**} with α^*, the demand for the risky asset when there is no background risk. For the sake of simplicity, we assume that the risk on labor income is independent of the portfolio risk. Obviously any correlation between the risks is important, but we aim to show that, even in the case of statistical independence, there is often a predictable effect on decision making. Intuition might suggest that

α^{**} should be smaller than α^*: independent risks should be substitutes. Since a risk averter is afraid of any bad luck with respect to the outcome of $\tilde{\varepsilon}$, he or she might try to compensate for the extra risk by behaving in a more cautious manner towards the level of endogenous risk $\tilde{y}$. Because $\tilde{\varepsilon}$ and $\tilde{y}$ are independent, the above problem can be rewritten as

$$\alpha^{**} \in \arg\max_{\alpha} Ev(w + \alpha\tilde{y}), \tag{4.6}$$

where the value function v is defined by $v(z) = Eu(z + \tilde{\varepsilon})$ for all z. This trick is very useful because we know the condition under which α^{**} (defined by (4.6)) is smaller than α^* (defined by (4.2)). Indeed, by Proposition 4.1, we just have to check whether v is more concave than u. In other words, the question becomes simply whether a zero-mean risk makes people more averse towards other independent risks. This is true if

$$-\frac{v''(z)}{v'(z)} = -\frac{Eu''(z + \tilde{\varepsilon})}{Eu'(z + \tilde{\varepsilon})} \geqslant -\frac{u''(z)}{u'(z)}, \tag{4.7}$$

for all $\tilde{\varepsilon}$ such that $E\tilde{\varepsilon} = 0$. This is equivalent to requiring that $Eh(z, \tilde{\varepsilon}) \leqslant 0$, where $h(z, \epsilon) = u''(z + \epsilon)u'(z) - u''(z)u'(z + \epsilon)$. This inequality holds if and only if h is concave in ϵ for all z. A necessary condition is that $h_{22}(z, 0)$ be negative, or, in the case where $u''' > 0$, that

$$-\frac{u''(z)}{u'(z)} \leqslant -\frac{u''''(z)}{u'''(z)} \tag{4.8}$$

for all z. This shows that this *a priori* simple and intuitive idea that independent risks must be substitutes requires a strong necessary condition on the fourth derivative of the utility function.

It can easily be shown that this condition is necessary but not sufficient to guarantee that any background risk makes investors more averse to other independent risks. We hereafter prove the following proposition, which provides a simple sufficient condition.

Proposition 4.3. *Consider the following three statements.*

1. *Any zero-mean background risk reduces the demand for other independent risks.*

2. *For all z, $-u''''(z)/u'''(z) \geqslant -u''(z)/u'(z)$.*

3. *Absolute risk aversion is decreasing and convex.*

Condition 2 is necessary for condition 1, under the assumption that u''' is positive. Condition 3 is sufficient for conditions 1 and 2.

Proof. It just remains to prove that condition 3 is sufficient for condition 1. If $A(\cdot)$ denotes absolute risk aversion, we can write that

$$-Eu''(z + \tilde{\varepsilon}) = E[A(z + \tilde{\varepsilon})u'(z + \tilde{\varepsilon})].$$

Under decreasing absolute risk aversion, we have that the right-hand side of this equality is larger than $EA(z+\tilde{\varepsilon})Eu'(z+\tilde{\varepsilon})$. Moreover, because A is convex, $EA(z+\tilde{\varepsilon})$ is larger than $A(z)$. Combining these three observations implies condition (4.7), which is necessary and sufficient for property 1 to hold.   □

Note that, once we accept that absolute risk aversion is decreasing, it is natural to accept that it also is convex. In particular, it could not be concave everywhere, since a function cannot be positive, decreasing and everywhere concave. But this argument does not exclude the case where A would be locally concave. Observe also that concave power utility functions all have an absolute risk aversion that is decreasing and convex, which implies that independent risks are substitutes for investors having these preferences. But it is easy to find utility functions for which this is not the case.

4.3   Portfolios of Risky Assets

4.3.1   *Diversification in the Expected-Utility Model*

Suppose now that risk-averse investors can invest their wealth in two assets that are risky. To keep the argument simple, let us assume that these two assets have the same distribution of returns $\tilde{x}_1$ and $\tilde{x}_2$ that are independent and identically distributed.[1] What should be the optimal structure of their portfolios? To answer this question, we must solve the following program:

$$\max_{\alpha} Eu(\alpha\tilde{x}_1 + (w - \alpha)\tilde{x}_2), \tag{4.9}$$

where α is the amount invested in the first risky asset. Under risk aversion, the objective function is concave in the decision variable. The first-order condition is

$$E(\tilde{x}_1 - \tilde{x}_2)u'(\alpha^*\tilde{x}_1 + (w - \alpha^*)\tilde{x}_2) = 0.$$

It is obvious that the unique root to this equation is $\alpha^* = \frac{1}{2}w$, since

$$E\tilde{x}_1 u'(\tfrac{1}{2}w(\tilde{x}_1 + \tilde{x}_2)) = E\tilde{x}_2 u'(\tfrac{1}{2}w(\tilde{x}_1 + \tilde{x}_2)),$$

because $\tilde{x}_1$ and $\tilde{x}_2$ can be interchanged because they are i.i.d. Thus it is optimal for all risk-averse investors to perfectly balance their portfolio in this case.

The mechanism behind this result is risk diversification. In fact, all other portfolios are second-order stochastically dominated by the balanced one. They are thus all rejected by risk-averse investors. This is easily seen by observing that $\alpha\tilde{x}_1 + (w - \alpha)\tilde{x}_2$ is distributed as

$$\frac{\tilde{x}_1 + \tilde{x}_2}{2} + \tilde{\varepsilon},$$

---

[1]The argument is easily extended to dependent but symmetric random variables.

where

$$\tilde{\varepsilon} \equiv (\alpha - \tfrac{1}{2})(\tilde{x}_1 - \tilde{x}_2).$$

Thus, the return of any portfolio α is distributed as the return of the balanced portfolio plus a pure noise $\tilde{\varepsilon}$ satisfying

$$E\left[\tilde{\varepsilon} \,\middle|\, \frac{\tilde{x}_1 + \tilde{x}_2}{2}\right] = 0.$$

This implies that accepting an unbalanced portfolio is equivalent to accepting zero-mean lotteries. To illustrate, let us consider two i.i.d. returns $\tilde{x}_1$ and $\tilde{x}_2$ that can take values of 0% or 20% with equal probabilities. A perfectly balanced portfolio would yield a return $\tilde{y}$ of either 0% with probability $\frac{1}{4}$, 10% with probability $\frac{1}{2}$, or 20% with probability $\frac{1}{4}$. One can check that the single asset portfolio has a distribution of returns that can be duplicated by taking the balanced portfolio plus a zero-mean lottery $(-10\%, \frac{1}{2}; +10\%, \frac{1}{2})$ conditional on obtaining 10% on the balanced portfolio.

In Chapter 1, we introduced the notion of risk aversion by showing that Sempronius is willing to diversify his assets, i.e. to share his wealth in two independent ships rather than in just one, if he has a concave utility function. This section formalizes the link between the preference for diversification and the more standard definition of risk aversion, which is to dislike zero-mean risks.

Most real-world investors do diversify their portfolios. However, the theory predicts that individual portfolios should be diversified internationally, which is often not the case. This is the so-called "international diversification puzzle," which stems in part from a penchant towards buying more local stocks, a phenomenon known as "home bias."

4.3.2 *Diversification in the Mean–Variance Model*

One simple measure of the beneficial effect of diversification is the reduction in the variance of the portfolio return that it generates. In the case of two i.i.d. assets, the variance of the portfolio return is minimized by selecting the perfectly balanced portfolio, which has a variance equaling the asset variance divided by a factor 2. Moreover, the expected return of the portfolio is independent of its composition. The 50:50 portfolio is optimal in our case, where the expected return is the same for the two assets. When the expected returns vary, the investor must trade off the risk against the expected performance of the portfolio. By adding more of an asset with a lower expected return, we have the obvious detrimental effect of lowering the expected return on the portfolio. However, this detrimental effect may be countered by the beneficial effects of diversification. Additional difficulties may arise when asset returns are correlated. In this section, we limit the analysis to a special case of EU, namely the mean–variance approach. Obviously, there are many limitations of this approach, as we discussed in Chapter 1. On the other hand, this approach works perfectly well in the case where investors have constant absolute risk aversion and asset returns are normally distributed. Let us also remind the reader that, in spite of several limitations, the mean–variance approach is still a cornerstone in the modern theory of finance.

Assume there are n risky assets, indexed by $i = 1, \ldots, n$. The return of asset i is denoted $\tilde{x}_i$, whose expectation is μ_i. The covariance between returns of assets i and j is denoted $\sigma_{ij} = E(\tilde{x}_i - \mu_i)(\tilde{x}_j - \mu_j)$. We assume that the variance–covariance matrix Σ can be inverted. There also exists a risk-free asset whose return is $r \equiv x_0$. If we normalize the initial wealth to unity, final wealth equals

$$\tilde{z} = 1 + x_0 \left(1 - \sum_{i=1}^{n} a_i \right) + \sum_{i=1}^{n} a_i \tilde{x}_i$$

$$= 1 + x_0 + \sum_{i=1}^{n} a_i (\tilde{x}_i - x_0), \qquad (4.10)$$

where a_i is the share of wealth invested in asset i. The evaluation of this risk follows a mean–variance approach, where the investor maximizes the certainty equivalent of final wealth which is approximated by $E\tilde{z} - \frac{1}{2} A \operatorname{var}[\tilde{z}]$. A is the index of absolute risk aversion of the investor. From equation (4.10), the mean and the variance of final wealth can be respectively written as

$$E\tilde{z} = 1 + x_0 + \sum_{i=1}^{n} a_i (\mu_i - x_0),$$

$$\operatorname{var}[\tilde{z}] = \sum_{i=1}^{n} \sum_{j=1}^{n} a_i a_j \sigma_{ij}.$$

Differentiating the certainty equivalent wealth with respect to the share a_i invested in asset i, and setting it equal to zero, yields

$$\mu_i - x_0 - A \sum_{j=1}^{n} a_j^* \sigma_{ij} = 0,$$

or, in matrix format,

$$\mu - x_0 = A a^* \Sigma, \qquad (4.11)$$

where $\mu - x_0$ is the vector of excess expected returns, and a^* is the vector of optimal shares invested in the risky assets. The solution of this system is

$$a^* = \frac{1}{A} \Sigma^{-1} (\mu - x_0). \qquad (4.12)$$

The investment in the risk-free asset corresponds to the remaining wealth

$$a_0^* = 1 - \sum_{j=1}^{n} a_j^*.$$

When returns are independently distributed, which implies that Σ and Σ^{-1} are diagonal matrices, this equation can be written as

$$a_i^* = \frac{1}{A} \frac{\mu_i - x_0}{\sigma_{ii}},$$

which extends equation (4.4) to the case of more than one risky asset. It should be noted that, in the independent case, the demand for a risky asset is independent of the opportunity to purchase other risky assets. Independence of returns implies independence of demands, which is one of the counterintuitive properties of the mean–variance model.

This solution has an important characteristic that much simplifies the operational advice that the modern theory of finance provides for investors. Namely, all investors, whatever their attitude to risk, should purchase the same portfolio of risky assets. To see this, define $\alpha^* = \Sigma^{-1}(\mu - x_0)$ as the optimal portfolio of risky assets of the investor with a degree of risk aversion A equaling unity. Then, solution (4.12) states that the investor with a degree of risk aversion $A = 0.5$ should purchase a portfolio of risky assets with twice the quantity of each of the risky assets contained in portfolio α^*. This is done by investing less in the risk-free asset. Thus, the structures of the two portfolios of risky assets are exactly the same. In short, all agents should purchase the same fund of risky assets. The only role of risk aversion is to affect the best balance between this fund and the risk-free asset. The common fund of risky assets is often referred to as a "mutual fund" and the fact that the choice can be narrowed down to investing in this mutual fund and the risk-free asset is referred to as the "mutual fund theorem" or the "two-fund separation theorem." Indeed, the result can also be proven in more general contexts than the mean–variance context we show here.

This result is extremely powerful. It suggests that portfolio management is a simple problem on which people should not spend too much time and energy. This, again, is counterfactual. However, it relies on two assumptions. First, it is assumed that financial markets are informationally efficient. This means that all information about future economic performances are already included in asset prices. Or, in other words, that all investors share the same information about risks. The second assumption is that investors have mean–variance preferences. We will come back to these two aspects of the "two-fund separation theorem" later.

4.4 Bibliographical References, Extensions and Exercises

The two-asset model was first examined by Arrow (1963, 1965, 1971). The effect of an increase in risk aversion on the demand for the risky asset is discussed by Pratt (1964). Extensive research on the effect of a change in the distribution of the return of the risky asset culminated in the paper by Gollier (1995), who obtained the necessary and sufficient condition. The effect of an independent background risk on choice under uncertainty was originally examined by Doherty and Schlesinger (1983). The effects were extended to the portfolio-choice problem, using more modern tools, by Kimball (1993), Gollier and Pratt (1996) and Eeckhoudt, Gollier and Schlesinger (1996). The benefit of diversification for risk-averse agents is best explained in Rothschild and Stiglitz (1971). The international diversification puzzle is stated in French and Poterba (1991) and Baxter and Jermann (1997). The standard reference for the equity premium puzzle is Mehra and Prescott (1985), which has been the source of a large amount of literature in which the simple two-asset model has been extended in several directions. Kocherlakota (1996) provides a survey of these lines of research.

Markowitz (1952) was the first to solve the static multiple assets problem in the mean–variance framework.

Chapter Bibliography

Arrow, K. J. 1963. Liquidity preference. Lecture VI in *Lecture Notes for Economics 285, The Economics of Uncertainty*, pp. 33-53, undated, Stanford University.

———. 1965. *Yrjo Jahnsson Lecture Notes*, Helsinki. (Reprinted in Arrow 1971).

———. 1971. *Essays in the theory of risk bearing*. Chicago: Markham Publishing Co.

Baxter, M. and U. J. Jermann. 1997. The international diversification puzzle is worse than you think. *American Economic Review* 87:170–180.

Doherty, N. and H. Schlesinger. (1983). Optimal insurance in incomplete markets. *Journal of Political Economy* 91: 1045–1054.

Eeckhoudt, L., C. Gollier, and H. Schlesinger. 1996. Changes in background risk and risk-taking behavior. *Econometrica* 64:683–690.

French, K. and J. Poterba. 1991. International diversification and international equity markets. *American Economic Review* 81:222–226.

Gollier, C. 1995. The comparative statics of changes in risk revisited. *Journal of Economic Theory* 66:522–536.

Gollier, C. and J. W. Pratt. 1996. Risk vulnerability and the tempering effect of background risk. *Econometrica* 64:1109–1124.

Kimball, M. S. 1993. Standard risk aversion. *Econometrica* 61:589–611.

Kocherlakota, N. R. 1996. The equity premium: it's still a puzzle. *Journal of Economic Literature* 34:42–71.

Markowitz, H. 1952. Portfolio selection. *Journal of Finance* 7:77–91.

Mehra, R. and E. Prescott. 1985. The equity premium: a puzzle. *Journal of Monetary Economics* 10:335–339.

Pratt, J. 1964. Risk aversion in the small and in the large. *Econometrica* 32:122–136.

Rothschild, M. and J. Stiglitz. 1971. Increasing risk. II. Its economic consequences. *Journal of Economic Theory* 3:66–84.

Exercises

(4.1) An individual with a utility function $u = \ln w$ has the opportunity to invest in a risky asset whose final payoff is distributed as $(1 + h, \frac{1}{2}; 1 - d, \frac{1}{2})$ with $h > d$. The risk-free return on bonds is zero. The initial price of the risky asset is normalized to unity.

   (a) Write the first order condition for α^* and solve it explicitly. Are you surprised by the result that α^* is a linear function of initial wealth?

   (b) Which property of the utility function generates the result that α^* is increasing in initial wealth?

   (c) Show that when d increases, α^* falls. Is this surprising? What about the impact on α^* of an increase in h?

   (d) Apply equation (4.4) to find the approximation for the proportion of wealth invested in the risky asset. Compare with the exact value you obtained under (a).

(4.2) Return to exercise 4.1. and assume that $w = 10$, $h = 0.10$ and $d = 0.08$. You should find that $\alpha^* = 12.5$. Now assume that, besides his wealth of 10, the decision maker faces a background risk $\tilde{\varepsilon}$ (independent of the other risk) distributed as $(+2, \frac{1}{2}; -2, \frac{1}{2})$.

   (a) Write the expected utility (Eu) of the decision maker.

   (b) Compute $dEu/d\alpha$, evaluate it at $\alpha = 12.5$. What does the sign imply for the comparison between α^* and α^{**} (the optimum when background risk is present)?

   (c) Verify that for $u = \ln w$ conditions 2 and 3 in Proposition 4.3 are indeed satisfied.

(4.3) An individual has to allocate his wealth w_0 between a safe asset paying a return r and a risky one paying a return $\tilde{x}$ with $E(\tilde{x}) > r$.

   If this individual has a utility function $u(w) = w - \beta w^2$ (with $\beta > 0$ and $1 - 2\beta w > 0$ for all the values taken by w so that marginal utility is positive).

   (a) Express the optimal value of α, the investment in the risky asset.

   (b) Explain why you obtain with this utility function that α^* is decreasing in w_0.

   (c) Compare the exact solution in (a) with the approximation proposed by Equation (4.4).

5
Static Portfolio Choices in an Arrow–Debreu Economy

In the previous chapter, we examined an economy in which the investment opportunity set was quite limited. Funds could be invested in portfolios containing only bonds and stocks. Suppose that an investor would like to take a bet on the event that the return on the Dow Jones this year will be larger than 10%. More precisely, suppose that he wants to sign a contract with a counterpart on financial markets that would give him $1 only if the return on the Dow Jones this year is larger than 10%, against the payment of a lump sum fee *ex ante*. He could be also willing to bet on other events, such as whether some specific asset will have a return in between two prespecified values, or whether the average temperature in Chicago will be higher than its level last year. Most of these types of investment opportunities were not available in the portfolio choice model presented in the previous chapter.

Both the strength and the weakness of the model presented in the previous section come from the linear relationship between final wealth and the return of each individual assets. It is a strength because this assumption yields simple operational advice for practitioners. It is a weakness because it artificially constrains the choice of investors. In particular, this model does not allow investors to purchase a wide variety of new financial instruments that have been developed by financial intermediaries worldwide over the last three decades. For example, assets called "options" have been developed that offer to their owners payoffs that are highly nonlinear in the return of the underlying assets. Many individual investors also favor the purchase of "portfolio insurance," a system in which a minimum return is guaranteed to the portfolio owners. In the following, we will assume that investors are allowed to take any such risk exposure. We will assume that investors can bet on any possible event. By enlarging the risk opportunity set, we can in fact "complete" financial markets. The portfolio choice problem in this economy was first examined by Arrow (1953) and Debreu (1959). We hereafter present the core of an Arrow–Debreu economy.

5.1 Arrow–Debreu Securities and Arbitrage Pricing

Let us assume that there are S possible states of nature at the end of the period that are indexed by $s = 0, \ldots, S - 1$. For the sake of a simple notation, we assume that there is a finite number of possible states. The probability of state s is denoted p_s. When the risk is limited to the randomness of assets returns, a state of nature is characterized by the vector of these realized returns. The assumption that markets are complete means that, for each possible state s, there is an asset which provides a unit payoff to its owner if and only if state s occurs and zero otherwise. These assets are called "Arrow–Debreu securities." Purchasing an Arrow–Debreu security associated to state s is equivalent to betting on that state.

In fact, what is important is not that Arrow–Debreu securities actually exist, but that they can be replicated with existing assets in the economy. Consider a simple example with two states of nature ($S = 2$), and a risky asset whose initial price is normalized to unity. Its final value in state s is P_s, $s = 0, 1$. In other words, the net asset return is $P_0 - 1$ in state 0, and $P_1 - 1$ in state 1. If, in addition, we assume that there exists a risk-free asset with return r in both states, then this is an example of an economy in which financial markets are complete. To see this, let us assume that $P_0 < 1 + r < P_1$; in other words the risky asset sometimes pays more and sometimes pays less than the risk-free asset.[1] Now, we can replicate the Arrow–Debreu security associated with state $s = 1$ by purchasing α units of the risky asset and by borrowing B at the risk-free rate, in such a way that

$$0 = \alpha P_0 - (1 + r)B,$$
$$1 = \alpha P_1 - (1 + r)B.$$

The first constraint states that this portfolio provides to its owner no revenue in state 0, whereas the second constraint means that the revenue in state 1 is one. The solution of this system is $\alpha = (P_1 - P_0)^{-1}$ and $B = P_0/(1 + r)(P_1 - P_0)$. We can think of one share of a mutual fund that invests in our portfolio of α units of the risky asset together with B borrowed at the risk-free rate. Since the payout of this mutual fund is exactly the same in each state as the Arrow–Debreu security associated with state 1, the principle of no arbitrage tells us that the total out-of-pocket expenditure for one share of this mutual fund must equal the price of the Arrow–Debreu security associated with state 1. Thus, investors can "bet" on state 1 occurring, by purchasing this mutual fund.

A similar exercise can be performed for the Arrow–Debreu security associated with state 0. In this example, there are two states, which implies that there are enough

---

[1] This is an equilibrium condition. If we suppose alternatively that $1 + r < P_0$ and $1 + r < P_1$, then purchasing an infinite number of the risky assets would be optimal, independent of the degree of risk aversion.

of two independent assets to "span" the entire set of all possible risk exposures. More generally, markets will be complete if there are at least as many assets whose vectors of state-contingent payoffs are linearly independent as there are number of states. Any set of assets with this property is said to "span the market." In any such market, we lose no generality and gain much simplicity by assuming that the Arrow–Debreu securities exist. Thus, investors can structure any set of state-contingent claims by investing in the appropriate portfolio of Arrow–Debreu securities.[2]

In this chapter, devoted to portfolio choice, the prices of contingent claims are taken as given. Let Π_s denote the price of the Arrow–Debreu security associated with state s. This is the price to be paid to obtain one monetary unit if and only if state s occurs. These prices can be inferred from the price of real assets from which contingent claims can be duplicated. To illustrate,

$$\Pi_1 = \alpha - B = \frac{1 - P_0/(1 + r)}{P_1 - P_0}$$

is the price of the Arrow–Debreu security associated with state $s = 1$ in our example above. Indeed, duplicating this asset requires purchasing α units of the risky asset whose price is 1, from which one must subtract a loan of B. By a simple arbitrage argument, Π_1 must be equal to the cost of building this portfolio, since it provides exactly the same state-contingent profile of revenue. By the way, this is the general idea followed in the important literature on arbitrage pricing, as initiated by Black and Scholes (1973). If we assume that $P_0 < P_1 - 1$, then the Arrow–Debreu security associated with state $s = 1$ in our example is a call option with strike price $P_1 - 1$.[3] In this example, we showed how to derive the price of this call option from the characteristics of the risk of its underlying asset, as did Black and Scholes (1973) in a much more complex environment.

Of course the implication works both ways: once we know the prices for our Arrow–Debreu securities, we can calculate the price of any financial asset by simply adding up the prices of Arrow–Debreu securities with the identical state payoffs. One particularly useful example is a risk-free bond with a payoff of 1 in each state of nature. The price of such a bond must be the discounted value of one unit of wealth, received with certainty at the end of the period:

$$P_B = (1 + r)^{-1}.$$

---

[2]Readers with a course in linear algebra will recognize that we only require a set of securities whose vector payoffs form a "basis" for the vector space of state-contingent payouts.

[3]A call option on a specific underlying asset provides to its owner the right to purchase this asset at a prespecified price (the "strike price") over a given period. Note that the option defined here would provide a gross payout of $P_1 - (P_1 - 1) = 1$ in state 1 and zero in state 0, since the owner of the option would not use it in state 0.

Moreover, holding a portfolio consisting of one unit of each and every Arrow–Debreu security also would have a risk-free payout of 1. Thus, using no-arbitrage arguments, we must have

$$\sum_{s=0}^{S-1} \Pi_s = P_B = (1 + r)^{-1}. \tag{5.1}$$

Define $\hat{p}_s \equiv \Pi_s(1 + r)$. If we consider the vector $(\hat{p}_0, \ldots, \hat{p}_{S-1})$ of S positive scalars, it follows from (5.1) that the elements of this set sum to one. As a result, we can view the elements of this set as probabilities in their own right. Indeed, $\hat{p}_s$ is often referred to as the risk-neutral probability for state s. By construction, in this manner, we see that the price of any asset in our complete market is simply its expected value, discounted at the risk-free rate, but with the expectation taken with respect to the risk-neutral probabilities $(\hat{p}_0, \ldots, \hat{p}_{S-1})$, rather than the true probabilities $(p_0, \ldots, p_{S-1})$. An asset with state-contingent payoffs $(y_0, y_1, \ldots, y_{S-1})$ can be duplicated by a portfolio containing y_s units of the Arrow–Debreu security associated to state s, $s = 1, \ldots, S$. By the standard no-arbitrage argument, its price must thus equal

$$P = \sum_{s=0}^{S-1} \Pi_s y_s = \frac{\sum_{s=0}^{S-1} \hat{p}_s y_s}{1 + r} = \frac{\hat{E}\tilde{y}}{1 + r}, \tag{5.2}$$

where $\hat{E}$ denotes the expectation operator with respect to probabilities $(\hat{p}_1, \ldots, \hat{p}_S)$. In a complete market economy with no arbitrage opportunity, there exists a "risk-neutral" probability distribution such that the price of any asset can be expressed as the discounted value of the risk-neutral expectation of its future payoffs. This is why risk-neutral probabilities are often referred to as stochastic discount factors. The search for this risk-neutral distribution is developed in another chapter.

5.2   Optimal Portfolios of Arrow–Debreu Securities

The problem for the investor is to determine the demand for each of the Arrow–Debreu securities. Let c_s be the investment in the Arrow–Debreu security associated with state s. By construction, it is also the final wealth of the agent in that state. The program of the investor can thus be written as

$$\max_{c_0, \ldots, c_{S-1}} \sum_{s=0}^{S-1} p_s u(c_s) \quad \text{subject to} \quad \sum_{s=0}^{S-1} \Pi_s c_s = w, \tag{5.3}$$

where w is the investor's initial wealth. In the following sections, we examine the properties of the optimal portfolio of Arrow–Debreu securities. Before proceeding, it is noteworthy that this decision problem is in general much more flexible for the investor than the one that we considered in the previous chapter. In the one-risky–one-risk-free-asset model, the state of nature is characterized by the realized excess return $s = y$, and the final wealth is constrained to be linear in it: $c_s = w + \alpha s$. In model (5.3), there is no such constraint, and the optimal risk exposure $\{c_s\}_{s=0,...,S-1}$ is constrained only by the budget constraint $\sum \Pi_s c_s = w$. It should also be observed that program (5.3) is a special case of the decision problem faced by consumers under certainty, as described in standard microeconomics textbooks. In an economy with S different goods, where Π_s denotes the price of good s, each consumer selects the bundle $(c_0, \ldots, c_{S-1})$ that maximizes his utility $U(c_0, \ldots, c_{S-1}) = \sum p_s u(c_s)$ under the standard budget constraint. The only specific attribute of the above program compared to the standard textbook problem is the additive nature of the objective function U.

Because the objective function in (5.3) is a sum of concave functions of the decision variables, the following first-order conditions are both necessary and sufficient for optimality:

$$u'(c_s^*) = \xi \frac{\Pi_s}{p_s} \quad \text{for all } s = 0, \ldots, S - 1, \tag{5.4}$$

where ξ is the Lagrange multiplier associated with (5.3), equal to the marginal utility of additional wealth. We see that the optimal consumption depends upon the state only through the ratio $\pi_s \equiv \Pi_s/p_s$ of the state price per unit of probability.[4] In other words, if there are two states with the same price per unit of probability for the associated contingent claims, it is optimal for the agent to purchase the same quantity of these claims. It is easy to check that not doing so would yield an increase in risk of final wealth. The intuition of this result is simple. Suppose, for example, that all π_s are the same. Since $\pi_s = (1 + r)^{-1}(\hat{p}_s/p_s)$, and since the $\{\hat{p}_s\}$ and the $\{p_s\}$ each sum to one, it follows that $\hat{p}_s = p_s \; \forall s$. Hence, contingent claims are actuarially priced in the sense that the price of any asset in such an economy equals the true expected value of its contingent payoff, discounted at the risk-free rate. It is then optimal to fully insure the risk, i.e. to purchase a risk-free portfolio: $c_s^* = w(1 + r)$ for all s. Purchasing a risky portfolio would here be equivalent to not insuring risk when insurance contracts are actuarially priced.

When some of the π_s are different, $\hat{p}_s$ and p_s are not identical for some s and there is a scope for an optimal risk exposure. We might expect that the investor will reduce the demand for contingent claims whose prices are large relative to the probability of the corresponding state. This means taking a risk. As stated above, equation (5.4) implies that we have a different level of consumption for each value of π_s and thus may write $c_s^* \equiv C(\pi_s)$ for all s. Since u' is decreasing due to risk

---

[4]Note that we can rewrite (5.2) using true expectations, rather than risk-neutral expectations, as $P = \sum_{s=0}^{S-1} p_s \pi_s y_s = E\tilde{\pi}\tilde{y}$. The set $\{\pi_s\}$ is often referred to in the finance literature as the pricing kernel.

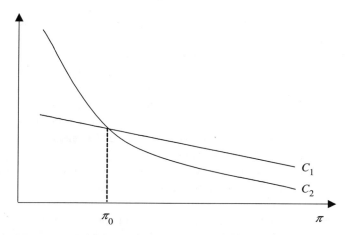

Figure 5.1. The more risk-tolerant agent 2 purchases a more risky portfolio.

aversion, the function C is well defined. It is characterized by $C(\pi) = u'^{-1}(\xi\pi)$ for all π. It is a non-increasing function: one consumes less in more expensive states. The absolute value of the slope of the C function is a local measure of the exposure to risk. At the limit, if C is a constant function, the agent does not take any risk. By fully differentiating the first-order condition $u'(C) = \xi\pi$ with respect to π, we obtain the result that

$$C'(\pi) = \frac{\xi}{u''(C)} = -\frac{T(C(\pi))}{\pi}, \tag{5.5}$$

where $T(C) = -u'(C)/u''(C)$ is the inverse of the measure of Arrow–Pratt risk aversion, often referred to as the local measure of absolute risk tolerance. Thus, more risk-tolerant people (i.e. less risk-averse people) will take more risk. In Figure 5.1, we compare the optimal portfolio C_1 of agent 1 to the optimal portfolio C_2 of agent 2, who is more risk-tolerant in the sense of Arrow and Pratt. Note that we cannot have either consumption curve totally above or below the other, since both must satisfy the same budget constraint in (5.3). Observe that equation (5.5) implies that at any crossing point, such as π_0, the slope of C_2 is larger than that of C_1 in absolute value. This further implies that we must get only a single crossing, as illustrated in the figure.

When the utility function exhibits constant relative risk aversion, one can solve the problem analytically. Suppose that $u'(C) = C^{-\gamma}$. Then the first-order condition yields $C(\pi) = \lambda\pi^{-1/\gamma}$, where λ equals $\xi^{-1/\gamma}$. The budget constraint, which can be rewritten as $E[\tilde{\pi}C(\tilde{\pi})] = w$, yields in turn

$$E[\tilde{\pi}C(\tilde{\pi})] = \lambda E\tilde{\pi}^{(\gamma-1)/\gamma}.$$

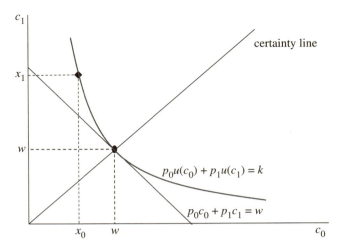

Figure 5.2. State-claims space, showing an iso-expected-value locus
and an indifference curve.

Thus, the optimal portfolio of an agent with constant relative risk aversion is such
that

$$C(\pi) = \left[\frac{\pi^{-1/\gamma}}{E\tilde{\pi}^{(\gamma-1)/\gamma}} \right] w. \tag{5.6}$$

Observe that, as in the one-risky–one-risk-free-asset model, the demand for assets
is proportional to wealth when relative risk aversion is constant.

5.3 A Simple Graphical Illustration

We return to the simple case of two states of nature, $S = 2$. In order to focus on the
risk aspects of the model, we assume that the risk-free rate is zero, $r = 0$. The set
of all possible contingent claims is represented by the positive orthant in Figure 5.2.
The 45° line represents the locus of claims with equal consumption in both states of
the world, which is referred to as the certainty line. The set of claims $\{(c_0, c_1)\}$ for
which $p_0 c_0 + p_1 c_1 = w$ for some positive scalar w represent an iso-expected-value
locus, i.e. the set of claims with mean wealth w. To analyze preferences, set the EU
equal to a constant k, $p_0 u(c_0) + p_1 u(c_1) = k$. The set of claims $\{(c_0, c_1)\}$ for which
EU is constant defines an indifference curve in state-claims space: $c_1 = f(c_0; k)$.

Using implicit differentiation, we can find the slope of the indifference curve
through any point in state-claims space,

$$\left. \frac{dc_1}{dc_0} \right|_{EU} = \frac{\partial f(c_0; k)}{\partial c_0} = -\frac{p_0 \, u'(c_0)}{p_1 \, u'(c_1)}.$$

The absolute value of dc_1/dc_0 is the marginal rate of substitution (MRS) between
states. It is the rate of trade-off, at the margin, between one unit of consumption

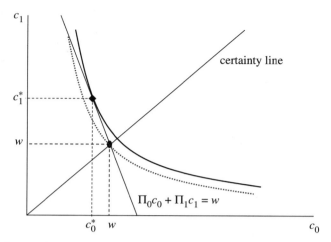

Figure 5.3.   Optimal contingent consumption involves selling state 0
claims and purchasing state 1 claims.

in state 0 and consumption in state 1, for which the consumer is just indifferent. If
we evaluate the MRS at claims for which we have certainty, $c_0 = c_1$, it follows that
the MRS $= p_0/p_1$ is independent of the preferences of the investor. This is another
expression of the fact that individuals are neutral to the introduction of small risk,
i.e. that there is second-order risk aversion under EU:

$$\frac{\partial^2 f(c_0; k)}{\partial c_0^2} = -\frac{p_0}{p_1}\left[\frac{u''(c_0)}{u'(c_1)} - \frac{u'(c_0)u''(c_1)}{(u'(c_1))^2}\frac{\partial f(c_0; k)}{\partial c_0}\right]$$

$$= \frac{p_0}{p_1}\frac{u'(c_0)}{u'(c_1)}\left[A(c_0) + A(c_1)\frac{p_0}{p_1}\frac{u'(c_0)}{u'(c_1)}\right],$$

where $A(c) = -u''(c)/u'(c)$ is absolute risk aversion. It implies that the indifference
curve is everywhere convex.

To operationalize the above information, consider the portfolio problem with
state prices equal to the probabilities for each state, $\Pi_0 = p_0$ and $\Pi_1 = p_1$. Since
$r = 0$, this implies that the line $p_0c_0 + p_1c_1 = w$ in Figure 5.2 represents the budget
constraint. It follows from the above graphical information that $c_0^* = c_1^* = w$ is the
optimal set of contingent claims on consumption. That is, the consumer should buy
w units of each of the two Arrow–Debreu securities.

Now let us suppose that $\Pi_0 > p_0$, which in turn implies here that $\Pi_1 < p_1$.
The budget line thus becomes $\Pi_0c_0 + \Pi_1c_1 = w$. As illustrated in Figure 5.3,
this new budget line will be steeper. Moreover, at $c_0 = c_1 = w$, we now have
MRS $= p_0/p_1 < \Pi_0/\Pi_1$. Thus, transferring contingent wealth from state 0 to
state 1 at market prices will increase the agent's EU. Indeed, the optimal level of
contingent consumption will be one for which $c_0^* < w < c_1^*$, such as that illustrated

in Figure 5.3, where MRS $= \Pi_0/\Pi_1$. If we consider the contingent claim (w, w) as the individual's initial endowment, the optimal set of trades is to sell $w - c_0^*$ units of the Arrow–Debreu security associated with state 0, and to use the proceeds to purchase $c_1^* - w$ units of the Arrow–Debreu security associated with state 1. Since

$$\pi_1 \equiv \frac{\Pi_1}{p_1} > 1 > \pi_0 \equiv \frac{\Pi_0}{p_0},$$

we see that $C(\pi)$ is decreasing in π, as predicted by our theory.

5.4 Bibliographical References, Extensions and Exercises

Arrow (1953) applied the general equilibrium theory developed by himself and Debreu (1959) to the case of financial markets under uncertainty. It is not the place here to present the developments that followed the discovery of the complete market framework. They span most of the modern theory of finance. The book by LeRoy and Werner (2001) provides a recent presentation of this theory.

Chapter Bibliography

Arrow, K. J. 1953. Le rôle des valeurs boursières pour la répartition la meilleure des risques. In *Econométrie*, pp. 41–48. Paris: Centre National de la Recherche Scientifique. (Translated as Arrow, K. J. 1964. The role of securities in the optimal allocation of risk-bearing. *Review of Economic Studies* 31:91–96.)

Debreu, G. 1959. *Theory of value*. Wiley.

LeRoy, S. and J. Werner. 2001. *Principles of financial economics*. Cambridge, UK: Cambridge University Press.

Exercises

(5.1) The Really Big Company, "RBC," has the following vector of state-contingent end-of-period earnings: $(100, 60, 40)$. State prices for the three states are Π_1, Π_2 and Π_3, respectively, where $\Pi_1 + \Pi_2 + \Pi_3 = (1 + r)^{-1}$. Here r denotes the risk-free rate for borrowing or lending.

    (a) Express the value of the unlevered firm (i.e. a firm with no debt) V^u in terms of state prices. Such a firm is called an all-equity firm, and the total value of the firm is owned by the shareholders.

    (b) Suppose that the RBC decides to use 20% debt financing. Further suppose that the RBC is able to make all debt payments without default. In other words, the RBC issues risk-free bonds to pay for 20% of the initial investment costs. The shareholders' claim is thus the residual firm value, after paying off the bonds. Find the value of the firm's debt and the firm's equity. Does the result of Modigliani and Miller (1958)—the value of the firm is the same both with and without this debt financing—hold in a world with no taxes? Explain.

    (c) Suppose that the RBC would default in state 3 if it used 50% debt financing. In this case, bondholders receive all of the firm's assets and the shareholders receive zero in state 3. Note that such a bond is not risk-free any longer. In a world with no taxes, does the result of Modigliani and Miller still hold? Explain.

(5.2) Consider a complete market with S states of nature. The pricing kernel is such that $\pi_1 < \pi_2 < \cdots < \pi_S$, where π_s is the state price for state s divided by the probability of state s (i.e. the "state-price density"). Prove the following result: an increase in a consumer's risk aversion will cause consumption in state 1 to fall, *ceteris paribus*.

(5.3) Consider an economy consisting of two risk-averse farmers, Mr. Doherty and Mr. Kessler. Both farmers plant soybeans but use different fertilization techniques. As a result of their differing techniques, only one plan is successful in any given year.

In state 1, Mr. Doherty achieves SSD ("Soybean Satisfaction and Delight") and has a crop yield of $X_1 > 0$. On the other hand, in state 2, Mr. Doherty achieves a yield of zero, while Mr. Kessler reaches a Soybean–Mash Equilibrium by having a yield of $X_2 > 0$. Unfortunately, Mr. Kessler's fertilizing strategy yields no soybeans at all in state 1.

A market for contingent claims develops (i.e. a market for soybeans specifying delivery contingent upon a particular state of nature) with price Π_i for contingent delivery of one unit of soybeans in state i, $i = 1, 2$. Both states of nature are equally likely.

    (a) Illustrate the core of this economy (i.e. Pareto efficient and individually rational allocations) using an Edgeworth box.

    (b) Which price will be higher, Π_1 or Π_2? Explain.

    (c) Suppose that instead of being risk-averse, Mr. Kessler were risk neutral. How would your answers to parts (a) and (b) change?

(5.4) Consider a market with three states of nature and three assets. The assets have the following state contingent vectors of payoffs:

$$
\begin{aligned}
\text{asset } A: \quad & (2, 5, 7), \\
\text{asset } B: \quad & (2, 4, 4), \\
\text{asset } C: \quad & (1, 0, 2).
\end{aligned}
$$

Assume that all assets may be sold short.

    (a) Show how to synthetically construct the Arrow–Debreu securities, as well as the risk-free asset using assets A, B and C.

    (b) A call option with exercise price X on an asset pays $\max(a_s - X, 0)$ in state s, where a_s is the asset payoff in state s. Suppose that only asset A exists in this market (not B or C), but that call options on asset A may also be bought or sold with any desired nonnegative exercise price X. Show how to synthetically construct the Arrow–Debreu securities, as well as the risk-free asset.

    (c) Show how your answer in part (b) fails to hold if we replace asset A with either asset B or with asset C. Explain why this cannot be done.

    (d) A put option with exercise price X on an asset pays $\max(X - a_s, 0)$ in state s, where a_s is the asset payoff in state s. Show how asset C together with the purchase or sale of put options can be used to synthetically construct the Arrow–Debreu securities. Explain why the same cannot be done if we replace asset C with asset B.

6

Consumption and Saving

Up to now, we have assumed that the decision maker lives for one period. This obscures the important intertemporal dimension of risk. In real life, agents can often postpone risk to the future. Indeed, this ability to postpone risky choices adds value of its own, usually referred to as a "real-option value." Decision makers can also choose to disseminate gains and losses from their current risk exposure over several periods, which is a type of time diversification of the effects of risk on their ultimate consumption. Alternatively, they might hope to recoup some of their current losses by taking on more risk in the future. In the extreme, this may lead to a type of "go-for-broke" strategy, such as a Las Vegas gambler who bets all of his small amount of remaining wealth on one last gamble in the hopes of recouping his large losses. Finally, agents can alter their planned levels of consumption and saving in the expectation of dealing with uncertainty in the future, such as saving a bit more in earlier periods as type of insurance against future risks. In this chapter and Chapter 7, we examine the relationship between risk and time. We first focus on the impact of risk on the optimal timing of consumption and saving.

6.1 Consumption and Saving under Certainty

As a benchmark case, we start with the characterization of optimal consumption under certainty. Assume that an agent lives for a known number of periods. We denote time by indexing the n dates $t = 0, \ldots, n - 1$. The agent is endowed with a flow of sure incomes y_t, where y_t denotes the revenue that is received with certainty at date t. We assume that there exists an efficient credit market with a constant risk-free interest rate r for both borrowing and lending. In each period, the agent decides how much to consume, which implicitly defines how much is saved or borrowed. If c_t denotes the consumption at date t, the dynamic budget constraint may be written as

$$z_{t+1} = (1 + r)[z_t + y_t - c_t], \quad t = 0, \ldots, n - 1, \tag{6.1}$$

where z_t is the cash transferred from date $t - 1$ to date t. This can also be interpreted as the accumulated saving at date t. We assume that the initial cash z_0 is zero.

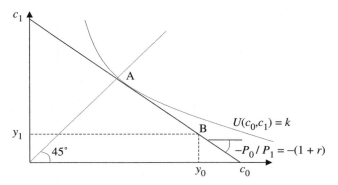

Figure 6.1. Lifetime decision problem of the consumer.

Because lenders will not agree to provide credit to agents that will not be able to repay their debt later on, there is an ultimate constraint $z_n \geqslant 0$: the agent cannot die with a negative net debt position. Recall that we are assuming certainty with regards to both wealth and income, so that this constraint may be imposed on debt financing. Using the dynamic budget constraint (6.1) recursively, condition $z_n \geqslant 0$ may be rewritten as

$$\sum_{t=0}^{n-1} \frac{y_t - c_t}{(1+r)^t} \geqslant 0. \tag{6.2}$$

This is the lifetime budget constraint of the agent. It states that the net present value of the flow of savings $y_t - c_t$ must be nonnegative; or equivalently that the present value of lifetime consumption cannot exceed the present value of lifetime income. More directly, we can write

$$\sum_{t=0}^{n-1} \Pi_t c_t \leqslant w_0, \tag{6.3}$$

where $\Pi_t \equiv (1+r)^{-t}$ and $w_0 \equiv \sum \Pi_t y_t$ is lifetime wealth, i.e. the net present value of the flow of revenues. Observe that Π_t is the price of a zero-coupon bond with maturity at date t, i.e. an asset that generates a unit cash flow only at date t. For a given value of w_0, the agent's objective is to choose an optimal consumption path (which in turn defines an optimal savings plan) across time.

We now describe the preferences of a young consumer over the set of all feasible lifetime consumption flows. Let $U(c_0, c_1, \ldots, c_{n-1})$ denote his lifetime utility if he selects consumption plan $c = (c_0, c_1, \ldots, c_{n-1})$. We assume that function U is increasing and concave. The optimal consumption is obtained by solving the following program:

$$\max_c U(c_0, c_1, \ldots, c_{n-1}) \quad \text{subject to budget constraint (6.3).} \tag{6.4}$$

This decision problem is described in Figure 6.1 in the case of two periods. The optimal consumption plan is characterized by point 'A', where the indifference curve is tangent to the budget line AB.

Before discussing the solution to this problem in a more analytical way, suppose that the agent can choose a revenue profile $(y_0, \ldots, y_{n-1})$ in a given opportunity set. This situation is typical of an investment problem in which an investor has several investment choices, each yielding a different set of cash flows. The structure of problem (6.4) obviously implies that the optimal revenue profile is the one that maximizes its net present value (NPV) $w_0 = \sum \Pi_t y_t$, independently of the temporal consumption preferences of the decision maker. This result is known as Fisher's Separation Theorem. It sustains the NPV rule, which is one of the most important rules in economics: every investor should choose the investment which maximizes the net present value $\sum y_t (1 + r)^{-t}$ of its cash flow.

Problem (6.4) is not much different from the static decision problem of an agent consuming n different physical goods in the classical theory of demand. The general properties of these demand functions are well known. We hereafter make an additional assumption on temporal preferences that enriches the model. Namely, we introduce an independence axiom stating that the preference order over the consumption pair (c_0, c_1) does not depend upon the consumption path over the remaining $n - 2$ periods.[1] This precludes phenomena such as the formation of consumption habits. This independence assumption implies that the utility function U must be separable, $U(c) \equiv \sum u_t(c_t)$, where u_t is the (intraperiod) utility of consumption at time t. To distinguish it from the intertemporal utility function U, we label u_t as the "felicity function" of consumption at date t. A common assumption is that felicity functions are proportional to each other: $u_t(\cdot) = p_t u(\cdot)$, for some increasing and concave function u and for some scalar $p_t > 0$. This set of assumptions has been adopted by most researchers over the last 50 years. Without loss of generality, we normalize p_0 to unity. Thus p_t can be interpreted as the discount factor for felicity $u(c_t)$ occurring at date t. If p_t is less than unity, it can be interpreted as a proportional loss of utility due to postponing consumption, i.e. it indicates a preference for consuming sooner rather than later. It is important to dissociate p_t, a psychological parameter, from r, a financial variable. Parameter p_t serves as a discount factor on felicity, whereas the interest rate r is only useful in discounting monetary flows, as we have seen above.

Using these restrictions, we can rewrite consumption problem (6.4) as

$$\max_c \sum_{t=0}^{n-1} p_t u(c_t) \quad \text{subject to} \quad \sum_{t=0}^{n-1} \Pi_t c_t = w_0. \tag{6.5}$$

---

[1] More precisely, if $(a, b, c_2, \ldots, c_{n-1})$ is preferred to $(d, e, c_2, \ldots, c_{n-1})$, then $(a, b, x_2, \ldots, x_{n-1})$ is preferred to $(d, e, x_2, \ldots, x_{n-1})$ for all $(x_2, \ldots, x_{n-1})$.

The first-order conditions for this problem may be written as

$$p_t u'(c_t) = \xi \Pi_t \quad \text{for } t = 0, \ldots, n-1, \qquad (6.6)$$

together with the budget constraint, where ξ is the Lagrange multiplier associated with problem (6.5). The Lagrange multiplier ξ is simply the marginal lifetime utility of an increase in the present value of wealth.

This problem is formally equivalent to the static Arrow–Debreu portfolio problem (5.3) of the previous chapter. We simply replace "states of nature" with dates, probabilities with discount factors, and Arrow–Debreu securities with zero-coupon bonds. This equivalence is striking between Figures 5.2 and 6.1. This equivalence has several important consequences for the remainder of this book. The most obvious ones are summarized below.

6.1.1 Aversion to Consumption Fluctuations over Time

First, we can interpret the concavity of the felicity function u in the context of the consumption–saving problem under certainty as an aversion to consumption fluctuation from period to period. The fact that marginal utility is decreasing with respect to consumption provides an incentive for the decision maker to smooth consumption over time. To see this, consider the special case with $p_t = 1$ for all t, and with $r = 0$, which implies that $\Pi_t = 1$ for all t. It follows from the first-order conditions (6.6) that $u'(c_t) = \xi$ in each period, so that the optimal consumption path does not exhibit any fluctuation in consumption from period to period: $c_t = w_0/n$ for all t. This is a situation where the optimal consumption plan A is on the 45° line in Figure 6.1. If incomes fluctuate over the life cycle of the consumer, the optimal saving strategy is to save any extra income above w_0/n, or to borrow the extra money in cases where the period income is smaller than w_0/n. The concavity of u implies that second-order conditions are satisfied, so that lifetime utility is maximized via consuming an equal amount in each period.[2] We conclude that when there is no impatience ($p_t = 1$), and a zero interest rate ($r = 0$), it is optimal to smooth consumption over time if the felicity function is concave. Thus, the assumption $u'' < 0$ expresses an aversion to consumption fluctuation over time. This result is a complete analogy with the aversion to consumption fluctuations across states of nature that we make in the static Arrow–Debreu portfolio problem. In the latter model, this implies that full insurance is optimal when asset prices are actuarially fair, i.e. when state prices equal probabilities in every state.

One can measure the intensity of the desire to smooth consumption over time by considering a situation without any credit market, so that $c_t = y_t$. Suppose that the income y_0 at date 0 is strictly less than the income y_1 at date 1. Since the

---

[2]If u were convex, this solution would yield a minimum lifetime utility, and it is easy to show that maximal utility is achieved by consuming only in one period.

marginal utility of consumption is larger at date 0 than at date 1, $u'(y_0) \geqslant u'(y_1)$, we know that the agent would not be willing to exchange one unit of consumption today for one unit of consumption tomorrow. Accepting such a deal would increase the discrepancy between date-0 and date-1 consumption, and would reduce his lifetime utility. If asked to sacrifice one unit of consumption today, the agent will demand more than one unit of consumption tomorrow as compensation. One way to measure the intensity of this resistance to trade today's consumption for consumption tomorrow is to define an additional reward $k > 0$ that must be given to the agent at date 1 to compensate for the loss in consumption at date 0. Assuming changes in the consumption level that are sufficiently small, k is defined by the following condition:

$$u'(y_0) = (1+k)u'(y_1).$$

The left-hand side of this equality is the marginal cost (in utils) of reducing consumption today, whereas the right-hand side is the marginal benefit (also in utils) of raising future consumption by a factor $1 + k$. In other words, k is defined so that the marginal utility loss by giving up one unit of consumption at date 0 must equal the marginal increase in utility by adding $1 + k$ units of consumption at date 1. If y_1 is close to y_0, we can use a first-order Taylor expansion of $u'(y_0)$ around y_1 to obtain

$$k \simeq \frac{y_1 - y_0}{y_1} \left[\frac{-y_1 u''(y_1)}{u'(y_1)} \right]. \tag{6.7}$$

The resistance to intertemporal substitution is approximately proportional to the growth rate of consumption. The multiplicative factor, $\gamma(y) \equiv -yu''(y)/u'(y)$, is hereafter called the measure of relative fluctuation aversion, or the relative degree of resistance to intertemporal substitution of consumption. Obviously, $\gamma(y)$ is an analogue to the Arrow–Pratt measure of relative risk aversion. Both measure the percentage decline in marginal utility relative to a small percentage increase in wealth (consumption). In our current setting, this is a local measure of the consumer's aversion to moving consumption from a date with lower consumption to a date with slightly higher consumption. Note also that there is an equivalence between the measures "in the small" and "in the large." That is, $\gamma(y)$ is related to the approximation of k (6.7) in exactly the same way that the Arrow–Pratt approximation for the risk premium is related to the measure of risk aversion. There has been much attention given to empirical estimates of $\gamma(y)$, which is widely believed to be somewhere between 1 and 5 for most consumers.

6.1.2 *Optimal Consumption Growth under Certainty*

In general, the real interest rate is not zero, and agents are impatient. Let us assume here that consumers use exponential discounting, $p_t = \beta^t$, for some scalar β less than unity. This yields a rate of pure preference for the present $\delta \equiv (1 - \beta)/\beta$ that is positive. In other words, $\beta = (1 + \delta)^{-1}$, and multiplying the felicity $u(c_t)$ by β^t is equivalent to discounting felicity at a constant rate δ per period. Using a constant rate to discount future utils is important for the time consistency of consumer decisions, as we will see in the last section of this chapter.

The presence of impatience and a positive return on savings presents two countervailing reasons not to smooth consumption completely over time. A higher level of impatience, i.e. a higher δ, induces agents to prefer consumption earlier in life. In other words, impatience tends to bias preferences in favor of consumption paths that decrease over time. On the other hand, a higher interest rate makes savings more attractive. It biases consumption choices in favor of consumption paths that are increasing over time. These two contradictory effects must be combined with the aversion to consumption fluctuations to characterize the optimal consumption growth under certainty.

As an illustration, we solve this problem analytically in the special case where the felicity function exhibits a constant relative degree of aversion to consumption fluctuations. Suppose that $u(c) = c^{1-\gamma}/(1 - \gamma)$, where γ is the constant degree of fluctuation aversion. Using the analogy with the Arrow–Debreu problem together with condition (5.6), or solving first-order conditions, (6.6) immediately yields the solution

$$c_t = c_0 a^t, \tag{6.8}$$

where

$$a = \left(\frac{1+r}{1+\delta}\right)^{1/\gamma},$$

and c_0 is some initial consumption that is selected to satisfy the lifetime budget constraint. Thus, when the psychological discount is exponential and relative aversion is constant, it is optimal for consumers to let their consumption grow at a constant rate g, where

$$g \equiv \left(\frac{1+r}{1+\delta}\right)^{1/\gamma} - 1 \simeq \frac{r - \delta}{\gamma}. \tag{6.9}$$

The approximation is closer when δ does not differ much from r. The optimal growth rate of consumption is positive when r is larger than δ. It is easy to check that this property holds independently of the specification of the felicity function. This is a case where the speculative motive for savings dominates the effect of impatience. We also see the intuitive effect of the aversion to fluctuations: an increase in γ reduces the optimal growth rate of consumption over time. But it is optimal to smooth consumption completely over the lifetime only when $r = \delta$, such as was the case in previous section where we had $r = \delta = 0$.

In the real world, consumption growth is subject to business cycles, which forces consumption to fluctuate over time. This has been the topic of much research over the last 30 years. This cycle around the secular trend has a negative impact on consumer welfare. Suppressing it, i.e. smoothing out business cycles, would be beneficial to consumers who dislike consumption fluctuations around the optimal growth rate g. However, Lucas (1987) showed that the importance of the effect of the business cycle on welfare has been largely overestimated by the profession. One can measure the cost of business cycle by the reduction in the growth rate of consumption that the representative agent would accept in exchange for the complete elimination of business cycles. Using data on consumption fluctuations in the US, Lucas showed that business cycles "cost" a reduction of much less than one-tenth of one percent in the annual growth rate of the US economy. This is totally insignificant! The reason is simple: exactly as risk aversion is a second-order effect in the additive EU model, the aversion to consumption fluctuations is a second-order effect in the time-additive lifecycle model. In other words, consumers have an extremely low aversion to small fluctuations in consumption. Lucas concluded that economists should concern themselves with the determinants of long-term growth rather than with the reduction of volatility.

6.2   Uncertainty and Precautionary Savings

Assuming that consumers have a sure income flow is clearly an unrealistic assumption. In this section, we introduce uncertainty into the picture. We consider a simple two-date model with a sure income y_0 in period 0, but an uncertain income $\tilde{y}_1$ in the second period. We assume that this risk is exogenous. For example, the consumer might plan for the future knowing that his future labor income is subject to changes that may be higher or lower than anticipated. Consumers select how much to save at date 0 in order to maximize their expected lifetime utility:

$$\max_s V(s) = u_0(y_0 - s) + Eu_1((1+r)s + \tilde{y}_1). \tag{6.10}$$

Observe that we do not need to assume at this stage that $u_1 = \beta u_0$, as we did in the previous section. Denote the optimal saving under uncertainty by s^*. The first-order condition for s^* is written as

$$u_0'(y_0 - s^*) = (1+r)Eu_1'((1+r)s^* + \tilde{y}_1). \tag{6.11}$$

It is important to observe that the willingness to save is determined by the expected marginal utility of future consumption.

The uncertainty affecting future incomes introduces a new motive for saving. The intuition is that it induces consumers to raise their wealth accumulation in order to forearm themselves to face future risk. This is the so-called precautionary motive for saving, and its relies on a prudent behavior. Its theoretical foundation can be derived by comparing s^* with the optimal saving $\hat{s}$ when the uncertain future income $\tilde{y}_1$ is replaced by its expectation:

$$\max_s \hat{V}(s) = u_0(y_0 - s) + u_1((1+r)s + E\tilde{y}_1).$$

Let $\hat{s}$ denote the solution to this maximization program. We want to determine whether the optimal saving under uncertainty is larger than when the uncertainty is removed: $s^* > \hat{s}$. Because $\hat{V}$ is concave in s, which is easily verified, this is the case if and only if $\hat{V}'(s^*)$ is negative. This condition means that reducing saving marginally from s^* raises lifetime utility under certainty. In other words, there will be a precautionary demand for savings if and only if

$$\begin{aligned}\hat{V}'(s^*) &= -u_0'(y_0 - s^*) + (1+r)u_1'((1+r)s^* + E\tilde{y}_1) \\ &= (1+r)[u_1'((1+r)s^* + E\tilde{y}_1) - Eu_1'((1+r)s^* + \tilde{y}_1)] \\ &\leqslant 0,\end{aligned}$$

where the second equality is obtained by using condition (6.11). Therefore, the level of precautionary saving is positive if and only if

$$Eu_1'((1+r)s^* + \tilde{y}_1) \geqslant u_1'((1+r)s^* + E\tilde{y}_1). \tag{6.12}$$

By Jensen's inequality, this follows whenever u_1' is convex, or equivalently whenever u_1''' is positive. This condition is referred to as "prudence," a concept that has already been introduced in the first chapter. Thus, prudence is necessary if we require that precautionary saving be positive for all possible distributions of the future risk. A consumer who has a concave marginal utility function, on the contrary, would reduce savings because of the future risk. This individual would exhibit what is called "imprudent behavior." Thus prudence corresponds to the positivity of the third derivative of the utility function, exactly as risk aversion relies on the negativity of its second derivative. An agent can exhibit a risk-averse and imprudent behavior, for example, by insuring risk at an unfair premium and by reducing its saving in the face of an non-insurable future risk. Or, following the definitions, a prudent person can be a risk-lover.

There is a link, however, between (decreasing) risk aversion and prudence. Recall from Chapter 1 that

$$A'(w) = A(w)[A(w) - P(w)],$$

where $A(w)$ is the Arrow–Pratt measure of absolute risk aversion and $P(w) = -u'''(w)/u''(w)$ is the measure of absolute prudence, which under risk aversion is positive only if $u''' > 0$. Thus, absolute risk aversion is decreasing if and only if $P(w) > A(w)$ for all w. Because we took decreasing absolute risk aversion (DARA) as a natural assumption, so too should we assume prudence.

One also can measure the intensity of the precautionary saving motive. This can be done by answering the following question: what would be the sure reduction in future income that would have the same effect on savings as the introduction of the future risk? Let ψ denote this "precautionary premium." It is defined implicitly by

$$Eu'_1(w + \tilde{y}_1) = u'_1(w + E\tilde{y}_1 - \psi), \tag{6.13}$$

where w is the accumulated wealth before the second date. This condition states that the willingness to save, which is measured by the expected marginal utility of future consumption, is not affected by the replacement of the risk by its expectation diminished by ψ. The precautionary premium is seen to be positive whenever the agent is prudent, i.e. whenever $u'''_1 > 0$. It is useful to observe at this stage that the precautionary premium is equivalent to the risk premium defined before, but where the utility function u_1 would be replaced by the marginal utility function $-u'_1$. The precautionary premium and the risk premium are the sure reductions in wealth that have the same effects as adding the risks to the expected marginal utility and to the EU, respectively. This implies that all results that we obtained previously for risk aversion and the risk premium can be transferred to prudence and the precautionary premium, by simply replacing u_1 with $-u'_1$.

For example, one can use the Arrow–Pratt approximation for the risk premium to obtain an equivalent one for the precautionary premium:

$$\psi \simeq \tfrac{1}{2}P(w + E\tilde{y}_1)\sigma^2_{\tilde{y}_1}, \tag{6.14}$$

where P is called the degree of absolute prudence. Recall from Chapter 1 that P is equivalently the index of absolute risk aversion for the utility function $v(w) = -u'_1(w)$, where v is risk averse whenever u_1 is prudent. This equivalence also follows since ψ is simply Pratt's risk premium for utility v. Similarly, the precautionary premium ψ is decreasing in wealth if and only if absolute prudence is decreasing in wealth.

To see how the precautionary premium affects savings more directly, consider the simple case where the risk-free rate of savings equals the discount rate for time preference, and set both equal to zero, i.e. $r = \delta = 0$. In particular, lifetime utility is assumed to be $U(c_0, c_1) = u(c_0) + u(c_1)$. We also assume that $E\tilde{y}_1 = y_0$, so that the individual has the same expected income at dates 0 and 1. Suppose first that $\tilde{y}_1$ is non-risky, with $\tilde{y}_1 \equiv y_0$. In this setting, the first-order condition (6.11) implies that $u'(y_0 - s) = u'(y_0 + s)$. As already observed, it follows that the optimal saving is zero, $s^* = 0$, since u is strictly concave. In other words, the consumer simply consumes his current income in each period: $c_0^* = c_1^* = y_0$.

Now suppose that $\tilde{y}_1$ is risky, so that the first-order condition is

$$u'(y_0 - s) = Eu'(E\tilde{y}_1 + s) = u'(y_0 + s - \psi).$$

The second equality above derives from our definition of the precautionary premium. Solving for the optimal savings, we obtain $s^* = \frac{1}{2}\psi$. Thus, if the consumer is prudent, there will be a precautionary demand for savings, $s^* > 0$. Moreover, an individual who is more prudent will have a higher value of the precautionary premium ψ, in the same way that an individual who is more risk averse has a higher risk premium. Consequently, a more prudent consumer will save more than his less prudent counterpart. It is also interesting to note that if the felicity function is quadratic, an assumption that is not uncommon in the finance literature, we have $\psi = 0$ and, hence, there is no precautionary savings motive.

6.3   Risky Savings and Precautionary Demand

In the previous section we considered only a labor-income risk. The individual had a risk-free savings alternative but was unsure about how much income would be earned at date 1. We now look at a model in which labor income is known, but the rate of return on savings is risky. We abstract from the portfolio problem of Chapter 4 and assume that there exists only one fund for risky savings, paying a return of $1 + \tilde{r}$, where $E\tilde{r} \equiv r_0 > 0$. We consider a consumer with an investment horizon of two periods. Since lifetime income is known with certainty, we assume without loss of generality that all income is paid at date $t = 0$. Letting w_0 denote this wealth, the consumer's objective is

$$\max_s V(s) \equiv u(w_0 - s) + \beta E u((1 + \tilde{r})s). \tag{6.15}$$

The first-order condition for this program is

$$u'(w_0 - s) = \beta E[(1 + \tilde{r})u'((1 + \tilde{r})s)]. \tag{6.16}$$

The second-order condition is easily shown to hold under risk aversion. In fact, the objective function $V(s)$ is easily seen to be concave in s.

Consider first the case with a risk-free savings rate of r_0, as in the previous section. The first-order condition in this case becomes

$$u'(w_0 - s) = \beta(1 + r_0)u'((1 + r_0)s).$$

In order to focus on the effects of risk, consider once again a simple case where the expected rate of return on savings equals the discount rate for time preference, i.e. $r = \delta$, so that $\beta = (1 + r_0)^{-1}$. Hence s^* satisfies $w_0 - s^* = (1 + r_0)s^*$. As expected, the optimal saving s^* is such that there is no fluctuation in consumption between dates: $c_0^* = c_1^*$. We next turn to the question of whether adding risk to the return on savings leads to a higher level of savings. It turns out in this setting that prudence alone is not sufficient to lead to an increase in the level of savings. In fact, there are two competing influences at work. On the one hand, the riskiness of returns makes savings less attractive than a risk-free rate with the same average return. But on the other hand, the date-1 risk will induce a precautionary motive to the prudent consumer. It turns out that we need a sufficiently high level of prudence in order to have the precautionary motive dominate, as we show next.

Since $V(s)$ is concave, it follows from (6.16) that uncertainty in the rate of return will cause the optimal level of savings to rise whenever

$$E[(1 + \tilde{r})u'((1 + \tilde{r})s)] > (1 + r_0)u'((1 + r_0)s).$$

This inequality will hold if the function $h(R) \equiv Ru'(Rs)$ is convex in R. Straightforward calculations show that $h''(R) = 2su''(Rs) + s^2 Ru'''(Rs)$. Assume that $u'' < 0$ and that savings are not zero, since c_1 would also be zero in that case. It follows that $h'' > 0$ if

$$\frac{-zu'''(z)}{u''(z)} > 2 \tag{6.17}$$

holds with $z = Rs$. The left-hand side of (6.17) is simply a measure of relative prudence, i.e. the absolute prudence measure $P(z)$ multiplied by the wealth level z. Thus, from (6.17) we obtain the following comparative static property of an increase in risk of the return on saving:

$$s^* \text{ will} \begin{cases} \text{increase} & \text{if relative prudence exceeds 2,} \\ \text{remain the same} & \text{if relative prudence equals 2,} \\ \text{decrease} & \text{if relative prudence is less than 2.} \end{cases}$$

Of course, relative prudence need not satisfy any of the above conditions. However, one case in which it does is that where the felicity function is of the CRRA type, namely $u(c) = c^{1-\gamma}/(1 - \gamma)$, where γ is the constant degree of risk aversion.[3] In this case, straightforward calculations show that relative prudence is equal to $\gamma + 1$. Hence, in the case of CRRA preferences, we have[4]

$$s^* \text{ will} \begin{cases} \text{increase} & \text{if relative risk aversion exceeds 1,} \\ \text{remain the same} & \text{if relative risk aversion equals 1,} \\ \text{decrease} & \text{if relative risk aversion is less than 1.} \end{cases}$$

6.4 Time Consistency

When the model contains only two consumption dates as in the previous two sections, every future action can be planned in advance at date 0, with no possibility to change

---

[3]We refer to "risk aversion" here rather than "fluctuation aversion" since our focus is on risk, and not on simply the timing of consumption in a risk-free setting. It is important to note that a problem with the approach we are using is its inability to fully distinguish between these two phenomena. This has been the focus of much research.

[4]The case for $\gamma = 1$ is found directly by assuming $u(c) = \ln c$.

one's mind. At the second date, the agent just consumes what he has in his savings account. When there are more than two dates, what has been planned at $t = 0$ can be revised at $t = 1$. If you decided at date $t = 0$ to purchase an expensive good that you planned to pay next period ($t = 1$), you may still decide at $t = 1$ to postpone the repayment in order to maintain your high consumption level. Thus, consumers may have a time-consistency problem. To see this, let us re-examine the consumption–saving problem under certainty that is described by (6.5) with $\Pi_t = (1 + r)^{-t}$ and $n \geqslant 3$. At $t = 0$, the consumer plans the consumption profile $(c_0, \ldots, c_{n-1})$ for his remaining lifetime that maximizes his lifetime utility $\sum_{t=0}^{n-1} p_t u(c_t)$ subject to his lifetime budget constraint $\sum_{t=0}^{n-1} \Pi_t c_t = w_0$. Remember that p_t is the factor that is used to discount the felicity occurring t dates from the current date. Using the first-order condition (6.6) for $t = 1$ and $t = 2$, a condition for the consumption plan to be optimal as seen from $t = 0$ is written as

$$\text{planned choice: } u'(c_2) = \frac{p_1}{(1+r)p_2} u'(c_1). \tag{6.18}$$

This consumption rule must be satisfied in order to spend efficiently the money saved from date $t = 0$. Anticipating how he will spend this money saved, the agent determines his optimal initial consumption c_0. Solving the system of equations (6.6) together with the budget constraint, the entire consumption profile

$$(c_0, c_1, c_2, \ldots, c_{n-1})$$

is selected.

Now, let us consider the situation that emerges at date $t = 1$. Wealth has been depleted by the initial consumption c_0, but it has also been augmented by return r on savings. At date $t = 0$, the agent planned to consume c_1 at $t = 1$. However, he is ready to reconsider this choice. His welfare for his remaining lifetime can be written as

$$\sum_{t=1}^{n-1} p_{t-1} u(c_t).$$

The indexes of the p parameters and the c variables are important here. Observe in particular that the felicity $u(c_2)$ occurring one period from the current date $t = 1$ is discounted at p_1, the discount factor for a one-period horizon. Maximizing this objective function with the budget constraint

$$\sum_{t=1}^{n-1} \Pi_{t-1} c_t = (w_0 - c_0)(1 + r)$$

yields the first-order condition

$$\text{actual choice: } u'(c_2) = \frac{p_0}{(1+r)p_1} u'(c_1). \tag{6.19}$$

Equations (6.18) and (6.19) are equivalent only if $p_1/p_2 = p_0/p_1$. This is equivalent to requiring that $p_t = \alpha\beta^t$ for $t = 0, 1, 2$, or that discounting be exponential.[5] Extending this condition for all t implies that the optimal consumption choice c_1 as actually selected at $t = 1$ is not different from the one that has been planned at $t = 0$. There is no time-consistency problem under exponential discounting.

The problem is more complex when the consumer does not use specification $p_t = \alpha\beta^t$ for the discount factors. Suppose, for example, that p_2 is larger than p_1^2/p_0. From (6.18) and (6.19), we derive that the consumption level c_1 that is actually selected at $t = 1$ is larger than that that was planned at $t = 0$. There is a time-consistency problem in that case. When determining his initial consumption, the agent cannot trust himself to limit his consumption in the future. This is typical of an addictive behavior: a smoker finds it beneficial to smoke today conditional on his commitment to stop smoking tomorrow. But when tomorrow arrives, the smoker finds it again beneficial to smoke, thereby postponing his decision to stop to the next day, and so on. We may suspect that such addictive behavior also arises for other goods, yielding a global consumption addiction problem. For people facing this problem, long-term saving plans with no possibility to withdraw may be welfare improving in spite of the lack of flexibility of these saving plans. The time-consistency problem may explain why a large fraction of the population in developed countries finds it acceptable to finance short-term consumption with credit card loans at rates as large as 20%, and still keeps money in long-term savings accounts with rates below 5%.

6.5 Bibliographical References, Extensions and Exercises

The understanding of consumption behavior is probably one of the most important challenges in modern macroeconomics. There have been many developments in this area of research since the seminal papers of Modigliani and Brumberg (1954) and Friedman (1957). These developments refer to the theory of real business cycles, which will not be covered here. Estimations of the relative degree of resistance to consumption fluctuations can be found in many different papers. Hall (1988) found an estimation around 10, whereas Epstein and Zin (1991) found values ranging from 1.25 to 5. An experiment on this has been performed by Barsky, Juster, Kimball and Shapiro (1997). The first formal analysis of precautionary savings is due to Leland (1968), Sandmo (1970) and Drèze and Modigliani (1972). Kimball (1990) coined the term of prudence, and examined the properties of the precautionary premium.

There is an important literature on the effect of liquidity constraints on optimal saving rates. If consumers cannot borrow money when there is a negative temporary

---

[5]This terminology comes from the fact that the continuous-time equivalent of this discount function is $p(t) = e^{-\delta t}$.

shock on their incomes, they will be more willing to accumulate wealth *ex ante*. This "buffer stock" leads to a new motive to save (Deaton 1991; Carroll 1997).

Strotz (1956) was the first to discuss the time-consistency problem of consumers using a discount factor that does not decrease exponentially with the time horizon. Pollack (1968) solved this time-consistency problem using a game-theoretic approach where the different players are the different selves of the consumer living at the different periods. Laibson (1997) re-examined this question to explain various facts on credit markets. There is now a wide and lively literature on "hyperbolic discounting."

Chapter Bibliography

Barsky, R. B., F. T. Juster, M. S. Kimball and M. Shapiro. 1997. Preference parameters and behavioral heterogeneity: an experimental approach in the health and retirement study. *Quarterly Journal of Economics* 112:537–579.

Carroll, C. D. 1997. Buffer-stock saving and the life cycle/permanent income hypothesis. *Quarterly Journal of Economics* 112:1–55.

Deaton, A. 1991. Saving and liquidity constraints. *Econometrica* 59:1221–1248.

Drèze, J. H. and F. Modigliani. 1972. Consumption decisions under uncertainty. *Journal of Economic Theory* 5:308–335.

Epstein, L. G. and S. Zin. 1991. Substitution, risk aversion and the temporal behavior of consumption and asset returns: an empirical framework. *Journal of Political Economy* 99:263–286.

Freidman, M. 1957. *A theory of the consumption function*. Princeton, NJ: Princeton University Press.

Hall, R. E. 1988. Intertemporal substitution of consumption. *Journal of Political Economy* 96:221–273.

Kimball, M. S. 1990. Precautionary savings in the small and in the large. *Econometrica* 58:53–73.

Laibson, D. 1997. Golden eggs and hyperbolic discounting. *Quarterly Journal of Economics* 62:443–477.

Leland, H. E. 1968. PhD dissertation. Stanford University, Stanford, CA, USA.

Modigliani, A. and R. Brumberg. 1954. Utility analysis and the consumption function: an interpretation of the cross-section data. In *Post-Keynesian economics*, ed. K. Kurihara. New Brunswick, NJ: Rutgers University Press.

Pollack, R. A. 1968. Consistent planning. *Review of Economic Studies* 35:201–208.

Sandmo, A. 1970. The effect of uncertainty on saving decisions. *Review of Economic Studies* 37:353–360.

Strotz, R. 1956. Myopia and inconsistency in dynamic utility maximization. *Review of Economic Studies* 23(3):165–180.

Exercises

(6.1) An individual has the following separable lifetime utility function

$$U = \ln c_0 + \ln c_1.$$

(a) If $y_0 = 10$ and $y_1 = 12$ and if there is no credit market, measure the value of the resistance to intertemporal substitution (k). Explain why it is equal in this case to the growth rate of income.

(b) Once there is a perfect credit market with a strictly positive interest rate, which income stream do you prefer:

$$y_0 = 10 \text{ and } y_1 = 12$$

or

$$y_0 = 12 \text{ and } y_1 = 10.$$

Is your answer affected by the features of U?

(c) With the income stream as in (a), what is the optimal value of c_0 when $r = 0$? What happens to c_0 when r becomes strictly positive?

(d) Suppose now that in the income stream of (a) there is labor income risk so that $y_1 = 12$ is replaced by a random variable $\tilde{y}_1$ given by $(10, \frac{1}{2}; 14, \frac{1}{2})$. Assuming that $r = 0$, what happens to the optimal value of c_0? (Hint: you will have to solve a second-degree equation in c_0. The fact that prudence is positive when U is logarithmic will help you to select the appropriate root between the two positive ones.)

(e) Answer questions (c) and (d) if the lifetime utility function becomes: $U = c_0 + \ln c_1$. Explain in words why the individual now wants to consume (much) more in the initial period.

(6.2) Assume to start with that $r = \delta = 0$ in a two-period model and that the utility function is quadratic, i.e.

$$u(c) = c - \beta c^2$$

with $\beta > 0$ and $1 - 2\beta c > 0$ so that marginal utility is positive for all relevant values of c.

(a) If y_0 and y_1 are certain, express the optimal values of s, c_0 and c_1. What happens if $y_0 = y_1$?

(b) Show that the results are not affected when y_1 becomes random with $E(\tilde{y}_1) = y_1$. Explain the result by reference to the notion of prudence.

(c) If y_1 is certain while r is now strictly positive, what is the optimal value of s? Assuming $y_0 = y_1$, compare with the optimal value found in (a). Is it intuitive that the optimal s becomes positive when r is positive? (Hint: in the proof you will need to use the condition that marginal utility of c is positive.)

(d) If r becomes random with $E(\tilde{r}) = r$, what happens to the optimal s? Interpret the result you observe by reference to the discussion following equation (6.16) in the text (the two opposite effects of a risky $\tilde{r}$ on savings).

(6.3) (Before solving this exercise, it pays to return to the solution of Exercise 4.3.)

An individual can allocate his saving between a safe asset (m) paying a return r and a risky one (α) with return $\tilde{x}$ ($E(\tilde{x}) > r$).

In order to avoid heavy computations assume that $y_0 = y_1 = y$ and that $\delta = 0$.

If this individual has a quadratic utility in c, compute the optimal values of s and its allocation between the two assets. (Hint: write Eu as a function of α and m. You will have two first-order conditions, one with respect to m and one with respect to α. Of course $s = \alpha + m$. Notice also that to find the optimal values of α and m you will have to solve a system of two linear equations in two unknowns.)

(6.4) Let us consider an economic agent who is going to live for two periods and who has the following utility function in each period:

$$u_t(c_t) = \begin{cases} c_t & \text{if } c_t \leqslant 1000, \\ 500 + \frac{1}{2}c_t & \text{if } c_t \geqslant 1000. \end{cases}$$

His current income is $y_0 = 1000$ and both r and δ are equal to zero.

How much will this agent save at time 0:

(a) if $y_1 = 1000$ with certainty;

(b) if $y_1 = 800$ with certainty;

(c) if $y_1 = 1200$ with certainty;

(d) if y_1 is a random variable defined by $\tilde{y}_1$ that is distributed as

$$(800, \tfrac{1}{2}; 1200, \tfrac{1}{2})?$$

For each case draw the $V(s)$ function. Comparing the answers in (a) and (d), what do you conclude about the level of precautionary saving?

(6.5) Consider a two-period model of consumption and savings. The individual has an initial wealth of w_0 and intertemporal preferences given by

$$U(c_0, c_1) = u(c_0) + (1 + \delta)^{-1} u(c_1),$$

where $\delta \geqslant 0$ and u is increasing and strictly concave.

Let $\tilde{r}_a$ and $\tilde{r}_b$ be two random rates of return on savings with $E\tilde{r}_a = E\tilde{r}_b = r_0$, and with the variances of $\tilde{r}_a$ and $\tilde{r}_b$ both strictly positive. Further suppose that $\tilde{r}_a$ is riskier than $\tilde{r}_b$ in the sense of Rothschild and Stiglitz.

Let s_0^*, s_a^* and s_b^* denote the optimal level of savings under return rates r_0, $\tilde{r}_a$ and $\tilde{r}_b$, respectively.

Prove that $s_0^* < s_b^* < s_a^*$ whenever relative prudence is greater than 2, thus extending our results in the text.

7

Dynamic Portfolio Management

Investors most often view their financial investments over a long period of time. In many instances, earlier investment decisions are not irreversible. This implies that investment management has an obvious dynamic nature. An important question is therefore whether the investment decisions that can be deduced from a static model, such as those developed in Chapters 4 and 5, can be used to determine the optimal dynamic portfolio strategy. In other words, the problem is to determine how future investment opportunities affect short-term investment choices. Similarly, one can be interested in determining the effect of one's investment horizon on the riskiness of his portfolio. Popular treatments suggest that short time horizons often lead to excessively conservative strategies. Thus, the decisions of corporate managers, graded on their quarterly earnings, are said to focus too much on safe, short-term strategies, with under-investment say in risky research and development projects. It is widely believed that privately held firms, which are not subjected to such short-term "report cards," secure substantial benefit from their ability to focus on longer-term projects. Mutual fund managers, who also get graded regularly, are similarly alleged to focus on strategies that will assure a satisfactory short-term return, with long-term expectations sacrificed. In the formal literature, the horizon-riskiness issue has received perhaps the greatest attention in addressing portfolio strategies appropriate to age.

Samuelson (1989) and several others have asked: "as you grow older and your investment horizon shortens, should you cut down your exposure to lucrative but risky equities?" Conventional wisdom answers affirmatively, stating that long-horizon investors can tolerate more risk because they have more time to recoup transient losses. This dictum has not received the backing of scientific theory, however. As Samuelson (1963, 1989) in particular points out, this "time-diversification" argument relies on a fallacious interpretation of the Law of Large Numbers: repeating an investment pattern over many periods does not cause risk to even out in the long run. This fallacy is illustrated by the following question, raised by Samuelson (1963).

> I offered some lunch colleagues to bet each $200 to $100 that the side of a coin they specified would not appear at the first toss. One distinguished

scholar $(\cdots)$ gave the following answer: "I won't bet because I would feel the \$100 loss more than the \$200 gain. But I'll take you on if you promise to let me make 100 such bets."

This story suggests that independent risks are complementary. However, Samuelson went ahead and asked why it would be optimal to accept 100 separately undesirable bets. The scholar answered:

"One toss is not enough to make it reasonably sure that the law of averages will turn out in my favor. But in a hundred tosses of a coin, the law of large numbers will make it a darn good bet."

Obviously, this scholar misinterprets the Law of Large Numbers! It is not by accepting a second independent lottery that one reduces the risk associated with the first one. If $\tilde{x}_1, \tilde{x}_2, \ldots, \tilde{x}_n$ are independent and identically distributed random wealth variables, $\tilde{x}_1 + \tilde{x}_2 + \cdots + \tilde{x}_n$ has a variance n times as large as the variance of each of these risks. What is stated by the Law of Large Numbers is that

$$\frac{1}{n} \sum_{i=1}^{n} \tilde{x}_i$$

(not $\sum_{i=1}^{n} \tilde{x}_i$) tends to $E\tilde{x}_1$ almost surely as n tends to infinity. It is by subdividing—not adding—risks that they are washed away by diversification.

7.1 Backward Induction

Solving dynamic decision problems requires an understanding of the method generally known as "backward induction." Suppose that you have to make a sequence of two decisions α_0 in period 0, and α_1 in period 1. Decision α_0 is about some risk exposure whose payoff $z(\alpha_0, x)$ depends upon the realization x of a random variable $\tilde{x}$. It is important to notice that x is observed after selecting α_0, but before decision α_1 is taken. Your objective *ex ante* is to maximize the expectation of a function U of $(\alpha_0, \alpha_1, \tilde{x})$:

$$\max_{\alpha_0, \alpha_1} EU(z(\alpha_0, \tilde{x}), \alpha_1). \tag{7.1}$$

Backward induction consists in first solving the second-period problem for each possible outcome that could prevail at the beginning of that period. This set of outcomes is entirely summarized by the payoff z obtained in the first period. The optimal strategy α_1^* in the second period will in general depend upon z, which is hereafter called the state variable of the dynamic program. This second-period problem contingent to "state z" is written as

$$v(z) = \max_{\alpha_1} U(z, \alpha_1). \tag{7.2}$$

The optimal value of the objective given z is denoted $v(z)$. Function v is called the value function, or the Bellman function. One then solves the first-period problem by selecting the risk exposure α_0 that maximizes the expectation of value function $Ev(z(\alpha_0, \tilde{x}))$. By doing so, the decision maker internalizes the effect of his future contingent strategy on his welfare U, given the definition of v. He is what we call "dynamically consistent." This technique transforms any dynamic problem into a sequence of static problems through the value function.

7.2 The Dynamic Investment Problem

In this section, we examine the effect of the opportunity to take risk in the future on the willingness to take risk in the short run. In other words, will an investor with a longer planning horizon be willing to invest a higher proportion of wealth in risky stocks as opposed to safer bonds? We assume that the investor has the objective of maximizing the EU of his accumulated wealth at a specific date. This is the case, for example, when the investment is targeted for retirement. This money is not used for intermediary consumption. In the standard terminology, this is called an investment problem. We will introduce intermediary consumption later on in this chapter. We also assume here that risks are independent over time, a condition that will be relaxed in the last section of this chapter.

One can illustrate the problem examined in this section as follows. Building on Samuelson's question, suppose that you are offered to bet on whether a fair coin will land "heads" (H) or "tails" (T). You get three times your stake if it lands H, and you lose it otherwise. Suppose that, given your risk aversion, you want to bet α on this single gamble. Now, suppose that you are told that you will be allowed to bet sequentially on two independent draws of the coin. How does this affect your bet α' on the initial draw of the coin? This question is equivalent to the effect of time horizon on the optimal investor's portfolio composition.

We consider the following more general problem. An investor who is endowed with wealth w_0 lives for two periods. At the beginning of each period, he has the opportunity to take some risk, the realization of which will be observed at the end of the corresponding period. It is important to notice that the investor will observe his loss or gain on the risk that he took in the first period before deciding how much risk to take in the second period. This makes the problem intrinsically dynamic, and it introduces flexibility, an essential element of dynamic risk management. To illustrate, under DARA, investors will take less risk in the second period if they suffered heavy losses on their portfolio in the first period.

To be more specific, we suppose that the second-period problem is an Arrow–Debreu portfolio decision. There are S possible states of nature $s = 0, \dots, S - 1$. The uncertainty prevailing over this second period is characterized by the vector of probabilities $(p_0, \dots, p_{S-1})$. Π_s is the unit price of the Arrow–Debreu security associated to state s. We assume that the risk-free rate is zero. This implies that a claim paying one euro in every state of nature must itself cost one euro; $\sum_s \Pi_s = 1$. In other words, if the investor does not take any risk in the second period, he will end up with the same final wealth as in the first period. Given the wealth z accumulated at the end of the first period, the investor selects a portfolio $(c_0, \ldots, c_{S-1})$ which maximizes the EU of his wealth at the end of the period subject to his budget constraint:

$$v(z) = \max_{c_0, \ldots, c_{S-1}} \sum_{s=0}^{S-1} p_s u(c_s) \quad \text{subject to} \sum_{s=0}^{S-1} \Pi_s c_s = z. \tag{7.3}$$

This is equivalent to problem (7.2) with $\alpha_1 = (c_1, \ldots, c_{S-1})$ and

$$U(z, \alpha_1) = p_0 u\left(\frac{z - \sum_{s=1}^{S-1} \Pi_s c_s}{\Pi_0}\right) + \sum_{s=1}^{S-1} p_s u(c_s).$$

In period zero, the investor must take a risky decision α_0 that yields a payoff $z(\alpha_0, x)$ which depends upon the realization x of some random variable $\tilde{x}$. In particular, this can be another portfolio choice problem. The optimal exposure to the risk in period 0 is obtained by solving the following program:

$$\alpha_0^* \in \arg\max_{\alpha_0} Ev(z(\alpha_0, \tilde{x})). \tag{7.4}$$

We want to determine the impact of the opportunity to take risk in the second period on the optimal exposure to risk in the first period. To do this, we compare the solution α_0^* obtained from the dynamic program (7.4) with the optimal exposure to risk in the first period when there is no such an option to take further risk in the second period. The short-lived investor, as well as the myopic investor would select the level $\hat{\alpha}_0$ that would maximize the EU of $z(\alpha_0, \tilde{x})$:

$$\hat{\alpha}_0 \in \arg\max_{\alpha_0} Eu(z(\alpha_0, \tilde{x})). \tag{7.5}$$

We see that the only difference between programs (7.5) and (7.4) is that the utility function u in the first program is replaced by the value function v in the second. It is another way to say that the effect of the future is entirely captured by the characteristics of the value function. In our context, the opportunity to take risk in the future raises the willingness to take risk today if v is less concave than u in the sense of Arrow–Pratt. This is a consequence of Proposition 4.1 in the case of a one-risky–one-risk-free-portfolio problem in the first period.

The optimal exposure to risk in the first period is larger than the myopic one if the value function v defined by program (7.3) is less concave than the original utility function u, i.e. v is more risk tolerant than u. The degree of absolute risk tolerance of v is characterized in the following proposition.

Proposition 7.1. *The value function for the Arrow–Debreu portfolio problem (7.3) has a degree of absolute risk tolerance given by*

$$T_v(z) = -\frac{v'(z)}{v''(z)} = \sum_{s=0}^{S-1} \Pi_s T(c_s^*),$$
(7.6)

where c^* is the optimal solution to problem (7.3) and $T(\cdot) = -u'(\cdot)/u''(\cdot)$ is the absolute risk tolerance for final consumption.

Proof. The optimal solution to program (7.3) is hereafter denoted $c^*(z)$. It satisfies the following first-order condition:

$$u'(c_s^*(z)) = \xi(z)\pi_s, \quad s = 0, \dots, S-1,$$
(7.7)

where $\pi_s = \Pi_s / p_s$ is the state price per unit of probability as developed in Chapter 5 and $\xi(z)$ is the Lagrange multiplier associated with (7.3) for a particular value of z. Fully differentiating condition (7.7) with respect to z and eliminating π_s yields

$$c_s^{*\prime}(z) = -\frac{\xi'(z)}{\xi(z)} T(c_s^*(z)).$$
(7.8)

Fully differentiating the budget constraint yields in turn

$$\sum_{s=0}^{S-1} \Pi_s c_s^{*\prime}(z) = 1.$$
(7.9)

Replacing $c_s^{*\prime}(z)$ by its expression in (7.8) implies that

$$-\frac{\xi'(z)}{\xi(z)} = \left[\sum_{s=0}^{S-1} \Pi_s T(c_s^*(z)) \right]^{-1}.$$
(7.10)

Finally, fully differentiating $v(z)$, which by definition equals $\sum_s p_s u(c_s^*(z))$, implies that

$$v'(z) = \sum_{s=0}^{S-1} p_s u'(c_s^*(z)) c_s^{*\prime}(z) = \xi(z) \sum_{s=0}^{S-1} \Pi_s c_s^{*\prime}(z) = \xi(z).$$

The second equality above follows from the first-order condition, whereas the third equality is due to (7.9). This confirms the classical result that the Lagrange multiplier associated to the budget constraint of the consumer equals the shadow price of wealth. From this result, we see that $v''(z) = \xi'(z)$ and $T_v(z) = -\xi(z)/\xi'(z)$. The proposition then follows immediately from equation (7.10). $\qquad\square$

Now, remember that we assumed that the risk-free rate in the second period is zero, in turn implying that $\sum_s \Pi_s = 1$. This assumption eliminated a potential wealth effect for those who are allowed to invest in the second period. Then, property (7.6) states that the absolute risk tolerance of the value function is a weighted average of the degree of risk tolerance of final consumption.[1] This property allows us to compare the degrees of concavity of u and v. Suppose, for example, that u exhibits "hyperbolic absolute risk aversion" (HARA), i.e. that T is linear in c. It implies that $T_v(z) = \sum_s \Pi_s T(c_s^*) = T(\sum_s \Pi_s c_s^*) = T(z)$. Thus, when u is HARA, the value function v has the same degree of concavity as u: $v(\cdot) = Ku(\cdot)$. This implies that the two programs (7.4) and (7.5) have exactly the same solution. In other words, under HARA preferences the option to take risk in the future has no effect on the optimal exposure to risk today: myopia is optimal. *Ceteris paribus*, young and old investors should select the same portfolio composition.

Suppose alternatively that the utility function u exhibits a convex absolute risk tolerance. Applying Jensen's inequality, it follows that $T_v(z) = \sum_s \Pi_s T(c_s^*) > T(\sum_s \Pi_s c_s^*) = T(z)$: the opportunity to take risk in the future raises the tolerance to current risks. The assumption that T'' is nonnegative is compatible with the intuition that a longer time horizon should induce more risk-taking.[2] On the other hand, if T'' is non-positive, a longer time horizon for investment should imply a more conservative investment in the short run.

Proposition 7.2. *Suppose that the risk-free rate is zero. In the dynamic Arrow–Debreu portfolio problem with serially independent returns, a longer time horizon raises (resp. reduces) the optimal exposure to risk in the short term if the absolute risk tolerance $T(\cdot) = -u'(\cdot)/u''(\cdot)$ is convex (resp. concave). In the HARA case, the time horizon has no effect on the optimal portfolio.*

When the long-term investment is targeted for consumption at a specific date, whether the investor should modify his risk exposure as the time horizon recedes is an empirical question which relies on the convexity, linearity or concavity of absolute risk tolerance. Of course none of these conditions on absolute risk tolerance need hold for all wealth levels. It is possible to have a risk tolerance that is sometimes convex and sometimes concave. For such an individual, we will not be able to predict the effect of a longer planning horizon on investment strategy. Depending on the circumstances, this individual sometimes will invest more in stocks and other times will invest more in bonds than would be invested under myopia.

One can think about the convexity/concavity of absolute risk tolerance by introspection. Remember that, by (4.4), the euro amount optimally invested in stocks is approximately proportional to T. Under DARA, it is increasing in wealth. The question is whether it is increasing at an increasing rate as wealth increases. If it is, this would be an argument for a convex T, and for a positive effect of time horizon length on risk taking. Most theoretical models in finance use HARA utility

---

[1] In the terminology of the theory of finance, it is a martingale.

[2] This assumption relies on the sign of the fourth derivative of the utility function.

functions. In these models, myopia is optimal, which simplifies much the analysis. One can, however, suspect that this assumption is made for simplicity rather than for realism. Econometric tests for HARA preferences are extremely scarce in the literature.

7.3 Time Diversification

In the investment problem, there is a single prespecified consumption date. This implies that all risks taken in life are borne on that date. In most instances however, investors will want to use their portfolios to finance consumption throughout their lifetimes.[3] This has an important advantage, which is to allocate current risks on wealth into small risks on consumption over a long time horizon. This produces an important time-diversification effect, which makes people with a longer planning horizon willing to take more risk.

To explain this, let us consider a simple model where the agent has the opportunity to take a risk at date $t = -1$. More specifically, we assume that the payoff for the initial risk-taking game is $z(\alpha_0, \tilde{x})$, where α_0 is a decision variable and $\tilde{x}$ is a random variable. The agent then consumes over the remaining n dates, numbered $t = 0, \ldots, n - 1$. We assume that the agent can save and borrow at a zero interest rate, and that he has no risk-taking opportunities from date $t = 0$ on. Moreover, in each period he earns a labor income y.

This problem exhibits the same dynamic structure as presented in Section 7.1. To determine the optimal exposure to risk in the first period, one needs first to solve the consumption–saving problem occurring after the risky outcome is revealed. For a given wealth z accumulated prior to date $t = 0$, we can write

$$v(z) = \max_c \sum_{t=0}^{n-1} p_t u(c_t) \quad \text{subject to} \quad \sum_{t=0}^{n-1} c_t = z + ny, \qquad (7.11)$$

where p_t is the discount factor associated to date t, and $z + ny$ is the lifetime wealth. With this value function v, one can determine the level of optimal initial risk taking by solving $\max_{\alpha_0} Ev(z(\alpha_0, \tilde{x}))$. This level of risk is increasing in the degree of risk tolerance of the value function v.

As already observed in the previous chapter, the structure of this consumption–saving problem is essentially the same as that of the static Arrow–Debreu portfolio problem in Proposition 7.1. The main difference main difference is that we do not have state prices, so that we need to assume here that $\Pi_s = 1$ for all s, i.e. a euro's worth of consumption at time t costs one euro today (since we assume that the

---

[3] Of course, the model presented here is overly simplified. For example, real-world tax incentives can work against this possibility.

risk-free rate is zero). Consequently, it follows from Proposition 7.1 that

$$T_v(z) = \sum_{t=0}^{n-1} T(c_t^*), \qquad (7.12)$$

where c_t^* is the optimal solution of problem (7.11). In the consumption–saving problem with certainty for dates $t = 0, n - 1$ and with a zero interest rate, the degree of tolerance to the risk on initial wealth equals the sum of the absolute tolerances to risk on consumption over the lifetime of the consumer.

We now want to examine the effect of an increase in n on $T_v(z)$. For simplicity, suppose that consumers are not impatient, so that $p_t = 1$ for all t. Then, it is optimal to smooth consumption completely: $c_t^* = y + (z/n)$ at every date t. In this setting, all gains and losses on the initial risk are allocated equally over the remaining n periods of consumption. Property (7.12) can thus be written as

$$T_v(z) = nT\left(y + \left(\frac{z}{n}\right)\right).$$

For a small initial risk (z small), the absolute tolerance to risk on wealth is proportional to the lifetime of the gambler. Thus, an agent who expects to live twice as long as another agent with the same yearly income would invest approximately twice as much in stocks as his shorter-lived counterpart at date $t = -1$. This is the real meaning that should be given to the notion of "time diversification."

Of course, we assumed here that there is only a single point in time when consumers may take a risk. In the real world, consumers can own stocks and take risks at any time. This more realistic assumption would not change our result in the HARA case. Indeed, using backward induction together with Proposition 7.2, adding the opportunity to take a risk in the future would not change the concavity of the value function at any specific date when HARA is assumed. Agents are myopic to future risks in this case and property (7.12) would still hold.

Another consideration in a more realistic setting is the existence of liquidity constraints. Time diversification works well only if consumers are allowed to borrow money at an acceptable loan rate when they face an adverse shock on their incomes and their cash on-hand is depleted. This is an unrealistic assumption. Agents with no liquidity reserve typically cannot smooth a negative income shock by borrowing money from their bank. They cannot fully time-diversify. Such liquidity constraints imply that agents should be much more averse to income risks. This is an additional argument in favor of decreasing absolute risk aversion.

7.4   Portfolio Management with Predictable Returns

In Section 7.2, we examined a portfolio-decision problem in which the opportunity set for investment was invariant over time. In the real world, it is often the case that this opportunity set is stochastic and that there is some predictability in its changes. Predictability can come, for example, from the existence of serial correlation in stock returns. The existence of mean-reversion in stocks returns has recently been recognized: a high return of the risky portfolio today generally implies a lower expected portfolio return tomorrow. Receiving some good news today often means bad news for the future opportunity set.

In this section, we consider the effect of such predictability on the optimal dynamic portfolio. Obviously, investors will follow a flexible strategy where the optimal risk exposure is made conditional on the opportunity set. But investors also will try to anticipate any shocks to this set. More specifically, investors can consider the possibility of hedging against any bad news about their future opportunity set. Of course, this is easier to accomplish if shifts are statistically related to current returns. The demand for stocks which is due to this anticipation is called the "hedging demand" for stocks. Because stocks are thought to be safer in the long run than in the short run, intuition suggests that an investor with a longer planning horizon will take more risks early in life.

For the sake of simplicity, we limit the analysis here to the case of constant relative risk aversion γ with a two-period time horizon. Constant relative risk aversion implies myopia with respect to the time horizon in the absence of predictability. We assume that the economy has one risk-free asset with a zero return and one risky asset whose return in period t is denoted by $\tilde{x}_t$, $t = 0, 1$. The opportunity set in the second period is thus completely described by $\tilde{x}_1$. Predictability comes from an assumption that the distribution of $\tilde{x}_1$ is correlated to $\tilde{x}_0$. We assume that $E\tilde{x}_0 > 0$. Investors invest only for their retirement at the end of the second period, so that there is no intermediate consumption.

In order to determine the optimal demand for the risky asset in the first period, and in particular its hedging component, it is necessary to follow the method presented in Section 7.1. We begin with solving the problem faced by investors in the second period for each possible situation. What is new here is that a situation is described not only by the wealth z accumulated at that time, but also by the realized return x_0 of the risky asset in the first period. More specifically, the value function v is defined by

$$v(z, x_0) = \max_{\alpha} E\left[\frac{(z + \alpha\tilde{x}_1)^{1-\gamma}}{1 - \gamma} \,\bigg|\, x_0\right]. \tag{7.13}$$

From Proposition 4.2, we know that the optimal solution of this program is a separable function $\alpha_1(z, x_0) = a(x_0)z$. This implies in turn that the value function is separable, with $v(z, x_0) = h(x_0)z^{1-\gamma}/(1 - \gamma)$, where

$$h(x_0) = E[(1 + a(x_0)\tilde{x}_1)^{1-\gamma} \mid x_0].$$

We can now turn to the first-period decision problem. This can be written as

$$\alpha_0^* = \arg\max_\alpha H(\alpha) = E\left[h(\tilde{x}_0) \frac{(w_0 + \alpha\tilde{x}_0)^{1-\gamma}}{1 - \gamma} \right]. \tag{7.14}$$

In order to determine the hedging component of the demand for the risky asset, we compare α_0^* against the demand for the risky asset when there is no predictability, i.e. when $\tilde{x}_1$ is independent of $\tilde{x}_0$. In this case, we know that myopia is optimal. Thus, without predictability, investors solve

$$\alpha_0^m = \arg\max_\alpha E\left[\frac{(w_0 + \alpha\tilde{x}_0)^{1-\gamma}}{1 - \gamma} \right].$$

When returns are somewhat predictable, the hedging demand is defined as $\alpha_0^* - \alpha_0^m$. This hedging demand will be positive if the derivative of H evaluated at α_0^m is positive. In other words, the hedging demand for the risky asset is positive if

$$H'(\alpha_0^m) = E[\tilde{x}_0 h(\tilde{x}_0)(w_0 + \alpha_0^m \tilde{x}_0)^{-\gamma}] \geqslant 0$$

whenever $E[\tilde{x}_0(w_0 + \alpha_0^m \tilde{x}_0)^{-\gamma}] = 0$.

To consider a specific type of predictability, we examine the case where an increase in x_0 deteriorates the distribution of $\tilde{x}_1$ in the sense of first-order stochastic dominance (FSD). A special case is when the stochastic process $(\tilde{x}_0, \tilde{x}_1)$ exhibits mean-reversion.[4] For example, suppose that the conditional distribution of $\tilde{x}_1$ can be written as $\tilde{x}_1 \mid x_0 = -kx_0 + \tilde{\varepsilon}$, where $\tilde{\varepsilon}$ is assumed to be independent of $\tilde{x}_0$ and where k is a positive scalar. Because any FSD shift in $\tilde{x}_1$ reduces the EU of final wealth, this assumption implies that $\partial v / \partial x_0$ is negative. Since $v(z, x_0) = h(x_0)z^{1-\gamma}/(1 - \gamma)$, it follows that h' must be negative when $\gamma < 1$, and h' must be positive when $\gamma > 1$.

Suppose first that relative risk aversion γ is larger than unity. Because h' must be positive in this case, it follows that for all x_0,

$$x_0 h(x_0)(w_0 + \alpha_0^m x_0)^{-\gamma} \geqslant x_0 h(0)(w_0 + \alpha_0^m x_0)^{-\gamma}.$$

Taking expectations on both sides, it follows in turn that

$$H'(\alpha_0^m) \geqslant h(0)E[\tilde{x}_0(w_0 + \alpha_0^m \tilde{x}_0)^{-\gamma}] = 0.$$

Thus, the hedging demand is positive when the relative risk aversion is larger than unity. If instead we have relative risk aversion less than unity, $\gamma < 1$, then h' is negative, and the above inequality is reversed. This result is summarized in the following proposition.

---

[4]Of course one could model the opposite effect, in which an increase in x_0 improves the distribution of $\tilde{x}_1$ by FSD. Such an assumption would imply a positive serial correlation of returns, which is consistent with so-called "momentum" arguments concerning the distributions of returns in the finance literature.

Proposition 7.3. *Suppose that an increase in the first-period return deteriorates the distribution of the second-period return in the sense of first-order stochastic dominance. Then, the hedging demand for the risky asset is positive (resp. negative) if constant relative risk aversion is larger (resp. smaller) than unity.*

Another way to interpret this result is that, when relative risk aversion is constant and larger than unity, a longer time horizon should induce investors to take more risk. The contrary is true if constant relative risk aversion is less than unity. Notice that when investors have a logarithmic utility function ($\gamma = 1$), myopia is still optimal in the presence of predictability.

The choice of the initial portfolio risk is driven by the slope of the marginal value of wealth at the end of the initial period. This marginal value of wealth depends upon the future opportunity set. If predictability reduces the marginal value of wealth in states where it is large, and raises it in states where it is small, then predictability has the same effect as a reduction in risk aversion: it raises the optimal level of risk in the portfolio. Consequently, we see that the central step of the analysis is to determine the effect that our FSD-deteriorating shift in the return of the risky asset will have on the marginal value of wealth. In the special case of mean-reversion, we can see two different effects of an increase in x_0. The first effect is a wealth effect: because the expected return in the second period becomes smaller, so is the expected final wealth. This raises the marginal value of wealth, since v is concave in z. The second effect is a precautionary effect: investors will invest less in the risky asset, thereby reducing the exposure to the risk. Under prudence, this reduces the marginal value of wealth. The global effect of an increase in x_0 on the marginal value of wealth is thus ambiguous. When relative risk aversion is constant and larger than unity,[5] the wealth effect always dominates the precautionary effect, and the hedging demand is positive. When relative risk aversion is less than unity, the wealth effect is dominated by the precautionary effect.

7.5 Learning about the Distribution of Excess Returns: a Numerical Illustration

Up to now, we have assumed that the distribution of excess returns is perfectly known to the investor. Relaxing this assumption introduces a new form of predictability that affects the optimal dynamic portfolio strategy. To illustrate this, we consider the following numerical example. Suppose that the risk-free rate is zero. We assume that there are two equally likely distributions of excess returns: either $(2, \frac{9}{10}; -1, \frac{1}{10})$ or $(2, \frac{1}{10}; -1, \frac{9}{10})$. Without any other information, the prior distribution of excess

---

[5]Notice that constant relative risk aversion is larger than unity if and only if absolute prudence is smaller than twice the absolute risk aversion. This explains why this condition implies that the precautionary effect is dominated by the wealth effect.

returns is thus $(2, \frac{1}{2}; -1, \frac{1}{2})$. By observing realized returns over time, investors will be able to update their beliefs about the true distribution of excess returns using Bayes's rule. We examine the effect of this learning process on the optimal dynamic portfolio management. Intuition suggests that investors will be cautious before learning about the riskiness of stocks. That is, they would take fewer risks than if they knew with certainty that the distribution is $(2, \frac{1}{2}; -1, \frac{1}{2})$.[6]

In the case of mean reversion that we examined in the previous section, a high return in the first period was bad news for the second-period investment opportunity set. Just the opposite is true in the presence of a learning process: a high return in the first period is good news for the second period. Let us now verify this specific claim. When the high return $x_0 = 2$ is observed during the first period, Bayes's rule implies that the probability of the favorable distribution goes up from $\frac{1}{2}$ to $\frac{9}{10}$. This implies that the expected probability of the high return goes up from $\frac{1}{2}$ to $0.9(\frac{9}{10}) + 0.1(\frac{1}{10}) = 0.82$. Thus, our revised *ex post* distribution of the excess returns is $(2, 0.82; -1, 0.18)$. On the other hand, when the low return $x_0 = -1$ is observed in the first period, Bayes's rule implies that the *ex post* distribution of the excess return equals $(2, 0.18; -1, 0.82)$. We see that observing the high return in the first period improves the distribution of excess return in the second period in the sense of first-order stochastic dominance, which is indeed good news for the investor. Using the same arguments as we used to prove Proposition 7.3, we obtain the following result.

Proposition 7.4. *Suppose that, as in the Bayesian learning process, an increase in the first-period return improves the distribution of the second-period return in the sense of first-order stochastic dominance. Then, the hedging demand for the risky asset is negative (resp. positive) if constant relative risk aversion is larger (resp. smaller) than unity.*

Suppose that relative risk aversion is constant and equal to $\gamma = 2$. Let us solve the portfolio choice problem in the second period conditional on each of the two possible observations made in the first period. If a high return is observed in the first period, straightforward calculations show that the investor should invest $a(2) = 40.22\%$ of his wealth in the risky asset during the second period. The value function $v(z, 2)$ equals $0.76u(z)$ in this case. On the other hand, if the low return is observed in the first period, the investor's optimal second-period investment should entail $a(-1) = -12.67\%$ of his wealth invested in the risky asset, and the value function $v(z, -1)$ equals $0.97u(z)$.

---

[6]This type of uncertainty is often referred to as "parameter uncertainty" and "ambiguity." In a one period model, such uncertainty does not affect decisions made using the EU criterion. Here we show how the same non-effect does not hold in an intertemporal setting. In the last chapter in this book, we consider an alternative to EU that allows ambiguity to influence single-period decision making.

Turning now to the first-period problem, the investor solves the following problem:

$$\max_{\alpha} \tfrac{1}{2}0.76u(w_0 + 2\alpha) + \tfrac{1}{2}0.97u(w_0 - \alpha).$$

This yields an optimal demand for the risky asset in the first period of $\alpha_0^* = 7.66\%$ of initial wealth w_0. It is easy to check that the myopic agent would invest $\alpha_0^m = 12.13\%$ of his wealth in the risky asset. Therefore, the hedging demand $\alpha_0^* - \alpha_0^m$ is negative, thereby showing that the learning process tends to induce a prudent investment behavior in the early stages of the learning process.

7.6 Bibliographical References, Extensions and Exercises

Merton (1969) and Samuelson (1969) were the first to solve the dynamic portfolio problem in a continuous-time economy with HARA utility functions. Mossin (1968) proved that HARA functions are the only ones for which myopia is optimal when there is no serial correlation in returns. Deaton (1991) and Carroll (1997) examine the effect of liquidity constraints on the optimal saving behavior.

The book by Campbell, Lo and MacKinlay (1997) provides an extensive analysis of stock returns. Barberis (2000) estimates significant predictability of US stocks returns. The implied standard deviation of ten-year returns is 23.7%, much smaller than the 45.2% value implied by the standard deviation of monthly returns. Kim and Omberg (1996) showed that this is indeed the case if constant relative risk aversion is larger than unity. Campbell and Viciera (1999) and Barberis (2000) estimate this hedging demand numerically. The effect of the return predictability on the optimal structure of the initial portfolio is surprisingly large. For an agent with a relative risk aversion equaling 10 and a ten-year time horizon, the optimal investment in stocks is about 40% of current wealth without predictability. It goes up to 100% when mean-reversion is taken into account. Kandel and Stambaugh (1996) solve a model in which there is mean-reversion in stock returns, but with some estimation risk on the parameters of the mean-reversion. Detemple (1986) is the first to examine the problem of asset demand under incomplete information and learning.

Chapter Bibliography

Barberis, N. 2000. Investing for the long run when returns are predictable. *Journal of Finance* 55:225–264.

Campbell, J. Y., A. W. Lo, and A. C. MacKinlay. 1997. *The econometrics of financial markets*. Princeton, NJ: Princeton University Press.

Campbell, J. and L. Viciera. 1999. Consumption and portfolio decisions when expected returns are time varying. *Quarterly Journal of Economics* 114:433–95.

Carroll, C. D. 1997. Buffer-stock saving and the life cycle/permanent income hypothesis. *Quarterly Journal of Economics* 112:1–55.

Deaton, A. 1991. Saving and liquidity constraints. *Econometrica* 59:1221–1248.

Detemple, J. B. 1986. Asset pricing in an economy with incomplete information. *Journal of Finance* 61:383–392.

Kandel, S. and R. Stambaugh. 1996. On the predictability of stock returns: an asset allocation perspective. *Journal of Finance* 51:385–424.

Kim, T. S. and E. Omberg. 1996. Dynamic nonmyopic portfolio behavior. *Review of Financial Studies* 9:141–161.

Merton, R. C. 1969. Lifetime portfolio selection under uncertainty: the continuous-time case. *Review of Economics and Statistics* 51:247–257.

Mossin, J. 1968. Optimal multiperiod portfolio policies. *Journal of Business* 41:215–229.

Samuelson, P. A. 1963. Risk and uncertainty: the fallacy of the Law of Large Numbers. *Scientia* 98: 108–113.

Samuelson, P. A. 1969. Lifetime portfolio selection by dynamic stochastic programming. *Review of Economics and Statistics* 51:239–246.

Samuelson, P. A. 1989. The judgement of economic science on rational portfolio management: indexing, timing and and long-horizon effects. *Journal of Portfolio Management* (Fall issue): 3–12.

Exercises

(7.1) An individual is endowed with a wealth of 100. In addition, she owns the gamble $\tilde{x}_1:(+20, \frac{1}{2}; -20, \frac{1}{2})$.

    (a) If her utility function is $u = \sqrt{W}$, compute her expected utility.

    (b) What happens to this expected utility if gamble $\tilde{x}_1$ is played twice, with independent draws? What happens if it is played three times with independent draws? Can you claim that the addition of independent draws makes the situation less risky while keeping the mean constant? (Instead of making the computation, you might wish to graph the cumulative distributions of final wealth for each number of draws.)

    (c) Contrast this result with the situation where the payoff of two draws is $\frac{1}{2}(\tilde{x}_1 + \tilde{x}_2)$, while it is $\frac{1}{3}(\tilde{x}_1 + \tilde{x}_2 + \tilde{x}_3)$ for three draws.

(7.2) An individual with initial wealth equaling 100 has the following utility function:

$$u = \begin{cases} W & \text{for } W \leqslant 100, \\ 50 + \frac{1}{2}W & \text{for } W \geqslant 100. \end{cases}$$

    (a) Should she accept a gamble $\tilde{x}$ described by $(+20, \frac{1}{2}; -11, \frac{1}{2})$?

    (b) Now this individual is told that when the result of the first gamble is known, she may participate in another gamble $\tilde{y}$, distributed as

$$(+56, \tfrac{1}{4}; -16, \tfrac{3}{4}),$$

    provided that she has first taken part in $\tilde{x}$. Does this additional opportunity induce the individual to accept $\tilde{x}$ first?

    (c) Now assume the individual is first offered $\tilde{y}$. Should she accept it?

    (d) What will she do if she is now offered the opportunity to take $\tilde{x}$ after the result of $\tilde{y}$ is known?

The results you obtain should convince you that the order in which the gambles are offered matters for risk-averse individuals.

(7.3) Consider a two-period model of investment with Bayesian learning. The individual has an initial wealth of w_0 and preferences are CRRA and we assume that $\delta = r = 0$. The individual must choose to invest in the risky and riskless assets at time $t = 0$ and $t = 1$. Assume that short selling of the risky asset is allowed.

Let $\tilde{r}_t$ be the distribution of excess returns at time t. The distribution is i.i.d. in the true distribution at each point in time, but there is an equally likely chance that the true distribution is either $(2, 0.8; -1, 0.2)$ or $(2, 0.2; -1, 0.8)$.

(a) Suppose that $r_0 = 2$. What is the posterior distribution of $\tilde{r}_1$? Suppose that $r_0 = -1$. What is the posterior distribution of $\tilde{r}_1$?

(b) Find the optimal investment in the risky asset at date $t = 0$ if relative risk aversion $\gamma = \frac{1}{2}$ under myopic behavior. (Either the consumer spends her wealth after the first period, or equivalently the consumer does not "learn" about the distribution following date $t = 0$.)

(c) Determine the hedging demand for the risky asset at date $t = 0$ when there is Bayesian learning and verify that it is positive, coinciding with the results of our proposition in the text.

(d) How would your answer to parts (b) and (c) above change if we do not allow short selling of the risky asset? (In other words, only a nonnegative level of the risky asset may be held.)

(e) How would your answer to parts (b) and (c) above change if the level of relative risk aversion were $\gamma = 2$?

8

Risk and Information

The nature of risks is to be sensitive to the arrival of new information. My beliefs about my life expectancy may be much affected if I tested positive for some defective genes. I may change my beliefs about the frequency of floods in my area because of new scientific information relative to global warming. Every day, financial news emerges that affects my perception of the riskiness of my investments.

Information is useful because of the Bayesian updating of the risk that it generates. Information is also useful because it allows for Bayesian updating of probability distributions, so that better decisions can be made than in the case where no information is available. For example, if you hear the weather forecast in the morning, predicting that it will likely rain, you might carry your umbrella with you to work. But if your office has a window and it is sunny at lunchtime, you might decide not to carry your umbrella to lunch. Compare this to your lunch companion, who took her umbrella to lunch only because she had no window in her office and did not have the same information with which to update her forecast. Young people might observe signals about their future productivity which allow them to better select their education. I can treat the disease for which I have been tested positive. Entrepreneurs can obtain information linked to the probability of success for their investment project. Policy-makers may wait for better scientific knowledge about a risk, such as global warming, before committing a large amount of funding to a potential solution. Technological innovations provide information to economic forecasters about the prospect of future growth of the economy. A common feature of these examples is that informative signals might be observed before the observer is required to make a final decision about the exposure to some risk.

Expecting better information should affect both the welfare of the decision maker and the optimal management of risk. First we examine the effect of information on welfare, and then we address the problem of risk management with information.

8.1 The Value of Information

8.1.1 An Example

Information is valuable because it allows for a better management of risk. To illustrate this point, consider a simple static insurance problem. Sempronius has an initial wealth of 4000 ducats. If his ship crosses the ocean safely, his wealth will be increased by 8000 ducats. Sempronius, who is risk-averse, is contemplating the possibility of purchasing insurance. To simplify the problem, we assume that the insurance company offers a single contract. The contract stipulates that if Sempronius's ship is sunk, an indemnity of 8000 ducats will be paid. The premium associated to this full insurance contract is 4400 ducats. If the probability of damage is $\frac{1}{2}$, this premium corresponds to a loading factor of 10%, as in the illustration presented in Section 3.1.

Sempronius's utility function is $u(z) = \sqrt{z}$. If he purchases the full insurance contract, his EU equals $\sqrt{12\,000 - 4400} = 87.178$. Because of full insurance, this is independent of Sempronius's beliefs about the likelihood of an accident. Let $p = p^0$ denote Sempronius's subjective probability of success in the absence of any information. At this stage, it is useful to leave p^0 unspecified. If he decides not to purchase any insurance, his EU equals

$$p^0\sqrt{12\,000} + (1 - p^0)\sqrt{4000} = 46.299p^0 + 63.246.$$

His decision problem can thus be written as

$$V^0 = V(p^0) = \max\{87.178, 46.299p^0 + 63.246\}, \tag{8.1}$$

where V^0 is Sempronius's maximum EU in the absence of information. It is a function $V(p^0)$ of his subjective probability of success. This problem can be solved by looking at Figure 8.1. As long as the subjective probability of success p is less than a threshold $p_c = 0.517$, it is optimal to fully insure the risk because $87.178 > 46.299p + 63.246$. Otherwise, no insurance is optimal. Remember that, in this simple example, there is no possibility of partially insuring the risk. This implies that the optimal expected utility $V(p)$ as a function of the probability of success p is piecewise linear. However, the essential property of the maximum EU is that it is convex in the probability of success. If the subjective probability of success equals $p^0 = 0.5$ when Sempronius has no information, his optimal strategy is to leave his shipment uninsured.

Suppose now that Sempronius can obtain information for free before determining to insure or not. For example, his fellows can give him information about pirates on the route, or about the weather. Suppose also that the insurer is unaware of the existence of such information as is available to its customer. Before getting information, Sempronius expects either a bad signal or a good signal about the success of his enterprise, with probabilities q and $1 - q$, respectively. Using Bayes's rule, he computes that the posterior probability of success is either $p^g > p^0$ if he receives the good signal, or $p^b < p^0$ if he receives the bad signal. Of course, we have that $qp^g + (1 - q)p^b = p^0$. It means that, prior to observing the signal, the probability of success is as before. We will hereafter suppose that $p^0 = 0.5, q = 0.5$,

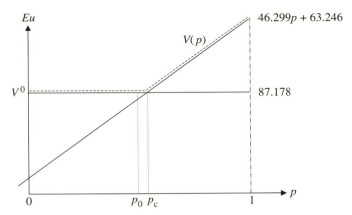

Figure 8.1. V^0 is the maximum expected utility when the probability of success is p^0. The dashed piecewise linear curve $V(p)$ is the maximum expected utility as a function of the probability p of success.

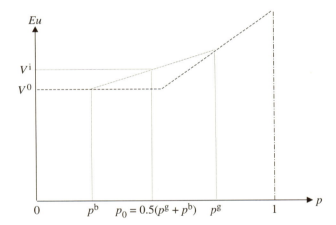

Figure 8.2. The maximum expected utility V^i with information.

$p^g = 0.75$ and $p^b = 0.25$. We want to determine whether expecting this information makes the decision maker better off *ex ante*.

To answer this question, we need to apply backward induction, as presented in Section 7.1. We first solve the decision problem for each possible signal received by the agent. We then use these contingent solutions to compute the EU prior to the observation of the signal. Contingent on a given signal, this problem is solved exactly as in (8.1), where we replace p^0 by either p^g or p^b. This solution has been described earlier using the dashed curve in Figure 8.1. When the signal is bad, the probability of success is only $p^b = 0.25$, which implies that it is optimal to fully insure the risk. It yields a certain final wealth equaling $12\,000 - 4400 = 7600$, and a final utility equaling $V(p^b) = 87.178$ with certainty. In contrast, if a good signal is perceived, the probability of success $p^g = 0.75$ is large enough to induce Sempronius not to insure the risk. In fact, the implicit loading of the premium becomes so large with such beliefs that insurance becomes undesirable. It implies an EU equaling $V(p^g) = 46.299 \times 0.75 + 63.246 = 97.970$. This is illustrated in Figure 8.2. The unconditional EU, i.e. the EU before observing the signal, is then simply $V^i = qV(p^g) + (1-q)V(p^b) = 92.574$. This is depicted as V^i in Figure 8.2.

Information is equivalent to introducing a mean-preserving spread in the probability of success. Because, as seen in Figure 8.1, the maximum expected utility V is a convex function of the probability of success p, information raises welfare:

$$V^i = qV(p^g) + (1-q)V(p^b) > V_0.$$

Figure 8.2 illustrates why. The investor has the option to not insure, if he receives the good signal. In this case, it is optimal to exercise this option, allowing him to raise his EU. Information combined with flexibility is valuable to the decision maker. In our numerical example, information has a monetary value equaling $\kappa = 970$ ducats, since

$$V^i = u(12\,000 - 4400 + \kappa),$$

i.e. Sempronius is indifferent between getting the information or receiving κ ducats.

It is important to see that information is valuable only because of the sensitiveness of the *ex post* decision to the signal. Suppose that, contrary to what we have illustrated in Figure 8.2, both p^g and p^b are both smaller than p_c. In this case, $p^t u(12\,000) + (1-p^t)u(4000)$ is smaller than $u(7600)$ both for $t = $ g and for $t = $ b. Hence, because of the linearity of V in interval $[p^b, p^g]$,

$$\begin{aligned} V^i &= qV(p^g) + (1-q)V(p^b) \\ &= V(qp^g + (1-q)p^b) \\ &= V^0, \end{aligned}$$

so that it would be optimal to not exercise this option. That is, Sempronius should insure the risk regardless of which signal is received. If this occurs, the information would be useless and the agent would not be willing to pay for such information. Information is valuable only if observing some of the possible signals would reverse your decision. To illustrate, the value of a genetic test would be zero if no treatment is available to cure the illness, or even to stabilize it.

8.1.2 A General Model

The property that the value of information is nonnegative is a general result that does not depend upon the particular decision problem or upon the information structure. Consider any decision problem where the final utility $U(s, \alpha)$ is a function of the state of the world s and of a decision variable α. Suppose that there are S possible states of nature. The uncertainty can thus be described by a vector of probabilities, $P = (p_1, \ldots, p_s, \ldots, p_S)$, where $\sum_s p_s = 1$. Now we can define the indirect utility function as

$$V(P) = \max_{\alpha} \sum_{s=1}^{S} p_s U(s, \alpha). \tag{8.2}$$

One can describe the decision problem without information as determining $V^0 \equiv V(P^0)$, the maximum EU given the distribution P^0 of the states of nature.

We now wish to compare this environment without information with an environment where the decision maker can observe a signal before choosing α. Suppose that there can be M possible messages $m = 1, \ldots, M$. The probability of receiving message m is denoted by q^m, with $\sum_m q^m = 1$. The posterior probability distribution of the states of nature given message m is denoted $P^m = (p_1^m, \ldots, p_S^m)$. Notice that the unconditional probability of state s is $\sum_m q^m p_s^m$. We assume that this is equal to the probability p_s^0 of state s in the environment without information. Using a vector notation, this means that

$$P^0 = \sum_{m=1}^{M} q^m P^m. \tag{8.3}$$

This states that the underlying risk is the same in the two environments. The maximum EU of the decision maker, who must decide upon α before observing the informative message, can be written as

$$V^i = \sum_{m=1}^{M} q^m \max_{\alpha} \sum_{s=1}^{S} p_s^m U(s, \alpha) = \sum_{m=1}^{M} q^m V(P^m). \tag{8.4}$$

The value of information will be nonnegative whenever V^i is at least as great as V^0, i.e.

$$\sum_{m=1}^{M} q^m V(P^m) \geqslant V\left(\sum_{m=1}^{M} q^m P^m\right). \tag{8.5}$$

Obviously, this will be true for all possible information structures if and only if the function V, which is defined by equation (8.2), is convex in P. Observe that, by definition, V is the upper envelope of linear functions $\sum_s p_s U(s, \alpha)$ of $(p_1, \ldots, p_S)$. This must be convex. We thus obtain the following proposition.

Proposition 8.1. *In the EU model, the value of information is always nonnegative:* $V^i \geqslant V^0$.

Proof. Let α^0 and α^m denote the optimal decision respectively without information and conditional to signal m. Observe that $V(P^m)$ is larger than

$$\sum_{s=1}^{S} p_s^m U(s, \alpha^0).$$

Otherwise α^0 would be a better decision than α^m when signal m is received. Because this must be true for all $m = 1, \ldots, M$, it implies that

$$V^i = \sum_{m=1}^{M} q^m V(P^m)$$

$$\geqslant \sum_{m=1}^{M} q^m \sum_{s=1}^{S} p_s^m U(s, \alpha^0)$$

$$= \sum_{s=1}^{S} \left(\sum_{m=1}^{M} q^m p_s^m \right) U(s, \alpha^0)$$

$$= \sum_{s=1}^{S} p_s^0 U(s, \alpha^0) = V^0.$$

This concludes the proof. It means that V is convex.   □

This proof provides a simple intuition to this result. An informed decision maker can always do at least as well as an uninformed decision maker by deciding to ignore the information. This shows once again that the value of information comes from the ability of the informed decision maker to adapt the decision to the circumstances in a more efficient way. It is worth noting that the linearity of EU with respect to probabilities is an essential ingredient for this result to hold. Interestingly, risk aversion does not play any role here. The information always has a nonnegative value, even to a risk-loving decision maker.

Up to now, we have compared a situation with some available information with a situation with no information. There is an extensive literature on comparing two information structures, where the question is to determine whether one is unambiguously better than the other. We will not examine this topic here, except to note that Figure 8.2 is very helpful for thinking about this in the framework of our example. It is apparent from this figure that, if the posterior probabilities p^b and p^g are "spread" further away from the mean p^0, then the value of information will increase. More generally, because V is convex, any mean-preserving spread of the information structure in the space of posterior probabilities will make all EU maximizers better off.

8.1.3 Value of Information and Risk Aversion

Because information allows for a better management of the risk, it would seem intuitive that more risk-averse decision makers should value information more than those who are less risk-averse. However, this is not true in general. We can illustrate this by going back to the two-state example presented in Section 8.1.1. Let w^b and w^g denote the certainty-equivalent wealth levels of the decision maker when he receives the signals p^b and p^g, respectively. Also let w^0 and w^i denote the certainty equivalent respectively in the absence and in the presence of information. The monetary value κ of information can implicitly be defined by

$$u(w^0 + \kappa) = qu(w^g) + (1 - q)u(w^b) = u(w^i). \tag{8.6}$$

In other words, the agent is indifferent between being informed, or not being informed and getting a compensating premium κ. It means that $\kappa = w^i - w^0$. We examine the effect of an increase of the concavity of u on κ.

Suppose that p^0 is smaller than p_c, the critical probability of success below which it is optimal to fully insure the risk of failure. Without information, the agent does not take any risk and $w^0 = 7600$ ducats. Of course, if the bad signal is received, the willingness to insure is reinforced, and $w^b = w^0$. The only interesting case is when p^g is larger than p_c, in which case the arrival of a good signal induces the agent to self-insure. In this case, we can expand (8.6) to obtain

$$u(7600 + \kappa) = q[p^g u(12\,000) + (1 - p^g)u(4000)] + (1 - q)u(7600).$$

It follows that κ can be interpreted as the certainty equivalent of a lottery whose payoffs are 4400, -3600 and 0 with probabilities qp^g, $q(1 - p^g)$ and $1 - q$, respectively. As we know from Chapter 1, any increase in risk aversion reduces the certainty equivalent κ of this risk. Thus, this is an example where an increase in risk aversion *reduces* the value of information. The intuition is simple: we have a case where information induces the agent to take a risk that he would not take in the absence of information. In this case, it is clear that a more risk-averse agent would value the information less, because the benefit of the risk exposure is smaller.

In Figure 8.3, we plot the value of information κ as a function of the degree of relative risk aversion γ by assuming Sempronius's utility function is $u(z) = z^{(1-\gamma)}/(1 - \gamma)$. As before, we assume that $p^0 = 0.5$, $q = 0.5$, $p^g = 0.75$ and $p^b = 0.25$. In the absence of information, it is optimal to insure the risk if the relative risk aversion is larger than $\gamma^* = 0.375$. When a bad signal is observed with $p^b = 0.25$, the subjective loading factor perceived by Sempronius is negative, which implies that it is always optimal to fully insure the risk. When a good signal is

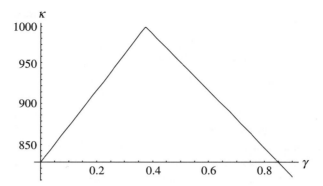

Figure 8.3. Value of information κ as a function of the degree of relative risk aversion γ.

observed ($p = p^g = 0.75$), the subjective loading factor is 120%. It can be computed that full insurance is optimal in that case only if relative risk aversion is larger than $\gamma = 2.390$, far outside the range of γ depicted in Figure 8.3.

As explained above, the value of information decreases with γ in the range $\gamma \geqslant \gamma^*$ of relative risk aversion. Suppose alternatively that $\gamma < \gamma^*$. For such low degrees of risk aversion, it is optimal to self-insure without information, because of the positive loading factor. In this range of smaller risk aversion, the risk exposure *ex ante* is larger without information than when information can be obtained, since it is still optimal to self-insure when a bad signal is observed. Symmetrically to the previous case, a bad signal induces the agent to insure a risk that he would have left uninsured in the absence of information. Here, information reduces the optimal risk exposure *ex ante*. It implies that an increase in risk aversion has a negative effect on w^0 that is larger than on w^i. It implies that $\kappa = w^i - w^0$ is positively affected by an increase in risk aversion. Globally, the value of information is hump-shaped in Figure 8.3.

8.2 Comparative Statics Analysis

Until now, we have examined the effect of information on welfare. We next examine the effect of information on behavior: how do these informative signals affect optimal actions that are to be taken *ex ante*, i.e. taken prior to the arrival of the signal? To answer this question, we consider the following two-period model:

$$\max_{\alpha_0} u(\alpha_0) + \sum_{m=1}^{M} q^m \max_{\alpha \in B(\alpha_0)} \sum_{s=1}^{S} p_s^m U(s, \alpha, \alpha_0). \qquad (8.7)$$

At date 0, the decision maker selects α_0, which yields felicity $u(\alpha_0)$ for this first period. At the beginning of the next period, the agent observes a signal m which affects his beliefs about the distribution of the states of nature $\tilde{s}$. He then chooses α to maximize his EU, conditional on having received signal m. The dynamic nature of this problem comes from the fact that the decision in the first period affects the second period in two ways. First, the choice set for α in the second period may be constrained by the initial choice of α_0. This is stipulated in (8.7) by the constraint $\alpha \in B(\alpha_0)$. Second, the initial choice of α_0 at date 0 might directly affect utility in the second period. This is why we assume in program (8.7) that U depends upon α_0.

The decision maker is in a situation of probabilistic uncertainty in the first period. He does not know which of the M probability distributions P^m, $m = 1, \ldots, M$, is the true one. However, he knows the probability distribution $(q^1, \ldots, q^M)$ over the set $\{P_m\}$. In short, he faces what is sometimes known as parameter risk: uncertainty about the parameters of the distribution for the risk that he must manage. He must make an initial decision prior to resolving this uncertainty. In real life, we are surrounded by these kinds of difficult decision problems. The timing of the decision is crucial when the uncertainty is evolving over time, i.e. when there is some resolution of the uncertainty over time.

For example, one can reinterpret the dynamic portfolio decision problem with predictability, as in Section 7.4, using our signaling terminology. Alternatively, a firm must decide to invest in new production capacities before knowing the future demand for its product. The firm knows that delaying the decision will allow it to get additional information, but it is costly to wait because of the lost revenues. Or consider a situation with scientific uncertainty such as the problem of the reduction of greenhouse gas emissions and the risk of global warming. We must decide whether to act immediately, without knowing the exact size of the risk, or to wait for scientific progress that might—or might not—confirm the level of danger. Many scientific advisers and environmentalists recommend that we use the precautionary principle in such a situation; in other words we should "play it safe."

We want to determine the effect of information on the choice of α_0. To do this, we compare the optimal α_0 of program 8.7 with the optimal initial decision when there is no early resolution of the uncertainty. We illustrate this general model with specific examples in the following two subsections.

8.2.1 Real-Option Value and Irreversibility

Early economic models of information considered the case where the selection of α_0 modified the opportunity set $B(\alpha_0)$ in the future, but had no direct effect on future utility ($U_{\alpha_0} \equiv 0$). Examples of this phenomenon abound in the real world. In many instances, investments are irreversible: a firm that invests in a new factory cannot easily decide to disinvest. Greenhouse gases emitted in the past can hardly be removed from the atmosphere by human intervention. Many genetically modified organisms cannot be eliminated once they have been introduced in the environment. Once a hydroelectric dam is built in a beautiful valley, one cannot go back and restore the valley to its initial state. Of course, this irreversibility might also preclude using newer and better technology: burying radioactive waste in reasonably secure containers today might not be considered if we had information that a new scientific method was on the horizon: one which would completely neutralize the radioactivity.

There is a clear link between information and irreversibility. Because new information may cause the decision maker to regret his initial decision, irreversibility is a problem. Stated differently, when beliefs are expected to evolve over time, it is often important to preserve some flexibility in decision making. In fact, flexibility has emerged recently as an essential aspect of risk management. To see why, we consider a very simple and still classical example.

A risk-neutral firm must determine if and when to invest in a risky project. The project generates a net cash flow of x_0 in period 0 and $\tilde{x}_1$ in period 1. We assume that $E\tilde{x}_1$ is positive. The investment is irreversible in the sense that if the investment is made in period 0 ($\alpha_0 = 1$), the firm cannot disinvest in period 1.[1] If α_t denotes the production capacity in period t, where $t = 0, 1$, this irreversibility means that $B(\alpha_0 = 0) = \{0, 1\}$, whereas $B(\alpha_0 = 1) = \{1\}$. This means that selecting not to invest in the project at date 0 ($\alpha_0 = 0$) allows for more flexibility in the future. "Not investing" is a reversible decision, whereas "investing" is an irreversible decision. The firm is assumed to discount future cash flows at rate r. We compare two cases. In the first case, the firm does not expect to receive any information about the distribution of $\tilde{x}_1$ before the end of period 1. In the second case, there is a complete early resolution of uncertainty at the end of the first period: x_1 is revealed with certainty.

Without any early resolution of uncertainty, it is optimal to invest immediately if and only if x_0 is positive. Indeed, the firm must compare the discounted expected cash flow $x_0 + (1 + r)^{-1}E\tilde{x}_1$ if it invests immediately to that which it will obtain if it delays the decision. Waiting to invest would yield a smaller net present value (NPV) of $(1 + r)^{-1}E\tilde{x}_1$.

We now turn to the optimal strategy when an early resolution of uncertainty is expected. In this case, it is optimal to invest immediately only if

$$x_0 + \frac{E\tilde{x}_1}{1 + r} \geq \frac{E\max(0, \tilde{x}_1)}{1 + r}. \tag{8.8}$$

The right-hand side of inequality (8.8) is the NPV when the firm decides not to invest in the first period and then follows a strategy of investing in the second period only when it is optimal to do so, conditional on the information, i.e. only when x_1 is positive. Thus, it might be optimal in this setting for the firm never to invest in the project. Inequality (8.8) may be rewritten as

$$x_0 \geq \frac{E\max(-\tilde{x}_1, 0)}{1 + r}. \tag{8.9}$$

---

[1] An extension of the irreversibility problem is the abandonment problem, in which the firm can reverse its decision, but only at some high cost.

The right-hand side, which is nonnegative, measures the benefit of waiting, which is the ability to avoid the loss $-x_1$ when x_1 is negative. Of course, the cost of this delay is the opportunity cost of receiving x_0.

The minimum value of x_0 that will cause the firm to invest immediately is larger when the uncertainty evolves over time. In other words, taking into account the resolution of the uncertainty causes the decision maker to value flexibility for the future. This is a very general result that holds for all decision problems (8.7) where $U_{\alpha_0} \equiv 0$. For example, in the real world, this value of flexibility tends to favor delaying the use of genetically modified foods, taking stronger early actions against global warming, and preserving environmental assets.

A firm that had to decide at date 0 whether or not to invest would usually decide to invest if and only if the NPV $x_0 + (1+r)^{-1}E\tilde{x}_1$ were positive. Indeed, in much of the finance literature, we often see this so-called "NPV rule" espoused. However, if delaying the decision is a possibility, and if some information will be revealed in the future, then the correct cost–benefit analysis is to use rule (8.8), which accounts for a premium $(1+r)^{-1}[E \max(0, \tilde{x}_1)]$ derived from the more flexible strategy. This premium is called the "real option value" of the ability to delay the decision. There is a large literature that provides various methods of computing these option values in a more realistic setting.

8.2.2 *Savings and the Early Resolution of Uncertainty*

Irreversibility is not the only element that affects the optimal early decision in the presence of an evolving uncertainty. Here we consider an example where the set B itself does not depend upon α_0. A consumer lives for three periods, $t = 0, 1, 2$, and has an initial wealth of w_0. There is a single asset whose return is risk free and is normalized to zero. We also assume that the agent is patient ($\beta = 1$). At the last date of consumption, the agent earns an uncertain income $\tilde{x}$. If there is no early resolution of uncertainty, i.e. when the realization of $\tilde{x}$ is observed only at the beginning of the third period, this decision problem can be written as

$$\max_{\alpha_0} \; u(w_0 - \alpha_0) + \max_{\alpha}[u(\alpha_0 - \alpha) + Eu(\alpha + \tilde{x})], \qquad (8.10)$$

where α_0 and α are the respective savings at the end of period 0 and period 1. Because the agent is averse to consumption fluctuations ($u'' < 0$), we know that it is optimal to smooth consumption over the first two periods: $w_0 - \alpha_0 = \alpha_0 - \alpha$. This implies that $\alpha = 2\alpha_0 - w_0$. Thus, the above problem can be rewritten as

$$\max_{\alpha_0} H(\alpha_0) = 2u(w_0 - \alpha_0) + Eu(2\alpha_0 - w_0 + \tilde{x}). \qquad (8.11)$$

We want to determine the effect of informative signals on the optimal savings decision, which must be made before this information is received. There is a simple tuition for why an earlier resolution of uncertainty might induce a smaller level of savings. Better information allows time for greater diversification of the future risk. This implicit reduction in risk provides an incentive for prudent agents to reduce their precautionary savings.

Suppose that the uncertainty is fully resolved at the end of the first period. It then is optimal for the agent to smooth his consumption perfectly over the remaining two periods. The problem at date 0 then becomes

$$\max_{\alpha_0} u(w_0 - \alpha_0) + 2Eu\left(\frac{\alpha_0 + \tilde{x}}{2}\right). \tag{8.12}$$

Its first-order condition for this problem is

$$u'(w_0 - \alpha_0^i) = Eu'\left(\frac{\alpha_0^i + \tilde{x}}{2}\right), \tag{8.13}$$

where α_0^i is the optimal saving of the informed agent, *ex ante*.

Since the function H is strictly concave in α_0, the optimal level of saving with a late resolution of uncertainty is larger than α_0^i if and only if $H'(\alpha_0^i)$ is positive. This condition can be rewritten as

$$Eu'(2\alpha_0^i - w_0 + \tilde{x}) \geqslant u'(w_0 - \alpha_0^i). \tag{8.14}$$

Now, let us make the following two changes in variables: let $z = w_0 - \alpha_0^i$ and let $\tilde{y} = 1.5\alpha_0^i - w_0 + \frac{1}{2}\tilde{x}$. Conditions (8.13) and (8.14) then can be rewritten respectively as

$$Eu'(z + \tilde{y}) = u'(z) \quad \text{and} \quad Eu'(z + 2\tilde{y}) \geqslant u'(z). \tag{8.15}$$

Let the function g be defined as $g(k) = Eu'(z + k\tilde{y}) - u'(z)$. We know from (8.15) that $g(0) = g(1) = 0$. Moreover, g will be convex whenever u is prudent. Consequently, $g(2)$ must be positive, as we wished to demonstrate. Thus, a complete early resolution of the income uncertainty at the end of the first period reduces the level of savings by all prudent agents. The result would be the opposite if the agents would be imprudent.

8.3 The Hirshleifer Effect

In the first section of this chapter, we explained that information always has a nonnegative value for the decision maker. In making this observation, it was assumed that the information does not affect the other parameters of the environment for the decision maker. In a sense, the information is private, not public. When the information is public, the story is quite different, as we see now in an illustrative example.

Suppose that, as in Section 3.2, all risk-averse agents face the idiosyncratic risk of a damage $\tilde{x}$. Suppose also that there is a competitive insurance market with no transaction cost ($\lambda = 0$) and no asymmetric information. We know that in this case that it is an equilibrium for agents to fully insure their risk at the actuarially fair premium $E\tilde{x}$. This is a first-best outcome, since all risk-averse agent are fully covered, and the aggregate risk is diversified away by the Law of Large Numbers.

Now suppose that a new technology is introduced that allows both parties to obtain information on $\tilde{x}$ at zero cost. To keep the presentation simple, let us assume that this technology provides perfect information. It will tell everyone—policyholders and insurers alike—who will suffer damage, together with the size of the damage. If insurance markets open only after this information is made available, there is nothing to insure anymore. From the point of view of the insurers, one cannot insure a realized risk. Viewed *ex ante*, this makes everyone worse off, because the possibility of insuring at fair price has been eliminated. The value of information is here negative. The cost of information equals the risk premium associated to $\tilde{x}$, since agents bear risk $\tilde{x}$ rather than its mean $E\tilde{x}$. This is the so-called Hirshleifer effect.

To see the problem here, let us suppose that exactly one half of the population will suffer a damage of size D, and the other half will suffer no damage. With no information, everyone can buy insurance based on a probability of damage of $p = \frac{1}{2}$. However, this perfect signal tells us that the "truth" is that exactly one-half of the population has $p = 0$ while the other half of the population has $p = 1$. In a sense, the no-information case allows one to buy insurance against being an unfavorable loss type (with $p = 1$). This possibility disappears once we know which individuals will suffer the loss and which will not.

What can we do against this? One possibility would be to organize insurance markets before information is available. The long-term insurance contract would then also insure against bad news. However, it may be difficult to guarantee that no one has the information at the time when the contract is signed. Otherwise, insurers would face the adverse selection problem that we explain later in this book. Also, it may be difficult to implement a system where policyholders obtaining good news will not be able to cancel their contracts. A second and more drastic solution would be to ban this new technology. This would be hard to organize in a globalized world. Also, this is highly likely to be counterproductive, as information has a positive value for organizing prevention more efficiently, for example. One can alternatively prohibit insurers the access to the information, but this also creates an adverse selection problem—only individuals who know they will have an accident demand insurance. Finally, one can socialize the risk through some form of compulsory insurance, in the fashion of a social security system or nationalized health care.

Let us debate the issue at a more prosaic level. Consider health insurance and the recent developments in biogenetics. It is expected that, in the near future, one will be able to predict the evolution of health for an individual. Even if not 100%

perfect, the information that a particular individual has a probability of say $p = 0.99$ of developing cancer in the next five years makes insurance a virtual impossibility *ex post*. Of course, suppressing these tests and hence this knowledge might deny the individual access to medical treatments, or to at least planning more optimally for his shorter expected life span. Being able to diagnose future diseases early is undoubtedly a noble project for medical research. But this might entail the undesired consequence of destroying the basis for health insurance, a crucial source of welfare in our modern societies. This is one of the reasons that genetic testing is such a controversial topic. Other examples abound, such as earthquake insurance, or life insurance.. All long-term insurance contracts, where individual risks evolve over time in a Markovian way, can be examined in light of the Hirshleifer argument.

8.4   Bibliographical References, Extensions and Exercises

Hirshleifer and Riley (1992) provide an extensive analysis of the value of information. In this chapter, we limited the analysis to the comparison of two situations, one of the two without any information. Blackwell (1951) was interested in the comparison of any pair of information structures. He raised the following question: under which condition does the second information structure make all decision makers better off than with the first structure, independent of both their attitude towards risk and the decision problem under scrutiny? Blackwell (1951) characterized such a restrictive notion of refined information structure, which is seldom satisfied. Cremer (1982) and Kihlstrom (1984) provided alternative proofs of Blackwell's characterization.

Treich (1997) and Persico (2000) examined the relationship between risk aversion and the value of information particularly for the portfolio decision problem. Persico obtains a positive relation with CARA preferences and normal returns. Treich obtains the same result without assuming CARA, but only in the case of small portfolio risks.

Epstein (1980) provides a general method for the comparative statics analysis of an early resolution of uncertainty. Arrow and Fischer (1974) and Henry (1974) were the first to stress the importance of irreversibility in cost–benefit analysis. The general result that more information induces the selection of a more flexible early action has been widely recognized in the modern theory of real investment. McDonald and Siegel (1984), Pindyck (1991) and Dixit and Pindyck (1994) show that it may be optimal to delay an investment with a positive marginal net present value (NPV) if more information is expected to come about the distribution of future cash flows. Eeckhoudt, Gollier and Treich (2004) derive the conditions under which information reduces precautionary savings.

Hirshleifer (1971) examined the effect of information in competitive markets. Schlee (2001) provides conditions on preferences that guarantee that all agents are made worse off by information in an Arrow–Debreu exchange economy.

Chapter Bibliography

Arrow, K. J. and A. C. Fischer. 1974. Environmental preservation, uncertainty and irreversibility. *Quarterly Journal of Economics* 88:312–319.

Blackwell, D. 1951. Comparison of experiments. In *Proceedings of the Second Berkeley Symposium on Mathematical Statistics and Probability*, ed. J. Neyman, pp. 93–102. Berkeley: University of California Press.

Cremer, J. 1982. A simple proof of Blackwell's "comparison of experiments" theorem. *Journal of Economic Theory* 27:439–443.

Dixit, A. K. and R. S. Pindyck. 1994. *Investment under uncertainty*. Princeton, NJ: Princeton University Press.

Eeckhoudt, L., C. Gollier, and N. Treich. 2004. Optimal consumption and the timing of the resolution of uncertainty. *European Economic Review*. (In the press.)

Epstein, L. S. 1980. Decision-making and the temporal resolution of uncertainty. *International Economic Review* 21:269–284.

Henry, C. 1974. Investment decisions under uncertainty: the irreversibility effect. *American Economic Review* 64:1006–1012.

Hirshleifer, J. 1971. The private and social value of information and the reward to inventive activity. *American Economic Review* 61:561–574.

Hirshleifer, J. and J. G. Riley. 1992. *The analytics of uncertainty and information*. Cambridge University Press.

Kihlstrom, R. E. 1984. A Bayesian exposition of Blackwell's theorem on the comparison of experiments. In *Bayesian models of economic theory*, ed. M. Boyer and R. E. Kihlstrom. Elsevier.

McDonald, R. and D. Siegel. 1984. The value of waiting to invest. *Quarterly Journal of Economics* 101:707–728.

Persico, N. 2000. Information acquisition in auctions. *Econometrica* 68:135-148.

Pindyck, R. 1991. Irreversibility, uncertainty and investment. *Journal of Economic Literature* 29:1110–1148.

Schlee, E. E. 2001. The value of information in efficient risk sharing arrangements. *American Economic Review* 91:509–524.

Treich, N. 1997. Risk tolerance and value of information in the standard portfolio model. *Economics Letters* 55:361–363.

Exercises

(8.1) A risk neutral firm has a very rigid production technology: either it does not produce or it produces a single quantity, say 50. Besides, because production takes time, the choice of the production level must be made before demand ($\tilde{D}$) is known. The level of demand is represented by a binary random variable (20, $1 - p$; 50, p), where p is the equivalent of the probability of success in the text. The economic data are as follows:

(1) fixed costs amount to 100;

(2) the output price per unit is 60 and it is independent of the production decision;

(3) constant average variable costs amount to 30.

Answer the following questions.

(a) What is the distribution of profits attached to each of the two production levels? Assume that any output that is produced and not sold has a salvage value of zero.

(b) Draw the expected profit attached to each decision as a function of p and characterize the optimal expected profit. Convince yourself that it is convex in p.

(c) What is the probability of success such that the expected profits attached to each decision are the same?

(d) Assume now that before making its output decision the firm can observe a signal that is perfectly correlated with the state of demand, i.e. the signal is good (g) whenever D is 50 and bad (b) whenever D is 20. How much should the firm produce when it receives a good signal? What should it do in the presence of a bad signal? Compute the expected profits with the signals when:

$$p = 0.10,$$
$$p = 0.16,$$
$$p = 0.50.$$

Then by comparison with the optimal expected profits without the signal compute the value of information at these three probabilities.

(e) Draw the value of perfect information as a function of p.

(f) Is this value of information influenced by a change in the fixed costs? By a change in the output price (say that the output price becomes 50)? Explain why these two changes have a different impact on the value of information.

(g) If the signals are imperfect because they are not perfectly correlated with the state of demand, show that the value of information falls for any p $(0 < p < 1)$. For instance assume that:

$$p(g \mid D = 50) = 0.9,$$
$$p(b \mid D = 20) = 0.7.$$

(8.2) A consumer who lives for two periods has the following intertemporal utility:

$$U = \ln c_0 + \ln c_1.$$

His current income is certain and equal to 10, but his future income is random and it is characterized by $\tilde{y}_1$ that is distributed as $(10, \frac{1}{2}; 14, \frac{1}{2})$.

(a) What are the optimal value of c_0 and the expected value of U when c_0 has to be chosen without any information on $\tilde{y}_1$?

(b) If perfect information is received about $\tilde{y}_1$, what happens to the expected value of U? Compute which share of y_0 this individual should be willing to give up in order to receive this perfect information.

(Hint: to avoid lengthy computations in the solution of (a), remember that the choice of the optimal c_0 has already been analyzed in Exercise 6.1 (d).)

9
Optimal Prevention

Up to now, our analysis has considered only financial decisions based upon risk. In many circumstances, it may be possible to alter the risk itself. Indeed, one reads in the newspaper most every week about some new discovery with regards to genetic engineering. By manipulating DNA codes, scientists hope to one day alter the probabilities of diseases. Of course, we can think of more mundane examples of engineering designed to mitigate risk. Consider a firm, for example, that in addition to fire insurance can use fireproof materials in construction and/or invest in a fire sprinkler system. This type of investment alters the risk distribution itself as opposed to insurance, which simply alters the financing of a risk's consequences. These types of risk-reducing activities in general are often referred to as loss control. Exactly how the distribution is altered might be rather complex. Plus, the engineering devices themselves might entail risks of their own. Perhaps our fireproof building material contains some toxic substance and will suffer the fate of asbestos, leading to long-term liability losses. Or perhaps our sprinkler system will erroneously be triggered even though there is no fire, leading to losses stemming from water damage. In this chapter we look at one type of loss control.

Loss prevention—or "self-protection"—is an effort undertaken to reduce the probability of an untoward event. What is the level of effort that would maximize the EU of the representative agent in the economy? In many instances, the cost–benefit analysis of prevention is examined under the assumption of risk neutrality. However, this implies that only reductions in the average size of the loss matter: there is no desire to reduce the variability of losses if this entails a slightly higher average loss. In reality, and most especially for most catastrophic risks like global warming, earthquakes or epidemic diseases, the assumption of risk neutrality is not reasonable. We should take into account risk aversion in the cost–benefit analysis of preventive actions. For example, potential severe losses due to possible future lawsuits might lead a pharmaceutical firm to conclude that a new drug is not worth bringing to the marketplace at all. The most extreme case of loss prevention is to avoid a risk completely.

9.1 Prevention under Risk Neutrality

As a base case, let us first consider a risk-neutral agent who faces the risk of losing an amount L with probability p. The agent can invest in preventive measures that reduce the probability of damage. If e is the amount of money invested in prevention, the probability of damage L is $p(e)$. We assume that p is a twice differentiable, decreasing and convex function: $p' < 0$ and $p'' \geq 0$. The convexity condition means that the preventive activity exhibits decreasing marginal productivity. The decision problem of the risk-neutral agent is to select e to minimize the net expected cost of the risk, taking into account of the cost of prevention. This objective may be written as

$$e^n \in \arg \min_{e \geq 0} C(e) \equiv e + p(e)L. \tag{9.1}$$

Because C is convex in e, the first-order condition $C'(e^n) = 0$ is both necessary and sufficient for a minimum. Finally, assume that $C'(0) < 0$, so that constraint $e \geq 0$ is not binding.

The optimal preventive investment e^n for the risk-neutral agent, assuming an interior solution, is defined by

$$-p'(e^n)L = 1. \tag{9.2}$$

The left-hand side of the equality is the marginal benefit of prevention. This is simply the reduction in the expected loss generated by one more euro invested in prevention. Thus, equation (9.2) is the classical optimality condition stating that the marginal cost must equal the marginal benefit. Typically, this yields a positive probability of damage ($p(e^n) > 0$), because the full elimination of the risk is usually extremely costly. This is the case, for example, when $p'(e) < 0$ for all e and $\lim_{e \to \infty} p'(e) = 0$. This is a situation where zero-risk (i.e. avoidance), even if technically attainable, is not economically feasible.

9.2 Risk Aversion and Optimal Prevention

The risk neutrality hypothesis is a good approximation only when the risk is small, or when it can be diversified away by the market. In this section, we consider the more general framework of risk aversion. Consider an EU maximizer who is endowed with wealth w_0 and who faces the risk of losing the amount L with probability $p(e)$. The decision problem now can be written as

$$e^* \in \arg \max_{e \geq 0} V(e) = p(e)u(w_0 - e - L) + (1 - p(e))u(w_0 - e). \tag{9.3}$$

With probability $p(e)$, final wealth is $w_0 - e - L$, otherwise it is $w_0 - e$. Notice that, when u is linear, program (9.1) and (9.3) are equivalent, since $V(e) = a - bC(e)$ for pair $(a, b > 0)$. We want to compare the optimal prevention e^* of the EU-maximizer with e^n, the optimal prevention of the risk-neutral decision maker. It might seem that risk-averse agents should invest more in risk prevention, and risk-loving ones should invest less. We hereafter show that this is not necessarily the case.

Before doing so, however, we need to say a few words about the second-order condition, which is not necessarily satisfied even under risk aversion. We have

$$V''(e) = -p''[u(w_0 - e) - u(w_0 - e - L)]$$
$$+ 2p'[u'(w_0 - e) - u'(w_0 - e - L)] + Eu'',$$

where $Eu'' = pu''(w_0 - e - L) + (1 - p)u''(w_0 - e)$. The first term is negative, whereas, under risk aversion, the second and third terms are respectively positive and negative. It turns out that one cannot guarantee that V is concave without placing additional restrictions on u and p. We hereafter assume that V is concave without examining these restrictions explicitly.

Because we assume that V is concave, e^* will be larger than e^n if and only if $V'(e^n)$ is positive. Evaluating this derivative yields

$$V'(e^n) = -p'(e^n)[u(w_0 - e) - u(w_0 - e - L)] - Eu',$$

where $Eu' = pu'(w_0 - e - L) + (1 - p)u'(w_0 - e)$. Using condition (9.2), we see that $V'(e^n)$ is positive if and only if

$$\frac{u(z) - u(z - L)}{L} \geq p(e^n)u'(z - L) + (1 - p(e^n))u'(z), \qquad (9.4)$$

where $z = w_0 - e^n$. This condition can be rewritten as

$$-p(e^n)[u'(z) - u'(z - L)] \leq \frac{u(z) - u(z - L)}{L} - u'(z). \qquad (9.5)$$

It is easy to check that the right-hand side of this inequality is positive under risk aversion. Because $[u'(z) - u'(z - L)]$ is negative under the same assumption, we obtain that risk aversion raises the optimal investment in prevention if and only if the probability of loss that is optimal for the risk-neutral agent is smaller than some critical threshold $\bar{p}$, where

$$\bar{p} \equiv \left(\frac{1}{L}[u(z) - u(z - L)] - u'(z) \right) [u'(z - L) - u'(z)]^{-1}.$$

There is in fact a simple intuition for why risk aversion does not necessarily raise the optimal investment in prevention. Introducing any form of risk aversion would always raise prevention only if more prevention yielded a second-order dominant shift in the distribution of final wealth. However, this can never be the case, since more prevention yields a reduction in wealth in the worst case (when damage L occurs). Indeed, prevention reduces wealth in both states of the world. The benefit of prevention comes from making the better of the two states more likely. Sufficiently risk-averse agents will find lowering wealth in the worst state to be extremely painful (in terms of utility loss). Among them is the infinitely risk-averse agent who wants to maximize the minimum final wealth. This agent will *never* invest in loss prevention.

It is easy to check that the critical threshold $\overline{p}$ equals $\frac{1}{2}$ if the utility function is quadratic, i.e. when the degree of prudence is zero. This is also easy to understand. The quadratic agent measures risk by its variance $\sigma^2 = p(1 - p)L^2$, which has a maximum at $p = \frac{1}{2}$. If p^n is less than $\frac{1}{2}$, an increase in loss prevention reduces both p and σ^2, which is desirable for risk-averse quadratic agents. Thus, when $p^n < \frac{1}{2}$, quadratic risk aversion comes to reinforce the willingness to spend effort for prevention. But if p^n is larger than $\frac{1}{2}$, an increase in loss prevention reduces p, but it raises σ^2. In this case, quadratic risk aversion tends to reduce risk prevention. In the limit case where the risk-neutral agent selects $p^n = \frac{1}{2}$, the effect on the variance is nil for small changes in prevention. It follows that all quadratic agents will also select $p^* = \frac{1}{2}$ in this case. But other risk-averse agents without a quadratic utility function may behave differently. The difficulty is that the critical threshold $\overline{p}$ is utility-dependent, and thus varies from agent to agent. In the next section, we examine conditions on preferences that makes $\overline{p}$ smaller or larger than $\frac{1}{2}$.

9.3   Prudence and Optimal Prevention

Common wisdom would seem to suggest that prudent people should invest more in prevention. This is quite the opposite in fact, as we show now. To isolate the effect of prudence ($u''' > 0$) or imprudence ($u''' < 0$), we limit the analysis to the case where the risk-neutral agents select $p^n = \frac{1}{2}$. As we have just seen, this implies that risk aversion does not affect the optimal investment in prevention for quadratic utility, since quadratic preferences exhibit zero prudence, $u''' = 0$. In such a situation, would a prudent agent invest more in prevention than the risk neutral agent? Using the analysis from the previous section, more prevention is optimal if condition (9.5) with $p^n = \frac{1}{2}$ is satisfied, i.e. if

$$\frac{u'(z - L) + u'(z)}{2} \leqslant \frac{u(z) - u(z - L)}{L}. \tag{9.6}$$

We know that for the agent with quadratic utility, (9.6) is satisfied via an equality. Suppose that the agent is imprudent ($u''' < 0$). Then, using Jensen's inequality for each possible value of the integrand below, we obtain that

$$u(z) - u(z - L) = \int_{z-L}^{z} u'(x)\, dx \geqslant \int_{z-L}^{z} \left[\frac{z - x}{L} u'(z - L) + \frac{x - z + L}{L} u'(z) \right] dx.$$

Solving the integral yields

$$u(z) - u(z - L) \geqslant \tfrac{1}{2} L[u'(z - L) + u'(z)],$$

which is equivalent to condition (9.6) for e^* to be larger than e^n. In the case of prudence ($u''' > 0$), we obtain the opposite result.

Proposition 9.1. *Suppose that the risk-neutral agent optimally selects an effort e^n such that the probability of loss p^n is equal to $\frac{1}{2}$. Then, all prudent agents select a level of effort smaller than e^n, whereas all imprudent agents select a level of effort larger than e^n.*

The intuition is that prudence raises the marginal value of wealth, thereby reducing the willingness to consume wealth in order to finance prevention. In other words, the prudent agent has a higher value for precautionary savings, and thus prefers to save more as a protection against loss (and consequently invest less in loss prevention) that an imprudent agent.

9.4 Bibliographical References, Extensions and Exercises

The optimality of loss-prevention activities was first examined by Ehrlich and Becker (1972), who termed such activity "self-protection." They also showed that insurance and prevention could be either complements or substitutes. The effects of the potential risks in loss-prevention activities themselves were examined by Briys, Schlesinger and Schulenburg (1991). Dionne and Eeckhoudt (1985) showed that an increase in risk aversion has an ambiguous effect on the optimal level of effort. Briys and Schlesinger (1990) showed that this effect is ambiguous because more prevention does not generate a reduction of risk in the sense of Rothschild and Stiglitz. Jullien, Salanié and Salanié (1999) showed that an increase in risk aversion raises the optimal level of effort if and only if the initially optimal probability of loss is less than a utility-dependent threshold. Chiu (2000) is the first to show that the third derivative of the utility function plays a role in the determination of this threshold. Jewitt (1989) and Athey (2002) examine the effect of risk aversion on the optimal choice for more general decision problems, that include prevention as a special case.

Chapter Bibliography

Athey, S. 2002. Monotone comparative statics under uncertainty. *Quarterly Journal of Economics* 117:187–223.

Briys, E. and H. Schlesinger. 1990. Risk aversion and the propensities for self-insurance and self-protection. *Southern Economic Journal* 57:458–467.

Briys, E., H. Schlesinger, and J.-M. Schulenburg. 1990. Reliability of risk management: market insurance, self-insurance and self-protection reconsidered. *Geneva Papers on Risk and Insurance Theory* 16:45–59.

Chiu, W. H. 2000. On the propensity to self-protect. *Journal of Risk and Insurance* 67:555–578.

Dionne, G. and L. Eeckhoudt. 1985. Self-insurance, self-protection and increased risk aversion. *Economics Letters* 17:39–42.

Ehrlich, I. and G. Becker. 1972. Market insurance, self insurance and self protection. *Journal of Political Economy* 80:623–648.

Jewitt, I. 1989. Choosing between risky prospects: the characterization of comparative statics results, and location independent risk. *Management Science* 35:60–70.

Jullien, B., B. Salanié, and F. Salanié. 1999. Should more risk-averse agents exert more effort? *Geneva Papers on Risk and Insurance Theory* 24:19–28.

Exercises

(9.1) Two neighbors, Sempronius and Caïus, have the same initial wealth of 10, which is subjected to the risk of a potential loss equal to 8. However, they greatly differ in the probability of occurrence of the loss. For Sempronius the loss has a probability of 0.40, while it is much higher for Caïus and amounts to 0.95.

Both Sempronius and Caïus have the opportunity to buy a safety device that costs 1 but reduces the probability of occurrence of the loss by 0.15.

(a) Show that if both Sempronius and Caïus are risk neutral they should both buy the device. Explain why.

(b) If they are equally risk averse with a utility function $u(w) = w - 0.04w^2$ identical for each of them, show that their opinion about the interest of the safety device will diverge.

(c) Once you have done the computations in (b), explain the results intuitively. In other words, why is Caïus now reluctant to buy the safety device?

(9.2) Our discussion on prevention has many points in common with the abundant literature on the "willingness to pay (WTP[1])" to reduce the probability of an accident". The WTP notion is important in cost-benefit analyses especially in the fields of health and environmental economics. This exercise and the following one build a bridge between the notions of prevention, the certainty equivalent and WTP.

Suppose that Julius has the utility function $u(w) = \sqrt{w}$. His initial wealth is 16 but he can lose 12 with a probability of 0.20, In short, he faces the lottery $(4, 0.2; 16, 0.8)$.

(a) Compute the certainty equivalent and the risk premium attached to this lottery as you did in Chapter 1.

(b) If Julius is offered a safety device that reduces the probability of loss to zero, should he accept it:

(i) if it costs 4.00?

(ii) if it costs 2.40?

(iii) if it costs 2.00?

---

[1] To be complete let us indicate that this notion was originally developed in the context of state-dependent utility, but it can be accommodated in an EU world.

(c) Explain your results intuitively by considering the amount that a risk-neutral decision maker would pay for such a safety device.

(d) Find the maximum price Julius should be willing to pay for the safety device and relate it to the results obtained for the certainty equivalent in (a).

(e) Now consider a different safety device that reduces the probability of loss from 0.20 to 0.10. Should Julius accept it:

(i) if it costs 2.00?

(ii) if it costs 1.20?

(iii) if it costs 1.00?

Again justify your answer by considering how much a risk neutral agent would pay.

(f) By successive approximations, try to obtain the maximum price that Julius should be willing to pay for the safety device.

(Hint. If the maximum price is denoted a, its value is obtained by solving:

$$(0.10)\sqrt{4 - a} + (0.90)\sqrt{16 - a} = (0.20)\sqrt{4} + (0.80)\sqrt{16} = 3.60.)$$

(g) Show that the true value of a you have just obtained is approximated by the following procedure:

(i) compute the certainty equivalent of the initial lottery, (E_1), as you did in (a);

(ii) compute the certainty equivalent, (E_2), of the final lottery if the safety device is free.

Then convince yourself that

$$a \cong E_2 - E_1.$$

Can you justify intuitively why this approximation makes sense?

(9.3) Formally, the notion of WTP is obtained by fully differentiating the following equation, which implicitly defines an indifference curve for expected utility:

$$pu(w - L) + (1 - p)u(w) = C \text{ (a constant)}.$$

Total differentiation yields:

$$\text{WTP} \equiv \frac{dw}{dp} = \frac{u(w) - u(w - L)}{pu'(w - L) + (1 - p)u'(w)}.$$

WTP is the marginal rate of substitution between wealth and the probability of loss: it indicates how much w can be decreased if p is slightly reduced while keeping the expected utility constant.

(a) Compute the value of WTP for Julius in Exercise 9.2.

(b) Show how it can be used to approximate the value of a in Exercise 9.2, i.e. the true value for a "nonmarginal" change in the probability of loss (from 0.20 to 0.10).

Part III

Risk Sharing

10
Efficient Allocations of Risks

This chapter examines the efficient allocation of risk within an economy. Up to now, we have mostly considered individual decisions related to risk and time. In order to focus on the properties of the risk sharing itself, we will assume that there are no transaction costs associated with the transfer of risk. One can easily characterize efficient risk sharing in two particular exchange economies. In the first economy, an infinite number of risk-averse individuals bear an independent and identically distributed risk. Suppose that these individuals create a mutual agreement whereby everyone would transfer his own risk to the pool in exchange for the mean outcome. By the Law of Large Numbers, this arrangement is technically feasible. Furthermore, this outcome is obviously a Pareto-efficient allocation of risk: everyone exchanges a risky wealth for its mean, i.e. all risk-averse individuals are fully insured. Alternatively, consider an economy in which all risk-averse agents have the same attitude toward risk and where they bear the same perfectly correlated risk. In this economy there are no possible gains from risk sharing. Thus autarky is Pareto efficient, and it is a competitive allocation.

More realistically, agents are not alike and individual risks are hopefully not perfectly correlated, but they are not completely idiosyncratic either. People are not completely alike, as they do not have the same wealth, and it is likely that there is some heterogeneity in their degree of risk aversion. In such a heterogenous economy, it is essential that agents be allowed to trade their risk. In this chapter, we describe the set of allocations that are Pareto efficient. We do not address the question of whether decentralized economies are able to attain such desirable allocations of risks. Whether such a market mechanism exists and how it works are topics left for the next chapter.

10.1 Risk Sharing: an Illustration

Let us go back to the Bernoullian story. Suppose that Sempronius and Jacobus both have a shipment that is expected to come back to London later this month. Sempronius's boat comes from the East Indies, whereas Jacobus's boat brings spices back from Cuba. There is a common belief that each boat has a probability of being sunk equaling $\frac{1}{2}$, and that these two possible events would be independent. Each owner is expecting a benefit of 8000 ducats in the event of success of their own enterprise. Let $\tilde{x}_S$ and $\tilde{x}_J$ be the random benefit of Sempronius and Jacobus, respectively. They are independent and distributed as $(0, \frac{1}{2}; 8000, \frac{1}{2})$.

Suppose that Sempronius and Jacobus decide to create a joint venture. The contract stipulates that the two entrepreneurs would bring the spices from their own shipment (conditional to its success) in the warehouse of the new company. The revenue generated by selling the spices contained in the warehouse would be spilt equally between the two shareholders. Would this sharing of the individual risk be acceptable for both parties? This question has been answered in Chapter 1, where we showed that Sempronius is better off by diversifying his investment in two ships rather than in one. This result is independent of the exact shape of Sempronius's utility function, as long as it is concave. The joint venture has the effect to replace the distribution of Sempronius's benefit from $\tilde{x}_S$ to $(\tilde{x}_S + \tilde{x}_J)/2$. This yields a mean-preserving reduction in risk in the sense of Rothschild and Stiglitz, as shown in Section 2.1.4. The symmetric argument can be made for Jacobus. This risk-sharing arrangement, which consists in a risk pooling, is Pareto-improving.

Suppose that Sempronius and Jacobus have mean–variance preferences with

$$U_S = E\tilde{c}_S - \tfrac{1}{2}A_S \operatorname{var}(\tilde{c}_S)$$

and

$$U_J = E\tilde{c}_J - \tfrac{1}{2}A_J \operatorname{var}(\tilde{c}_J),$$

where $\tilde{c}_i$ is the final benefit of agent i, and A_i is his absolute risk aversion. These preferences can be interpreted as an Arrow–Pratt approximation of the true preferences of the two investors. Under these specifications, the social surplus of the risk-sharing contract presented above equals

$$\frac{4000^2}{4}[A_S + A_J].$$

We now show that the contract presented above is not efficient if the two investors have different degrees of risk aversion. Suppose, for example, that Sempronius is more risk-averse than Jacobus: $A_S > A_J$. The initial situation is such that the two agents have 50% of the shares of the joint venture. Jacobus can propose that Sempronius purchase an additional 1% of the firm against a lump sum payment P. What is the minimum price $P_{\min}$ that Sempronius is going to ask for this transfer of property rights? It is given by

$$4000 - (4 \times 10^6 A_S) = 3920 + P_{\min} - (3.84 \times 10^6 A_S),$$

or

$$P_{\min} = 80 - 0.16 \times 10^6 A_S.$$

Similarly, the maximum price that Jacobus is ready to pay to get this additional 1% of shares is such that

$$4000 - (4 \times 10^6 A_J) = 4080 - P_{max} - (4.16 \times 10^6 A_J),$$

or

$$P_{max} = 80 - (0.16 \times 10^6 A_J).$$

Because A_J is smaller than A_S, we conclude that P_{max} is larger than P_{min}. This means that any exchange of this 1% share for a price between P_{min} and P_{max} is Pareto-improving. From an initial fifty–fifty sharing of the aggregate risk, it is socially efficient to transfer some of the aggregate risk to the less risk-averse agent.

It is interesting to determine the efficient sharing of the aggregate risk between Sempronius and Jacobus. Consider a contract in which member i would get a share α_i of the total benefit of the products brought back from the Colonies by those of the two boats that return safely to London. Of course, $\alpha_S + \alpha_J = 1$. Moreover, the contract stipulates that agent i gets a lump sum P_i from the company in addition to his share of the benefit. Because the company has no free cash, it must be that $P_S + P_J = 0$. We determine the feasible contract $(\alpha_S, \alpha_J, P_S, P_J)$ that maximizes the sum of the two agents' *ex ante* utility $U_S + U_J$. Using conditions $\alpha_J = 1 - \alpha_S$ and $P_J = -P_S$, this sum equals

$$8000 - 16 \times 10^6 [\alpha_S^2 A_S + (1 - \alpha_S)^2 A_J].$$

It is maximized with

$$\alpha_S^* = \frac{T_S}{T_S + T_J},$$

where $T_i = 1/A_i$ is agent i's degree of absolute risk tolerance. For example, if Jacobus's risk tolerance is twice as large as Sempronius's risk tolerance, Jacobus should bear two-third of the joint venture risk. The risk pooling and the bias of the sharing of the aggregate risk towards those who are more risk-tolerant are the two characteristics of an efficient risk sharing, as shown in the remainder of this chapter.

10.2 Description of the Economy and Definition

We consider a simple static exchange economy with n risk-averse agents. Individual i has a twice differentiable increasing and concave utility function $u_i, i = 1, \ldots, n$. The description of the uncertainty in the economy is as described in Chapter 5. At the beginning of the period, nobody knows which state of nature will prevail at the end of the period. Agent i is endowed with $\omega_i(s)$ units of a single consumption good in state s. Thus, agent i faces risk if there exists at least one pair of states of nature (s, s') such that $\omega_i(s) \neq \omega_i(s')$. Because he is risk-averse, the agent seeks insurance at an actuarially reasonable price. But he is also willing to accept risk from other

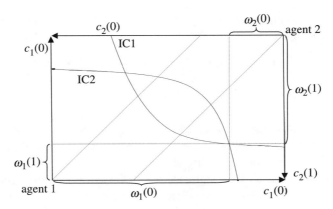

Figure 10.1.   The Edgeworth box with two agents and two states of nature.

consumers if he gets a good expected return on this activity. We assume that there is an agreed-upon probability distribution over the states.

To examine which risk allocations and which risk transfers are socially efficient, we take the broadest view possible and allow for any kind of contingent transfers, as long as they are socially feasible. The set of possible risk contracts is complete. An allocation is characterized by n functions $c_1(\cdot), \ldots, c_n(\cdot)$, where $c_i(s)$ is the consumption of agent i in state s. An allocation of risk is socially feasible if, in each possible state of nature, the aggregate consumption equals the total wealth $z(s) = \sum_i \omega_i(s)$ available in that state:

$$\sum_{i=1}^{n} c_i(s) = z(s), \quad \text{for all } s \text{ in the support of } \tilde{s}. \tag{10.1}$$

In Figure 10.1, we describe an economy with two agents and two states of nature by using the Edgeworth box. The edges of the box measure the total quantity of the consumption good in the two states. Observe that there is some aggregate uncertainty, since there is more to consume in state $s = 0$ than in state $s = 1$. The set of allocations yielding full insurance for agent i is the 45° line starting from the origin of agent i. Because these two lines do not cross, there is no possibility of fully insuring the two agents against the macroeconomic risk. We also draw the indifference curve of the two agents, which contains their initial endowment. They describe their EU in autarchy. In a sense, Figure 10.1 combines two Figures 5.2, with the one corresponding to agent $i = 2$ being upside down. Any point in the Edgeworth box describes a feasible allocation of resources.

An allocation of risk is Pareto efficient if it is feasible and if there is no other feasible allocation that raises the EU of one consumer without reducing the EU of at least one of the others. In Figure 10.2, we describe the set of all Pareto-efficient allocations of risk in a two-agent two-state economy, the so-called "contract curve".

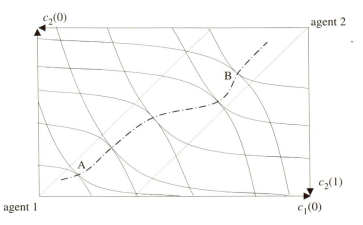

Figure 10.2.   The curve AB of Pareto-efficient allocations of risk in
the Edgeworth box with two agents and two states of nature.

As is well known, a Pareto-efficient allocation can be obtained by a maximization
procedure. Let $(\lambda_1, \ldots, \lambda_n)$ be a vector of positive scalars. Then, the solution to the
following program is a Pareto-efficient allocation:

$$\max_{c_1(\cdot),\ldots,c_n(\cdot)} \sum_{i=1}^{n} \lambda_i E u_i(c_i(\tilde{s})) \quad \text{subject to constraints (10.1),} \tag{10.2}$$

where $\tilde{s}$ describes the uncertainty about the state of nature. The proof of this result is
easily seen by contradiction. Suppose that the solution to (10.2) is not Pareto efficient.
Then, by definition, there would be another allocation satisfying constraints (10.1)
that would increase $E u_i(c_i(\tilde{s}))$ for some i without reducing the $E u_j(c_j(\tilde{s}))$ of the
other $j \neq i$. But this would contradict the assumption that the initial allocation
maximizes $\sum_i \lambda_i E u_i$.

It also can be shown that any Pareto-efficient allocation of risk can be expressed
as the solution of program (10.2) for some vector $(\lambda_1, \ldots, \lambda_n)$. In the following, we
take this vector as given. This means that we consider a specific efficient allocation,
i.e. a specific point along the contract curve AB in Figure 10.2. But the properties
that we examine are common to all efficient allocations.

10.3   Characterization of Efficient Allocations of Risk

An important insight into this problem comes from switching the sum and the expectation in program (10.2) so that it can be rewritten as

$$\max_{c_1(\cdot),\ldots,c_n(\cdot)} E\left[\sum_{i=1}^{n} \lambda_i u_i(c_i(\tilde{s}))\right] \quad \text{subject to} \sum_{i=1}^{n} c_i(s) = z(s), \text{ for all } s. \tag{10.3}$$

This is the consequence of the EU hypothesis, which makes the objective additive with respect to states. Obviously, the optimal solution to this problem can be obtained by solving it state by state, i.e. by solving the following sequence of much simpler programs:

$$\max_{c_1(s),\ldots,c_n(s)} \sum_{i=1}^{n} \lambda_i u_i(c_i(s)) \quad \text{subject to} \quad \sum_{i=1}^{n} c_i(s) = z(s), \qquad (10.4)$$

for each s. Program (10.4) can be interpreted as a decision problem under certainty in which the group must share a cake of size $z(s)$ in order to maximize a weighted sum of the members' utility. The proof that the optimal solution $c_1^*(\cdot), \ldots, c_n^*(\cdot)$ generated by the sequence of cake-sharing programs (10.4) is the optimal solution of program (10.3) can be obtained by contradiction. Suppose that this is not the case: there is a feasible allocation $\hat{c}_1(\cdot), \ldots, \hat{c}_n(\cdot)$ other than the one generated by the sequence (10.4) that yields a larger value for $E[\sum_i \lambda_i u_i(c_i(\tilde{s}))]$. That is obviously not possible, since it would mean that, for at least one state of nature s, this alternative allocation would yield $\sum_i \lambda_i u_i(\hat{c}_i(s))$, which is larger than what can optimally be attained in state s with solution $c_1^*(\cdot), \ldots, c_n^*(\cdot)$. This is a contradiction. It also is noteworthy that program (10.4) has an objective function that is concave in the decision variables. Therefore, its solution is unique and its first-order conditions together with the feasibility constraint are both necessary and sufficient for efficiency. Observe that the probability distribution of $\tilde{s}$ completely disappears from the picture describing the set of efficient allocations of risk.

The first-order conditions for program (10.4) can thus be written as

$$\lambda_i u_i'(c_i(s)) = \mu(s), \qquad (10.5)$$

for all $i = 1, \ldots, n$, and for all possible s. The Lagrange multiplier μ associated to the feasibility constraint is a function of the parameter s of the corresponding program. Condition (10.5) can be rewritten as

$$\frac{u_i'(c_i(s))}{u_i'(c_i(s'))} = \frac{u_j'(c_j(s))}{u_j'(c_j(s'))} \qquad (10.6)$$

for all pairs (i, j) and (s, s'). The two sides of the above equality correspond to the marginal rates of substitution of consumption in states s and s', respectively, for agents i and j. Condition (10.6) is the classical efficiency condition, stating that marginal rates of substitution must be equalized across agents. Graphically, it means that indifference curves in Figure 10.2 must be tangent at an efficient allocation.

The simplification allowed by program (10.4) allows us to more easily characterize efficient risk-sharing allocations. In particular, we will examine in sequence the two main components of efficiency. The first is the mutuality principle, which states that all diversifiable risks must be "washed out" by a mutual arrangement. This principle leads to full insurance for the case of independent and identically distributed risks. The second principle deals with sharing the socially undiversifiable risk. So long as $z(s)$ is not a constant, full insurance for everyone is not feasible.

10.3.1 The Mutuality Principle

The mutuality principle is easy to obtain from the sequence of state-contingent cake-sharing programs (10.4). What is it that differentiates the program associated with state s from the one associated with state s'? The only difference comes from the possibility that the aggregate wealth levels $z(s)$ and $z(s')$ are different. Thus, if two states have the same aggregate wealth, $z(s) = z(s')$, then the solutions of the programs for states s and s' must be identical: $c_i(s) = c_i(s')$, for all $i = 1, \ldots, n$. In other words, if there are two states with the same aggregate wealth, then, for any consumer, the same amount of the consumption good is optimal in each these two states. The following proposition states the mutuality principle.

Proposition 10.1. *A necessary condition for an allocation of risk to be Pareto efficient is that whenever two states of nature s and s' have the same level of aggregate wealth, $z(s) = z(s')$, then for each agent i consumption in state s must be the same as in state $s' : c_i(s) = c_i(s')$ for $i = 1, \ldots, n$.*

The simplest illustration of this property is when there is no aggregate uncertainty in the economy. When $z(s) = z$ for all s, all agents should enjoy a state-independent consumption plan, i.e. they should be fully insured. In other words, when individual risk can be completely diversified away, it is socially efficient to do so. Quite an obvious recommendation indeed. Figure 10.3 illustrates such a situation. The Edgeworth box is a square and the two 45° lines coincide when there is no macroeconomic risk. The set of all Pareto-efficient allocations corresponds to this line.[1] In autarchy, the risk borne by agent 1 is perfectly negatively correlated with the risk borne by agent 2. This is as if the two agents with an initially sure endowment would gamble against each other on the occurrence of a spot on the Sun this year, or on whether a coin will land head or tail up. The mutuality principle states that it is Pareto optimal to withdraw the gamble, or equivalently, that an insurer fully covers the risk borne by the two players.

The mutuality principle, however, says much more than that in fact. It states that Pareto-efficient consumption of any agent i in state s does not depend directly upon the individual's wealth $\omega_i(s)$ in that state. Rather, it only depends upon the aggregate wealth $z(s) = \sum_i \omega_i(s)$ in that state. This means that if individual endowments were socialized and the n members of the pool gave their endowment to the pool,

---

[1]The traditional tangency condition for efficiency is easy to check in this case. Indeed, remember from Section 5.3 that, along the 45° line, the marginal rate of substitution between $c_i(0)$ and $c_i(1)$ equals p_0/p_1 for the two agents $i = 1$ and 2.

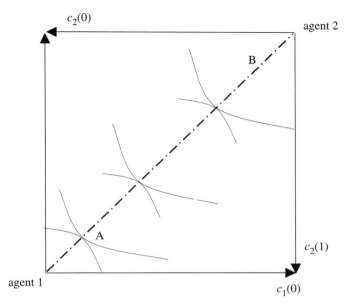

Figure 10.3.   The curve AB of Pareto-efficient allocations of risk
when there is no macroeconomic risk: $z(0) = z(1)$.

the planner could achieve an efficient allocation by reallocating the collected wealth according to a rule that does not depend upon who gave how much to the pool. In short, a Pareto-efficient c_i depends upon s only through $z(s)$. Of course, market considerations such as those in the next chapter rely upon more than just Pareto efficiency. For example, if participation in any reallocation scheme is voluntary, we would also need to add a constraint that the agent is at least as well off by participating as he would be by not participating. This additional constraint would restrict the set of Pareto-efficient allocations.

The mutuality principle tells us that risks that can be fully diversified must be completely washed out. In the real world, mutualizing risks does not typically diversify the risk completely. A social risk or macroeconomic risk remains, which comes from the fact that the aggregate wealth z is in general not independent of the state of nature. The economy faces random events that generate phases of recession or expansion. The mutuality principle leaves unanswered the question of how to share the undiversifiable risk. The next section deals with the problem of how to share this inescapable type of macroeconomic risk.

10.3.2   Sharing of the Macroeconomic Risk

Before examining the efficient allocation of the undiversifiable risk, it is noteworthy that program (10.4) shares the same structure as programs (5.3) and (6.5). It should not be surprising then that we will encounter results in this chapter that are quite similar to results that were obtained in previous chapters. Only the context and the terminology will change.

We normalize states in such a way that $z(s) = s$ for all s. From the mutuality principle, this is without loss of generality. Indeed, if we have two states with the same aggregate wealth, the social planner should allocate it in exactly the same way. The first-order conditions for program (10.4) can thus be rewritten as

$$\lambda_i u_i'(c_i(z)) = \mu(z), \tag{10.7}$$

for all $i = 1, \ldots, n$, and for all possible z. What is of interest here is the relationship between c_i and z. If c_i is independent of z, this means *ex ante* that agent i would be fully covered against fluctuations of the aggregate wealth z. On the other hand, if $c_i'(z) = 1$, this means that agent i bears all of the macroeconomic risk, and that he insures all other consumers. Thus, the derivative of c_i with respect to z measures the share of the macroeconomic risk borne by agent i. Fully differentiating the first-order condition (10.7) yields

$$\lambda_i u_i''(c_i) c_i'(z) = \mu'(z).$$

Eliminating λ_i in this equation, using condition (10.7), implies that

$$c_i'(z) = T_i(c_i(z)) \frac{-\mu'(z)}{\mu(z)},$$

where $T_i(c) = -u_i'(c)/u_i''(c)$ is the absolute risk tolerance of agent i. Now, observe that fully differentiating the feasibility constraint

$$\sum_j c_j(z) = z$$

implies that

$$\sum_j c_j'(z) = 1.$$

Combining this with the above equation implies that

$$\frac{-\mu'(z)}{\mu(z)} \sum_{j=1}^N T_j(c_j(z)) = 1. \tag{10.8}$$

Finally, these last two equations together imply that

$$c_i'(z) = \frac{T_i(c_i(z))}{\sum_{j=1}^N T_j(c_j(z))}. \tag{10.9}$$

This is an important result. It is very intuitive. To understand it, let us first digress as to what risk tolerance for an individual describes.

Recall that risk aversion represents the rate of decline in marginal utility that would occur for a 1 euro increase in wealth. Thus risk tolerance is just the inverse: risk tolerance equals 100 times the number of euros it would take to yield a 1% decline in marginal utility. The aggregate risk tolerance is the sum of individual risk tolerances,

$$\sum_{j=1}^{N} T_j(c_j(z)).$$

Thus, aggregate risk tolerance is 100 times the amount of aggregate wealth it would take to make all consumers experience a 1% drop in marginal utility. Equation (10.9) thus states that the share of the undiversifiable risk borne by each agent equals the share of his own risk tolerance in the aggregate risk tolerance. The larger the risk tolerance of agent i relative to the aggregate risk tolerance of the group, the larger the risk agent i should bear. Notice that condition (10.9), which is a differential equation, must hold for all $i = 1, \ldots, n$. Thus, condition (10.9) is in fact a system of differential equations. Solving it requires n initial conditions, say $c_1(0), \ldots, c_n(0)$. Once again there is an infinite number of efficient allocations that can be identified either by this set of initial conditions or by the weighting vector $(\lambda_1, \ldots, \lambda_n)$.

Note that (10.9) implies that $c_i'(z) > 0$ for all i if individuals are all risk-averse. This implies that each agent must have more wealth in state s than in state s' whenever $z(s) > z(s')$. This property of Pareto efficiency is known as co-monotonicity. Graphically, it implies that the set of Pareto-efficient solutions is in between the two $45°$ lines in Figure 10.2: everyone should consume more in state 0 than in state 1, since $z(0) > z(1)$. It implies unanimous agreement among all agents as to which state is the best state, which state is the second-best state, and so on. Of course, this is not typically the case in the real world. The state in which you win a lottery is better for you than the state in which your neighbor wins the same lottery, for example. However, lotteries and other types of market transactions are not based solely on efficient risk sharing. From a risk sharing perspective, it makes sense that everyone will agree on the ranking of the states.

Several particular cases are worth examining. Suppose, for example, that there exists one risk neutral agent, say $i = 1$, in the economy: $T_1(c) \to \infty$. Condition (10.9) directly implies that $c_1'(z) = 1$, and that $c_i'(z) = 0$ for all $i \neq 1$. All risk-averse agents are fully insured against individual risks by this single risk-neutral agent.

Another interesting example is when all agents have a constant degree of absolute risk tolerance (CARA): $T_i(c) = t_i$ for all c. The system of differential equations is here particularly simple to solve, since the right-hand side of (10.9) does not depend

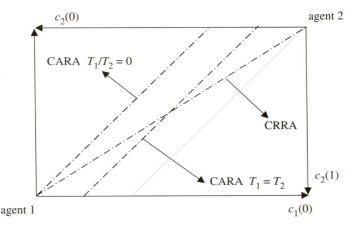

Figure 10.4. The curve of efficient allocations in the CRRA case and in the CARA case.

upon z. It follows that

$$c_i(z) = c_{i0} + \frac{t_i}{\sum_j t_j} z, \qquad (10.10)$$

for some vector $(c_{10}, \dots, c_{n0})$ of lump-sum transfers, with $\sum_i c_{i0} = 0$.

More generally, the system can be solved analytically if individual risk tolerances are linear in consumption (i.e. HARA utility) with the same slope. Let $T_i(c) = t_i + \alpha c$. Indeed, the system can then be rewritten as

$$c_i'(z) = \frac{t_i + \alpha c_i(z)}{t + \alpha z}, \qquad (10.11)$$

where we use the feasibility constraint together with $t = \sum_j t_j$. The reader can verify that the solution to this differential equation is simply

$$c_i(z) = c_{i0} + \frac{t_i + \alpha c_{i0}}{\sum_j t_j} z. \qquad (10.12)$$

The solution (10.12) is what is known as a linear sharing rule. In the special case where all consumers have the same constant relative risk aversion ($t_i = 0$ so that $T_i(c) = \alpha c$ for all i), condition (10.11) states that $c_i'(z) = z^{-1} c_i(z)$. It follows that each agent i should consume a constant share of the aggregate wealth $c_i(z) = k_i z$, where $\sum_j k_j = 1$. In the Edgeworth box of Figure 10.4, we draw the sets of efficient allocations of risk in these special cases.

10.4 Aggregation of Preferences

Suppose that a group of agents is in a position to implement an efficient sharing of risks among the group's members, characterized by a specific weighting vector

$(\lambda_1, \ldots, \lambda_n)$. This group faces a decision problem under uncertainty. In this section, we examine the attitude of this group towards risk. If the group is society as a whole, for example, we might need to decide upon some public policy such as how much to invest in global warming problems or how to structure a social security program. If the group is a firm, i.e. a set of shareholders, this might be a capital-budgeting decision as to which projects the firm should undertake. If the group is a household, the problem under scrutiny might be about job selection or the investment in education for the children. How should the fact that risks can be efficiently shared within the group affect the decision making of the group? In other words, can we assign a level of risk tolerance to the group?

As earlier in this chapter, the planner of the group's allocation of risk has the objective of maximizing the weighted sum of the members' EU. If this group can decide which risk it should select among different options, it should select the one that maximizes this weighted sum. Let us define function v as

$$v(z) = \sum_{i=1}^{n} \lambda_i u_i(c_i(z)), \qquad (10.13)$$

where $c_1(\cdot), \ldots, c_n(\cdot)$ is the efficient allocation associated to the weights $\lambda_1, \ldots, \lambda_n$. With this notation, the problem of the planner is just to select the aggregate risk that maximizes $Ev(\tilde{z})$. Observe that v will be increasing and concave if all of the individual utilities u_i are. Hence, the problem for the planner of a group of EU maximizers is itself an EU maximization problem.[2] In a certain sense, we can think of the planner as an individual representing the group, who makes decisions based upon the utility v. For this reason, we often refer to the planner as the "representative agent" for this group.

Observe also that the risk tolerance of the group, i.e. of the representative agent, can be measured by the function T_v, with $T_v(z) \equiv -v'(z)/v''(z)$. We can link the degree of risk tolerance of the representative agent to the distribution of risk tolerances in the group by observing that

$$v'(z) = \sum_{i=1}^{n} \lambda_i u_i'(c_i(z)) c_i'(z) = \mu(z), \qquad (10.14)$$

since $\lambda_i u_i'(c_i(z)) = \mu(z)$ and $\sum_i c_i'(z) = 1$. Thus, we obtain that

$$T_v(z) = -\frac{\mu(z)}{\mu'(z)} = \sum_{i=1}^{N} T_i(c_i(z)), \qquad (10.15)$$

because of condition (10.8). The absolute risk tolerance of an efficient group equals the sum of individual risk tolerances in the corresponding state. Note that, in general,

---

[2]This is not necessarily the case outside the world of Arrow and Debreu.

the choice of the weighting vector $(\lambda_1, \ldots, \lambda_n)$ will affect the risk tolerance of the group through variations in the allocation of consumption.

Let us consider the special case of HARA utility for the individuals in the group, so that all individual degrees of absolute risk tolerance are linear with the same slope: $T_i(c) = t_i + \alpha c$. Equation (10.15) implies in this case that $T_v(z) = t + \alpha z$. This is an example where the choice of the allocation of risk among the set of all efficient ones, i.e. the choice of $(\lambda_1, \ldots, \lambda_n)$ does not matter for determining the attitude towards risk of this group. The inequity in the wealth distribution does not affect the group's willingness to take risk. Under DARA, for example, the larger risk tolerance of wealthier agents just compensates the smaller risk tolerance of the poorer ones. If we assume more specifically that all agents have the same constant relative risk aversion γ, i.e. if $t_i = 0$ and $\alpha = \gamma^{-1}$, we obtain that the representative agent also has a constant relative risk aversion γ.

This is also an example where there is unanimity within the group about the group's attitude to risk. To see this, consider the attitude of agent i to the group's risk $\tilde{z}$ given the transfer $c_i(\tilde{z})$ of this aggregate risk to agent i. This can be measured by the degree of concavity of the implicit utility function v_i, where $v_i(z) \equiv u_i(c_i(z))$ for all z. This is how agent i calculates his final utility in a given state z. Given that

$$v_i'(z) = u_i'(c_i(z))c_i'(z) = u_i'\left(c_{i0} + \frac{t_i + \alpha c_{i0}}{\sum_j t_j} z\right)\frac{t_i + \alpha c_{i0}}{\sum_j t_j},$$

the degree of concavity of v_i is inversely proportional to

$$-\frac{v_i'(z)}{v_i''(z)} = -\left(u_i'(c_i)\frac{t_i + \alpha c_{i0}}{\sum_j t_j}\right)\left(u_i''(c_i)\left[\frac{t_i + \alpha c_{i0}}{\sum_j t_j}\right]^2\right)^{-1}$$

$$= (t_i + \alpha c_i)\frac{t_i + \alpha c_{i0}}{\sum_j t_j}$$

$$= t + \alpha z = T_v(z).$$

Thus, the attitude towards the aggregate risk of each member of the pool is identical. Therefore, there is unanimity on the management of risk followed by the planner. It happens that these two important properties hold only in this special case of linear risk tolerances with the same slope. For groups where preferences do not satisfy this condition, it is always possible to find a risky choice problem for which some members of the pool disagree on the risk policy followed by the planner.

10.5 Bibliographical References, Extensions and Exercises

Borch (1962) was the first to examine the efficient allocations of risk in an economy of risk-averse agents. Wilson (1968), Rubinstein (1974) and Constantinides (1982) demonstrated the mutuality principle, and they showed how to share the undiversifiable risk in the economy. Leland (1980) and Varian (1985) were more specifically interested in the characterization of efficient risk sharing and collective preferences when consumers have heterogeneous beliefs. Arrow and Lind (1970) discussed whether society should be neutral towards risk. Finally, transaction costs have been introduced into the efficient risk-sharing model by Arrow (1971) and Raviv (1979), as discussed in the chapter on insurance decisions. Townsend (1984) tests the existence of efficient allocations of risk in small villages of developing countries.

Chapter Bibliography

Arrow, K. J. 1971. *Essays in the theory of risk bearing*. Chicago: Markham Publishing Co.
Arrow, K. J. and R. C. Lind. 1970. Uncertainty and the evaluation of public investment decision. *American Economic Review* 60:364–378.
Borch, K. 1962. Equilibrium in a reinsurance market. *Econometrica* 30:424–444.
Constantinides, G. M. 1982. Intertemporal asset pricing with heterogeneous consumers and without demand aggregation. *Journal of Business* 55:253–267.
Leland, H. E. 1980. Who should buy portfolio insurance? *Journal of Finance* 35:581–596.
Raviv, A. 1979. The design of an optimal insurance policy. *American Economic Review* 69:84–96.
Townsend, R. M. 1984. Risk and insurance in village India. *Econometrica* 62:539–592.
Rubinstein, M. 1974. An aggregation theorem for securities markets. *Journal of Financial Economics* 1:225–244.
Varian, H. 1985. Divergence of opinion in complete markets. *Journal of Finance* 40:309–317.
Wilson, R. 1968. The theory of syndicates. *Econometrica* 36:113–132.

Exercises

(10.1) An economy consists of two individuals, Sempronius and Jacobus, each with logarithmic utility. There are two equally likely states of nature. Sempronius has an endowment of 10 ducats worth of consumption in both states. Jacobus has an endowment of a contingent claim for 15 ducats worth of consumption in state 1, but only 5 ducats worth of consumption in state 2. Jacobus offers Sempronius the following trade: Jacobus will give Sempronius 3 ducats worth of consumption in the event that state 1 occurs in exchange for a promise from Sempronius to provide Jacobus with 2 ducats worth of consumption in the event that state 2 occurs.

    (a) Are both individuals made better off by the proposed trade?

    (b) Is the final contingent-consumption allocation resulting from this trade Pareto efficient?

    (c) Describe the set of all Pareto-efficient allocations in this economy.

    (d) How would your answer to part (c) change if the probability of state 1 was $p = 0.4$, instead of 0.5?

(10.2) Consider an economy with n risk-averse agents in which each agent possesses a non-tradeable zero-mean background risk $\tilde{\varepsilon}_i$, for $i = 1, \ldots, n$. We further suppose that each $\tilde{\varepsilon}_i$ is independent of the aggregate tradeable wealth $z(\tilde{s})$ and that all agents have quadratic utility functions.

    (a) Show that Pareto-efficient allocation of the aggregate tradeable risk $z(\tilde{s})$ is not affected by the presence of the background risks.

    (b) Would the conclusion of (a) be true if all agents had CRRA preferences with the same degree of relative risk aversion? Why or why not?

(10.3) A planner allocates wealth among n consumers. The planner knows individual preferences and assigns equal weight to everyone's expected utility in making all decisions. Assume that currently the state-contingent distribution of consumption claims is Pareto efficient. Now suppose that the planner discovers that there will be twice as much aggregate wealth as previously expected in all states of nature. Will doubling the level of contingent consumption for each consumer in each state of nature lead to a Pareto-efficient allocation?

(10.4) Consider an economy with $n + 1$ agents. The first n agents have a constant relative risk aversion equaling 5, whereas the last agent is much less risk-averse since she has a logarithmic utility function. Explain why it is not socially efficient for this less risk-averse agent to bear all the macroeconomic risk.

(10.5) Consider n countries whose economies are asymmetrically affected by macro-economic risks. In each country, there is a social security system that diversifies away the idiosyncratic component of individual risks. These countries are considering forming a federation that would unify all national social security systems into a single federal system. From a risk-sharing perspective, could this reform be mutually advantageous for the different countries? If yes, describe the basic rules of a mutually advantageous federal system.

11
Asset Pricing

In the previous chapter, we assumed that there was a benevolent social planner in society who imposed an efficient allocation of risk. In this chapter, we turn to decentralized decision making by the individuals. Each individual has access to a complete set of competitive markets of Arrow–Debreu securities to exchange risk. Many questions can be raised about the functioning of this economy. Why do these individuals, all with their own self-interest in mind, find it worthwhile to trade with each other? How will assets be priced in this market? Can such decentralized decision making generate a Pareto-efficient allocation of risk? Can this model explain the large equity premium that has been observed in developed countries over the last century? Is it compatible with the observed low return on bonds over the same period? What is the shape of the yield curve in this economy? In this chapter, we will attempt to provide some answers to these important questions.

11.1 Competitive Markets for Arrow–Debreu Securities

In this section, we reconsider the economy that was defined in the past chapter by introducing markets for risk exchanges. There is some uncertainty about the state $\tilde{s}$ that will occur at the end of the period. We have n risk-averse agents, $i = 1, \ldots, n$, and agent i is endowed with an initial state-dependent wealth claim $\omega_i(\tilde{s})$. As in Chapter 5, we assume that agents can trade risk within a complete market. Let $\pi(s)$ denote the price per unit of probability of the Arrow–Debreu security associated with state s. If $p(s)$ denotes the probability of state s, this means that one must pay $p(s)\pi(s)$ to obtain one unit of the consumption good if and only if state s occurs.[1] The decision problem of agent i is to find a portfolio $c_i(\cdot)$ of Arrow–Debreu securities that maximizes his EU under a budget constraint. This can be written as

$$\max_{c_i(\cdot)} Eu_i(c_i(\tilde{s})) \qquad (11.1)$$

---

[1] Recall from Section 5.1 that the price for one unit of wealth contingent upon the occurrence of state s was defined as $\Pi(s) \equiv p(s)\pi(s)$. The set of prices defined per unit of probability, $\{\pi(s)\}$, is referred to as the pricing kernel for this economy.

subject to

$$E\pi(\tilde{s})c_i(\tilde{s}) = E\pi(\tilde{s})\omega_i(\tilde{s}). \tag{11.2}$$

Equation (11.2) is the budget constraint, which states that the value of the selected portfolio cannot exceed $E\pi(\tilde{s})\omega_i(\tilde{s})$, the market value of individual i's initial endowment. As was examined in Chapter 5, the first-order condition for this program can be written as

$$u_i'(c_i(s)) = \xi_i\pi(s), \tag{11.3}$$

for all s. Solving Equations (11.2) and (11.3) yields demand functions $c_i = C_i(\pi)$ whose main properties have been described before.

To complete the description of the model, we need to add the market clearing condition $\sum_i[c_i(s) - \omega_i(s)] = 0$, or equivalently,

$$\sum_{i=1}^{n} c_i(s) = \sum_{i=1}^{n} \omega_i(s) = z(s), \tag{11.4}$$

for all s. Condition (11.4) simply states that the aggregate consumption in state s cannot exceed what is available in that state, which is denoted $z(s)$. This condition is, in fact, the feasibility condition.

We should point out the main weakness of the complete-markets model, which is to assume that all individual risks can be traded on financial markets. More realistically, there are many risks that are not tradeable. Labor income risk typically cannot be traded. It is very difficult to transfer all of the risk associated with real estate, an important fraction of the households' wealth. More recently, we have found a lack of tradeability for much of the risk associated with terrorism. If all risks were indeed tradeable, this would imply that the total capitalization of financial markets, i.e. the market value of all assets traded, must equal the total wealth of the economy, which is very far from reality, even in the US economy. Still, the assumption that markets are complete remains a cornerstone of modern asset-pricing theory.

11.2   The First Theorem of Welfare Economics

All economists have somewhere in their background knowledge the essential result that, under certain conditions, a competitive allocation is Pareto efficient. These conditions are the absence of externalities and of asymmetric information, the completeness of market, and some additional technical conditions on preferences that are fulfilled for risk-averse EU maximizers. So, it is no surprise that this result also holds in the economy presented here. This can be seen directly by comparing conditions (10.7) and (11.3), as we explain below.

Let us start with the mutuality principle. We will take some liberty in notation and use "s" to denote both the state of nature and the Arrow–Debreu security associated

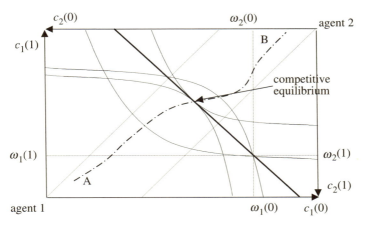

Figure 11.1. Competitive allocation of risk in the Edgeworth box. The thick straight line is the budget line of the two consumers. The dashed line is the set of Pareto-efficient allocations of risk.

with that state of nature. We have seen in Chapter 5 that the individual demand for a specific Arrow–Debreu security s depends only upon its relative price $\pi(s)$. Moreover, this individual demand is decreasing in π. Thus, if there are two states s and s' with the same price $\pi(s) = \pi(s')$, every agent must have the same demand for asset s and asset s', and thus the same consumption in these two states: $c_i(s) = c_i(s')$. Consequently, the aggregate consumption levels must be the same, which is possible only if $z(s) = z(s')$. In other words, if there are two states with the same aggregate wealth, the competitive state prices must be the same, and for any arbitrary i, agent i will consume the same amount of the consumption good in these two states. Thus, individual consumption at equilibrium and competitive state prices depend upon the state only through the aggregate wealth available in the corresponding state. This implies that the competitive allocation of risk satisfies the mutuality principle, and that all diversifiable risk is eliminated in equilibrium. As in the previous chapter, we hereafter denote $z(s) = z$, for all s.

Let us rewrite condition (11.3) as

$$\xi_i^{-1} u_i'(c_i(z)) = \pi(z). \tag{11.5}$$

This is equivalent to the first-order condition (10.7) for an efficient allocation of risk by taking $\xi_i^{-1} = \lambda_i$ for all i, and $\mu(\cdot) \equiv \pi(\cdot)$. We conclude that competitive markets allocate the macroeconomic risk in a Pareto-efficient manner: decentralized decision making yields efficient sharing. In the Edgeworth box of Figure 11.1, we draw the competitive equilibrium of an economy with two agents and two states of nature. We see that the competitive equilibrium lies on the curve AB of Pareto-efficient allocations. Moreover, both consumers are better off at the competitive equilibrium than in autarchy.

Recall that there is a "representative agent" for each efficient allocation of risk. This implies, in particular, that the attitude towards risk of any economy implementing a Pareto-efficient allocation can be duplicated by an economy with a single EU maximizing agent with concave utility function v. From the first theorem of welfare economics, we know that this must also be true in the special case of the competitive allocation.

The existence of a representative agent simplifies the analysis. From (10.14), the marginal utility of the representative agent in a given state equals the equilibrium state price itself: $v'(z) = \mu(z) \equiv \pi(z)$. From condition (10.15), recall that the risk tolerance of v evaluated at aggregate wealth z equals the sum of individual risk tolerances in that state:

$$T_v(z) = \sum_{i=1}^{N} T_i(c_i(z)).\tag{11.6}$$

We are now in a position to explore some characteristics of asset prices in such an economy.

11.3 The Equity Premium

In this section, we want to compare the prices and expected returns of two particular portfolios. The first portfolio is the risk-free portfolio, i.e. a portfolio that yields one unit of the consumption good in all states. We normalize its price to $E\pi(\tilde{z}) = 1$. This means that the risk-free rate in this economy is zero. Because our model is static at this stage, this is without loss of generality. Because we know that the pricing kernel $\pi(\cdot)$ is linked to the preferences of the representative agent through $\pi(\cdot) = v'(\cdot)$, this condition normalizes the representative utility function in such a way that $Ev'(\tilde{z}) = 1$.

The second portfolio provides a constant share α of the aggregate wealth in the economy. This means that the portfolio yields αz units of the consumption good in state z, for all z. Because the entire individual wealth is subject to trading, this portfolio can be interpreted as a fully diversified mutual fund of all assets of the economy. The price of this equity portfolio is equal to the sum of the values of the assets that it contains, i.e. it equals $E\alpha\tilde{z}\pi(\tilde{z})$. Its expected payoff is $E\alpha\tilde{z}$. The expected return, which is often called the return on equity, equals

$$\phi = \frac{E\tilde{z}}{E\tilde{z}\pi(\tilde{z})} - 1 = \frac{E\tilde{z}}{E\tilde{z}v'(\tilde{z})} - 1,\tag{11.7}$$

The difference between ϕ and the risk-free rate is called the equity premium. This is the amount of excess return (i.e. return in excess of the risk-free return) that is earned on average by holding the risky mutual fund. Because the risk-free rate here is assumed to be zero, ϕ is at the same time the return on equity as well as the equity premium.

Because agents are risk-averse, they will not invest in the stock market at all unless the average equity return is larger than the risk-free rate in the economy. But for this exchange economy to be in equilibrium it is necessary that the entire aggregate risk $\tilde{z}$ be borne by individuals, through their asset holdings. This is stated in the feasibility (or market-clearing) condition (11.4). Thus, the equity premium must be larger than the risk-free rate, large enough to induce voluntary assumption of the entire aggregate risk. But how large is large enough? Suppose that the aggregate consumption was z_0 in the previous period, and that the aggregate consumption at the end of the current period is a random variable $\tilde{z}$. Because each period is very short, $\tilde{z}$ is a small risk around z_0. Because the risk-free rate is zero, it must be that $1 = Ev'(\tilde{z}) \simeq v'(z_0)$. Using a first-order Taylor approximation similar to the one used to obtain equation (4.4), we derive that

$$E\tilde{z}v'(\tilde{z}) \simeq z_0 v'(z_0) + z_0^2 \sigma^2 v''(z_0) \simeq z_0[1 - \gamma\sigma^2],$$

where $\sigma^2 = \text{var}(\tilde{z}/z_0)$ is the variance of the growth rate of aggregate consumption, and $\gamma = -z_0 v''(z_0)/v'(z_0)$ is the relative risk aversion of the representative agent. Suppose that all agents in the economy have the same constant relative risk aversion γ. We know from the previous chapter that this implies that the representative agent also will have relative risk aversion γ. Using these approximations, we can rewrite equation (11.7) as

$$\phi \simeq \frac{z_0}{z_0[1 - \gamma\sigma^2]} - 1 \simeq \gamma\sigma^2. \tag{11.8}$$

The variance σ^2 of the yearly growth rate of gross domestic product (GDP) per capita has been around 0.0006, or 0.06% over the last century in the United States.[2] Thus, for empirically feasible levels of relative risk aversion between 1 and 4, the equity premium should be somewhere in between 0.06% and 0.24% per year.

Is this prediction about how risks should be priced in our economy compatible with the data? Let us review some historical data on financial returns, such as those presented by Kocherlakota (1996) and documented in Chapter 4. They provided statistics on asset returns for the US over the period from 1889 to 1978. We concluded that the observed equity premium has been equal to 6% over that period. This important difference between the value predicted by the model (less than one-quarter

---

[2]We consider the GDP per capita, rather than the GDP, to take into account of the important growth rate of the US population during the period.

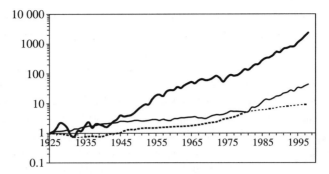

Figure 11.2. Value of a portfolio of $1 invested in 1925 in large US stocks (bold line) or in long-term bonds (thin line), respectively. Consumer price index (dashed line). Logarithmic scale. (Source: Ibbotson Associates.)

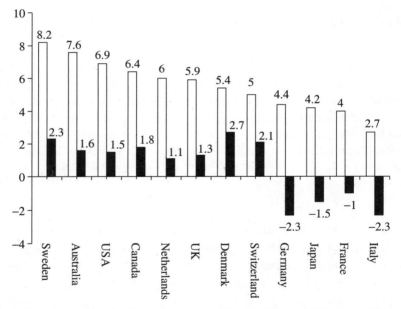

Figure 11.3. Average real stocks (white bars) and bonds (black bars) returns, 1900–1999. (Source: Dimson, Marsh and Staunton (2000).)

of a percent per year) and the observed value of 6% per year is what economists refer to the equity premium puzzle.[3]

---

[3]Not all empirical evidence is in agreement, however. For example, evidence by Jorion and Goetzmann (1999) shows that the equity premium might not be quite as high as is typically supposed. Thus, there may be an empirically smaller "puzzle" that actually needs to be rationalized by the theory.

This makes a huge difference in the long term. For example, Ibbotson Associates showed that $1 invested in the stock of large US companies in 1925 would have yielded a portfolio value of $2351 in 1998, assuming that all earned dividends are reinvested during this period. Compare this to the same dollar invested in long-term bonds over this period. The 1998 value of this bond would be only $44, including reinvested interest. True, holding stocks has been risky, in particular in the first half of the century, as shown in Figure 11.2. It has been shown that all investors with an investment horizon of 20 years always earned more from their portfolio by investing in stocks than by investing in bonds, independent of the time they entered the market during the century. Because of the small size of the sample, this does not prove first-order stochastic dominance, however. Indeed, it may be possible that we experienced luck during the period, with no big long downturns of the economy, in spite of the two world wars. We see in Figure 11.3 that other developed countries experienced similar patterns in their financial markets.

The level of relative risk aversion consistent with US data typically requires unrealistically high levels, such as 15 or 40. With relative risk aversion equal to 20, for example, a person with $100 of initial consumption would have a certainty equivalent of less than $3.50 for a lottery ticket paying a prize of $100 with a probability of $p = 0.5$. There has been an enormous effort over the last 15 years to understand and to solve the equity premium puzzle. Several explanations have been proposed for this high-equity premium: uninsurability of labor risks, the peso problem, habit formation, consumption externalities, violations of EU, liquidity constraints, transaction costs, participation costs, inequity in the distribution of wealth, persistence of pessimism, and many others. It appears that there is no single explanation of the puzzle, particularly if we want to solve it jointly with the other puzzle that we will see later in this chapter, namely, the risk-free rate puzzle.

11.4 The Capital Asset-Pricing Model

In the previous section, we priced a very specific portfolio, i.e. the fully diversified portfolio consisting of a fixed percentage claim on the aggregate equity available in the economy. We now examine the pricing of specific assets within this economy. Before going into details, we want first to stress an important characteristic of asset pricing when markets are complete. Consider a risky asset, i.e. an asset whose value depends upon the state of nature that will prevail at the end of the period. Suppose first that this risk is statistically independent of the market risk $\tilde{z}$. Also suppose, for example, that, whatever the GDP z, the firm generates a value q with probability p and zero otherwise. What should its market value be *ex ante*? Because of the mutuality principle, we know that the state prices depend only upon z and not upon the success of the specific firm. The *ex ante* value of the firm is thus equal to $E[\pi(\tilde{z})(qp+0(1-p))] = qp$, since we normalized $E\pi(\tilde{z})$ to unity. This means that individual risks that are not correlated to the market risks are actuarially priced. This result is a direct consequence of the fact that risk aversion is a second-order effect in the EU framework. Adding a small share ε of independent risk $(q, p; 0, 1 - p)$ to the market portfolio has the same effect on welfare as increasing wealth by $\varepsilon pq - 0.5\varepsilon^2 p(1 - p)q^2 A$, where A is absolute risk aversion. If ε is small, investors will value this investment at εpq, which is actuarially fair.

Observe that the actuarial fair pricing of diversifiable risks in the economy implies that all agents will fully insure against diversifiable risks in equilibrium. This is compatible with Pareto efficiency.

Let us now consider an asset whose return may be correlated with the aggregate risk. A risky asset is fully characterized by the payoff that it provides to its owner in each possible state of nature. Consider an asset q whose payoff in state z is $q(z)$. From the mutuality principle, we only need to know the relationship between z and q. If factors other than z influence the firm's final value, $q(z)$ represents the expected payoff of the firm conditional on z. The market value of this firm *ex ante* equals

$$P(q) = Eq(\tilde{z})\pi(\tilde{z}) = Eq(\tilde{z})v'(\tilde{z}). \tag{11.9}$$

This is the asset-pricing formula common to all models with complete markets. Using no-arbitrage arguments, we just need to know function $\pi \equiv v'$ to price any asset on the market. This is why the function π is often called the pricing kernel.

As in the previous section, one can obtain an approximation formula by assuming that $\tilde{z}$ is a small risk around some $z_0 : \tilde{z} = z_0 + k\tilde{\varepsilon}$, where we now assume that $E\tilde{\varepsilon} = 0$. By normalizing the risk-free rate to zero, so that $v'(z_0) = 1$, it follows that

$$P(q) \simeq Eq(\tilde{z}) - \frac{\gamma}{z_0} \operatorname{cov}(q(\tilde{z}), \tilde{z}), \tag{11.10}$$

where $\gamma = -z_0 v''(z_0)/v'(z_0)$ is the relative risk aversion of the representative agent measured at the expected level of aggregate wealth, and $\operatorname{cov}(q(\tilde{z}), \tilde{z})$ is the covariance of $q(\tilde{z})$ and $\tilde{z}$. This is a central equation for understanding the Capital Asset-Pricing Model, or "CAPM." It tells us that the current market value of an asset equals its future expected payoff minus a risk premium which takes the form of the product of risk aversion and a measure of the asset risk. This is reminiscent of the Arrow–Pratt formula. But the asset risk is here measured by the covariance of the future asset value and the aggregate wealth in the economy, not the variance of $q(\tilde{z})$. This is again the direct consequence of the mutuality principle. If the asset value is not correlated to the market value, the asset will be actuarially priced. Notice that the risk premium becomes negative for assets that are negatively correlated with aggregate wealth. These are assets whose integration in the market portfolio reduces the risk of the portfolio. This hedging property raises their attractiveness for risk-averse agents, and consequently increases their market values to levels above

Table 11.1. The estimated beta of a few existing assets.

firm	β
Moulinex	1.8
Renault	1.6
HSBC	1.5
Royal and SunAlliance	1.3
Pechiney	1.2
LVMH	0.8
British Telecom	0.7
Glaxo Wellcome	0.6
Carrefour	0.5
L'Oréal	0.4

their expected payoffs in equilibrium. In other words, these assets will have a rate of return less than the risk-free rate.

The statistical relationship between the asset return and the market return is often measured by the so-called beta of the asset, which is defined by

$$\beta(q) \equiv \frac{\operatorname{cov}(q(\tilde{z}), \tilde{z})}{\sigma_{\tilde{z}}^2}. \tag{11.11}$$

If we consider the special case where $q(\tilde{z}) = \tilde{z}$, equation (11.10) yields the price of our market portfolio:

$$P_{\mathrm{M}} \simeq E(\tilde{z}) - \frac{\gamma}{z_0}\sigma_{\tilde{z}}^2. \tag{11.12}$$

Solving (11.12) for γ/z_0 and using this together with (11.11) in equation (11.10) above yields

$$Eq(\tilde{z}) - P(q) = \beta(q)[E(\tilde{z}) - P_{\mathrm{M}}]. \tag{11.13}$$

This equation is essentially a modified version of the so-called security-market line from the CAPM.[4]

The beta of the market portfolio, of course, is unity. Fully diversifiable assets have a zero beta. Table 11.1 provides the estimated beta of a few existing assets.

11.5 Two-Fund Separation Theorem

One can re-examine the equilibrium allocation of risks in this framework. In equilibrium, people select portfolios whose final values are co-monotonic, as they depend

---

[4]If we concern ourselves with returns, rather than with prices, then we can assume that one share of each security has a price of 1, with the payoffs expressed now as the gross earnings per share. In this setting, equation (11.13) tells us that the return on asset q equals its beta times the expected return on the market portfolio. This is precisely the security-market-line equation whenever the risk-free rate is equal to zero.

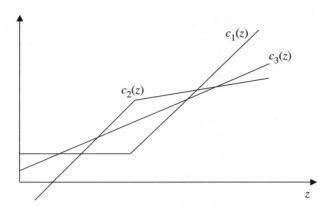

Figure 11.4. Agent 1 purchases portfolio insurance from agent 2. The portfolio of agent 3 contains only the risk-free asset and a share of the market portfolio.

in an increasing way upon the realization of a single random variable $\tilde{z}$. This dependence can be quite complex, however. But in the special case of linear risk tolerances $T_i(c) = t_i + \alpha c$, we know that this relationship is linear. Linearity has an important consequence in a decentralized economy. It implies that it is sufficient to limit asset supply to two funds. There would be a fund offering a risk-free portfolio in zero net supply. In addition, there would be another fully diversified fund of stocks. It would be a fund whose unique aim is to duplicate the market performance z, state by state. By allowing people to sell all their risk to the second fund, and to purchase shares of the two funds, one can obtain any consumption plan that depends linearly upon z. Thus, one can duplicate the equilibrium allocation with just these two funds. We do not need to organize complete contingent markets. This is the two-fund separation property, which holds under linear absolute risk tolerances. It is also sometimes referred to as a "mutual fund theorem," since it implies that all investors only require one mutual fund of risky stocks, together with a risk-free asset, for investment purposes. As mentioned before, linear risk tolerance is in fact the only case within an EU framework where the two-fund separation property holds.

Many investors, however, do not want linear consumption plans, such as the investors $i = 1$ and 2 whose optimal portfolios are illustrated in Figure 11.4, for example. In this case, agent 1 purchases what is known as portfolio insurance. This means that he gets a minimum guaranteed income from his portfolio. This can be done by buying put options whose underlying asset value is that of the mutual fund. Intuition might suggest that the most risk-averse agents would purchase that kind of instrument at equilibrium for much the same reason that risk averters prefer deductible insurance policies. However, this is not true when the two-fund separation property holds, i.e. when risk tolerances are linear with the same slope. More-risk-averse investors will rather purchase more of the risk-free asset. To sum up, portfolio insurance seems attractive for risk-averse investors. However, it should be noted that, to each investor purchasing portfolio insurance, there must be someone on the other side of the market who would be ready to sell portfolio insurance, a very risky business. At equilibrium with HARA preferences, the price of portfolio insurance would be too large for anyone to want to purchase it.

Still, it is possible to understand why such financial instruments are often traded in real-world markets. First, they are useful for helping agents to get rid of their individual risks that cannot be diversified away by the market. Indeed differences in these individual risks alone can be enough to cause some investors to sell options, while others buy options. Second, agents may have risk tolerances that are not linear, or which are linear but not with the same slope. Finally, contrary to what we implicitly assume here, people often form different beliefs on the probability distribution of the states of nature. One analyst's "hot stock" recommendation may be another analyst's "dog."

11.6 Bond Pricing

We normalized the risk-free rate to zero in our analysis above. In fact, because there is only one consumption date in the model, the notion of an interest rate has no meaning. We need to introduce saving in the model in order to discuss interest rates. It is easiest to extend the above model to two consumption dates. We do this in the next two sections. We then show how this framework easily extends to multiple periods.

11.6.1 The Risk-Free Rate

Agent i is now endowed with a fixed wealth of ω_{i0} units of the consumption good at date 0, and with the state contingent claim for $\omega_i(s)$ units at the second date in state s, for all s. We denote aggregate wealth at date 0 as $\omega_0 = \sum_i \omega_{i0}$. As in Chapter 6, it is assumed that the agent maximizes the discounted value of the flow of EU over his lifetime, i.e. he maximizes $u_i(c_{i0}) + \beta E u_i(c_i(\tilde{s}))$, where c_{i0} is consumption at date 0, $c_i(s)$ is consumption in date 1 in state s, and β is the discount factor.[5]

At date 0, consumers face both a saving decision and a portfolio decision. The numeraire is the consumption good. It costs $\pi(s)$ (per unity of probability) units of the consumption at date 0 to purchase a contract that guarantees the delivery of one unit of the good at date 1 if and only if state s occurs. Let $r = [E\pi(\tilde{s})]^{-1} - 1$ be the risk-free rate in the economy. Indeed, it costs $E\pi(\tilde{s}) = (1+r)^{-1}$ at date 0 to buy one unit of the good with certainty at date 1. The decision problem of agent i can now be written as

$$\max_{c_{i0}, c_i(\cdot)} u_i(c_{i0}) + \beta E u_i(c_i(\tilde{s})) \tag{11.14}$$

---

[5] The notation for β as used here is not to be confused with the beta from the CAPM.

subject to

$$c_{i0} + E\pi(\tilde{s})c_i(\tilde{s}) = \omega_{i0} + E\pi(\tilde{s})\omega_i(\tilde{s}). \tag{11.15}$$

The market clearing conditions are $\sum_i c_{i0} = \omega_0$ together with condition (11.4). We see that the additive nature of the problem is not affected by introducing an initial saving/consumption decision. Therefore, all properties that we examined previously, such as the mutuality principle and the sharing rule of the macro risk, still hold in this dynamic model. The only difference is due to the fact that we cannot normalize the risk-free rate to zero, since the numeraire has already been fixed to be the consumption good. The first-order conditions for this problem are given by $\beta u_i'(c_i(s)) = \xi_i \pi(s)$ together with $u_i'(c_{i0}) = \xi_i$ and the constraints. One can eliminate the Lagrangian multiplier ξ_i to write

$$\beta u_i'(c_i(s)) = u_i'(c_{i0})\pi(s) \quad \forall s. \tag{11.16}$$

Condition (11.16) states that the marginal gain in EU from having an extra date-1 unit of consumption in state s exactly equals the utility loss of financing this via current consumption. Since this is true for all states s, this condition implies that there is no possible gain for switching contingent consumption between the states at date 1, or for switching consumption between date 0 and date 1. This condition is often called the Euler equation.

In order to characterize the risk-free rate in this economy, it is necessary to use the representative agent. Because of the additive nature of the objective in (11.14), and because markets are complete, there must be a representative agent who behaves towards risk and time exactly as the economy as a whole does at the competitive equilibrium. Let v be the utility function of this representative agent. Preferences for our representative agent are fully characterized by the agent's risk tolerance as described in equation (11.6). As in (11.16), the first-order condition for the decision problem of the representative agent is written as

$$\beta v'(c(s)) = v'(c_0)\pi(s) \quad \forall s, \tag{11.17}$$

where $(c_0, c(\cdot))$ denotes the optimal consumption plan of the representative agent. Obviously we cannot interpret this condition in the same way as we did for (11.16). The representative agent consumes all wealth available at every date and state. It is thus the prices that must be adjusted correctly in (11.17). In other words, in order to have an equilibrium, we need in addition that $c_0 = z_0$, and $c(s) = z(s)$ for every state s. Combining all this, we get the equilibrium conditions

$$\pi(s) = \frac{\beta v'(z(s))}{v'(z_0)} \quad \forall s. \tag{11.18}$$

By taking the expectation, we obtain that

$$E\pi(\tilde{s}) = \frac{\beta E v'(\tilde{z})}{v'(z_0)}.$$

It thus follows that

$$r = \frac{v'(z_0)}{\beta E v'(\tilde{z})} - 1 = \frac{v'(z_0)}{\beta E v'(z_0(1 + \tilde{x}))} - 1, \qquad (11.19)$$

where $\tilde{x}$ is the growth rate of the economy. This is an important new pricing formula which allows us to determine the current market value of any asset whose future payoff is certain. The equilibrium risk-free rate r depends upon the rate of impatience β, on the concavity of the representative utility function, on the current level of aggregate wealth z_0, and on the distribution of future growth $\tilde{x}$. We examine this relationship in more detail in the next subsection.

11.6.2 Factors Affecting the Interest Rate

First of all, consider the case where future growth is identically zero $\tilde{x} \equiv 0$. If $\delta = \beta^{-1} - 1$ denotes the rate of pure preference for the present, then the equilibrium risk-free rate of interest will equal δ, $r = \delta$. Let $B_1 = (1 + r)^{-1}$ denote the price of a pure-discount bond, also called a zero-coupon bond, paying one unit of consumption with certainty at date 1. Thus, with zero growth in the economy, $B_1 = \beta$. If the expected growth rate is positive but certain, $\tilde{x} = g > 0$, it follows from (11.19) that we must have $B_1 < \beta$, i.e. $r > \delta$. This is because agents are averse to consumption fluctuations over time. Therefore, in order to induce them to accept a current consumption low enough to be compatible with current aggregate wealth, a larger interest rate is necessary. The larger the growth rate g, the larger the equilibrium risk-free rate. We call this the wealth effect. This explains why interest rates tend to go up during booms and down during recessions.

To illustrate, consider the case where individuals all have constant relative risk aversion γ. We have already seen that this is also true for the representative agent. We can thus write the zero-coupon bond price as

$$B_1 = \frac{\beta E v'(z_0(1 + \tilde{x}))}{v'(z_0)} = \beta E (1 + \tilde{x})^{-\gamma}. \qquad (11.20)$$

From (11.20) we can confirm the two results above: that $B_1 = \beta$ when $\tilde{x} \equiv 0$ and $B_1 = \beta(1 + g)^{-\gamma} < \beta$ when $\tilde{x} \equiv g > 0$. Moreover, note that B_1 is decreasing in the degree of risk aversion γ in the case where $\tilde{x} \equiv g$. A higher γ lowers the price of a zero-coupon bond, i.e. increases the equilibrium risk-free rate of interest. Since there is no risk at date 1 and since g is positive, we know that consumers consume more at date 1 than at date 0. An increase in the concavity of v would cause the ratio $v'(z_0(1 + g))/v'(z_0)$ to decrease. Thus, consumers would find it advantageous to shift some of their consumption from date 1 to date 0; they would purchase fewer zero-coupon bonds. Of course this not possible in equilibrium. Hence, the price of these bonds would need to fall to maintain our equilibrium.

Suppose now that $\tilde{x}$ is random with $E\tilde{x} \equiv 0$: there is zero growth on average but we may experience either expansion or recession with positive probabilities. Since constant relative risk aversion implies constant relative prudence $P^r = 1 + \gamma$, we know that $Ev'(\tilde{z}) = v'(E\tilde{z} - \psi)$, where ψ denotes the precautionary premium for $\tilde{z}$. It follows that $B_1 = \beta(1 - \psi)^{-\gamma} > \beta$. When the future growth of the economy is uncertain, prudent people tend to save more, due to their precautionary savings demand. At a fixed current aggregate wealth z_0, this cannot be an equilibrium. Therefore, the interest rate must be reduced in order to lower the demand for savings. This explains why the interest rate tends to go down when more uncertainty accumulates. We call this the precautionary effect.

If we have a positive rate of growth on average, $E\tilde{x} \equiv g > 0$, but this rate of growth is risky, we see that the wealth effect (to shift consumption from date 1 to date 0) and the precautionary effect (to shift wealth from date 0 to date 1) work in opposite directions: $B_1 = \beta(1 + g - \psi)^{-\gamma}$. We cannot tell *a priori* which of these effects might dominate. Moreover, the effect of an increase in γ is also ambiguous, since it also will also increase the precautionary premium ψ.

If we do not have constant relative risk aversion, of course the analysis is even more complex. However, if we assume that both the expected growth rate g and the level of risk are small, we can approximate the risk-free rate as[6]

$$r \simeq \delta + R[g - \tfrac{1}{2}\sigma^2 P^r], \tag{11.21}$$

where σ^2 is the variance of growth rate of aggregate consumption, R is relative risk aversion and P^r is relative prudence, both evaluated at the expected future wealth $\mu = z_0(1 + g)$. Here we see the various trade-offs between the average growth rate and its riskiness in determining the equilibrium risk-free rate of interest. Since any change in risk aversion necessitates a change in relative prudence, we should be cautious about predicting the effect about a change in risk aversion.

One can try to bring this theory to the data. The expected growth rate of the US economy was around 2% during the 20th century. So, the consumption smoothing term gR alone generates a risk-free rate between 2 and 8% per year, assuming a measure of relative risk aversion somewhere between 1 and 4. It is even larger if we add the effect of impatience. This is a problem, however, since the mean real interest rate of the US economy during this period has been much lower, around 1%. This illustrates the risk-free rate puzzle. One could hope that the precautionary effect helps in explaining this phenomenon, but this is not the case. The variance

---

[6]Let $\mu = z_0(1 + g)$. Since the risk is small, $Ev'(z_0(1 + \tilde{x}))$ is approximately equal to $v'(\mu)[1 + \tfrac{1}{2}z_0^2\sigma_{\tilde{x}}^2 A(\mu)P(\mu)]$, where $A(c) = -v''(c)/v'(c)$ and $P(c) = -v'''(c)/v''(c)$ are respectively absolute risk aversion and absolute prudence of the representative agent. Since the expected growth is small, we can approximate $v'(z_0)$ by $v'(\mu)[1 + z_0 g A(\mu)]$. We also use the approximation $(1 + y)^{-1} \simeq 1 - y$ for small y. Finally, we approximate $R = z_0(1 + g)A(\mu)$ by $z_0 A(\mu)$. This approximation can be shown to be exact in a continuous time framework.

of the growth rate of the economy has been relatively small, around 0.0006. This implies that one would need a very large degree of relative prudence to solve the puzzle. Observe that when relative risk aversion is a constant γ, relative prudence is a constant $\gamma + 1$. So, even with a large level of relative risk aversion $\gamma = 4$, the precautionary term $\frac{1}{2}\sigma_{\tilde{x}}^2 RP^r = \frac{1}{2}\sigma_{\tilde{x}}^2 \gamma(1 + \gamma)$ equals $0.006 = 0.6\%$ per year, a very small impact with respect to the consumption smoothing term $gR = 8\%$. Hence, the empirical risk-free rate remains a puzzle from a theoretical point of view.

11.6.3 The Yield Curve

Adding a longer time horizon to our model is not difficult. Up to now we have been interested in determining the risk-free rate for cash flows occurring within the next 12 months. We can perform the same exercise for cash flows obtained in 24 months' time. There is no reason *a priori* to believe that the risk-free rate will be independent of the time horizon. In reality, they differ. Both the expected growth and the uncertainty attached to it depend upon the time horizon that we consider. The so-called yield curve describes the relationship between the interest rate and time horizon.[7] Most of the time, the observed yield curve in the economy is increasing: one gets a better return when investing in long-term bonds than when investing in bonds with a shorter time to maturity. But it may be possible in some circumstances to have an inverted yield curve.

The expected growth of the economy over the next two years is larger than the expected growth rate over the next year alone. Thus, the positive wealth effect is larger over two years than over one year. Similarly, the uncertainty on the growth of the economy is larger over 24 months than over 12 months. It implies that the precautionary effect will also be larger. Because the wealth effect and the precautionary effect work in opposite directions, it is not clear whether the interest rate is increasing or decreasing with the maturity of the asset.

Let $\tilde{x}_{01}$ denote the random growth rate of the economy over the next 12 months, and $\tilde{x}_{12}$ denote the growth rate between months 12 and 24. Thus, the GDP per capita two years from now is fully described via the random variable $z_0(1 + \tilde{x}_{01})(1 + \tilde{x}_{12})$. If we assume that the representative agent is patient, ($\beta = 1$), the price for a zero-coupon bond maturing in one year, is as in equation (11.20):

$$B_1 = \frac{1}{1 + r_{01}} = \frac{Ev'(z_0(1 + \tilde{x}_{01}))}{v'(z_0)}.$$

Similarly, the price for a zero-coupon bond maturing in 2 years, B_2, satisfies the condition

$$B_2 = \frac{1}{(1 + r_{02})^2} = \frac{Ev'(z_0(1 + \tilde{x}_{01}))(1 + \tilde{x}_{12})}{v'(z_0)},$$

---

[7] In finance jargon this is also often called the zero curve, since it describes the interest rates used to price zero-coupon bonds.

where r_{02} denotes the rate of return *per year* for this bond. Suppose that $\tilde{x}_{01}$ and $\tilde{x}_{12}$ are independent and identically distributed, and that the representative agent has a constant relative risk aversion of γ. Then, we obtain that

$$
\begin{aligned}
B_2 &= \frac{1}{(1 + r_{02})^2} \\
&= \frac{E z_0^{-\gamma} (1 + \tilde{x}_{01})^{-\gamma} (1 + \tilde{x}_{12})^{-\gamma}}{z_0^{-\gamma}} = [E(1 + \tilde{x}_{01})^{-\gamma}]^2 \\
&= \left[\frac{E(z_0(1 + \tilde{x}_{01}))^{-\gamma}}{z_0^{-\gamma}} \right]^2 = \left[\frac{E v'(z_0(1 + \tilde{x}_{01}))}{v'(z_0)} \right]^2 = \frac{1}{(1 + r_{01})^2}.
\end{aligned}
$$

Thus, with constant relative risk aversion and no serial correlation in the growth rate of the economy, the yield curve is flat: $r_{01} = r_{02}$. There should be no reward for long-term investors. This is a case where the increased wealth effect and the increased precautionary effect counterbalance each other.

11.7 Bibliographical References, Extensions and Exercises

The building blocks of asset-pricing theory have been shaped by many different authors, such as Markowitz, Merton, Samuelson, Black, Scholes and many others. The list is too long to be presented here. Lucas (1978) proposes a very simple model of an exchange economy to solve the asset-pricing problem. Mehra and Prescott (1985) and Weil (1989) use Lucas's model to present the equity premium puzzle and the risk-free rate puzzle, respectively. Cass and Stiglitz (1970) prove that the two-fund separation property, which is a key requirement in the capital asset-pricing model, holds under EU only when absolute risk tolerances are linear with the same slope. Leland (1980) shows who should purchase portfolio insurance at equilibrium when linear risk tolerance does not hold. Franke, Stapleton and Subrahmanyam (1998) show how, even in an economy with linear risk tolerances, differences in background risks can be enough to cause some investors to sell options, while others buy them.

Cox, Ingersoll and Ross (1985) consider a very general economy with production to characterize the yield curve. Several models prior to 1985 proposed pricing formulas that relied on non-maximizing behaviors by investors.

Chapter Bibliography

Cass, D. and J. Stiglitz. 1970. The structure of investor preferences and asset returns, and separability in portfolio allocation. *Journal of Economic Theory* 2:122–160.

Cox, J., J. Ingersoll, and S. Ross. 1985. A theory of the term structure of interest rates. *Econometrica* 53:385–403.

Dimson, E., P. Marsh, and M. Staunton. 2002. *Triumph of the optimists: 101 years of global investment returns*. Princeton, NJ: Princeton University Press.

Franke, G., R. Stapleton and M. Subrahmanyam. 1998. Who buys and who sells options: the role of options in an economy with background risk. *Journal of Economic Theory* 82:89–109.

Ibbotson Associates. 1999. *Stocks, bonds, bills and inflation: 1999 yearbook*. Ibbotson Associates, Chicago, IL, USA.

Jorion, P. and W. N. Goetzmann. 1999. Global stock markets in the twentieth century. *Journal of Finance* 54:953–980.

Leland, H. E. 1980. Who should buy portfolio insurance? *Journal of Finance* 35:581–596.

Lucas, R. E. 1978. Asset prices in an exchange economy. *Econometrica* 46:1429–1446.

Mehra, R. and E. Prescott. 1985. The equity premium: a puzzle. *Journal of Monetary Economics* 10:335–339.

Weil, P. 1989. The equity premium puzzle and the risk free rate puzzle. *Journal of Monetary Economics* 24:401–421.

Exercises

(11.1) It can be shown that equation (11.9) also holds for the case where $\tilde{z}$ has a continuous distribution. Suppose that $(\tilde{z}, q(\tilde{z}))$ has a bivariate normal distribution. Stein's Lemma states that if $(\tilde{x}, \tilde{y})$ has a bivariate normal distribution and $h(\cdot)$ is a differentiable function, then $\text{cov}(\tilde{x}, h(\tilde{y})) = Eh'(\tilde{y}) \text{cov}(\tilde{x}, \tilde{y})$.

  (a) Use Stein's Lemma to show that the price of asset q satisfies

$$P(q) = Eq(\tilde{z}) + Ev''(\tilde{z}) \text{cov}(\tilde{z}, q(\tilde{z})).$$

  (b) What happens to your answer in (a) if $q(\cdot)$ is the identity function?

  (c) If $\tilde{R}_q$ denotes the gross return on asset q, then by definition $Eq(\tilde{z}) = P(q)E\tilde{R}_q$. Use this result to derive the so-called security market line equation from the CAPM (assuming that the risk-free rate is zero):

$$E\tilde{R}_q - 1 = \text{cov}(\tilde{R}_z, \tilde{R}_q)[\text{var } \tilde{R}_z]^{-1}[E\tilde{R}_z - 1].$$

(11.2) Consider an economy with n risk-averse consumers with CRRA preferences and the same degree of relative risk aversion γ. Aggregate wealth at date $t = 0$ is constant at z_0. At date $t = 1$, aggregate wealth is $z_1 = z_0(1 + \bar{g})$, where $\bar{g}$ is a strictly positive constant. At date $t = 2$ aggregate wealth is $\tilde{z}_2 = z_1(1 + \bar{g} + \tilde{\varepsilon})$, where $E\tilde{\varepsilon} = 0$, var $\tilde{\varepsilon} > 0$. Determine the shape of the yield curve in this economy.

(11.3) Consider an Arrow–Debreu economy with n agents and S states of nature. Suppose that all agents have HARA preferences with same slope: $T_i(c) = t_i + bc$ for $i = 1, \ldots, n$. Show that the equilibrium prices (i.e. the pricing kernel) is invariant to the distribution of initial claims.

(11.4) Consider an Arrow–Debreu economy with n agents and S "tradeable" states of nature. We assume that all agents have identical endowments and identical preferences. We differ here by assuming that there are S tradeable states of nature, but each agent also has a private *non-tradeable*, additive background risk $\tilde{\varepsilon}_i$. Assume that all of the background risks are mutually independent and are identically distributed. They are also independent from the random aggregate wealth $\tilde{z}$. We further assume that all agents are standard risk averse. (Standard risk aversion is equivalent to decreasing absolute risk aversion in tandem with decreasing absolute prudence.) Show that the equilibrium pricing kernel is more disperse with the background risks present. (Hint: what do you know about the derived utility functions in such as case?)

  If you cannot answer this question for the general case, try showing it for the simpler case with two agents and two states, $n = S = 2$.

(11.5) Both Sempronius and Jacobus have a logarithmic utility function and an initial wealth equaling 100. They both face the idiosyncratic risk of losing 50 with probability 0.5. There exists an external insurance company that offers full insurance contracts at an actuarially unfair price.

(a) Suppose initially that they are unable to share risk efficiently. How much is Jacobus ready to pay to fully insure his risk? Now answer the same question for Sempronius.

(b) Suppose that Sempronius and Jacobus accept to share their individual risk efficiently. How much should the group be ready to pay to fully insure their risk?

(c) Compare the answers to questions (a) and (b). How can you explain the difference?

Part IV

Extensions

12
Asymmetric Information

Until now we have maintained an assumption of complete information by all agents in the market place. Of course in many situations people might have different information on which to base their economic decisions. In this chapter we focus on the case where some market participants have private information (information that is known only to themselves). Sometimes this information is difficult, if not impossible, to fully reveal to others. For example, it would be easy for you to convince someone that you know how to play the piano, assuming that you do know how. Thus "playing the piano" would be information that can be easily verified. However, suppose a local store offered a free piano to you if you could prove to them that you do not know how to play the piano? How would you convince them that you are not a gifted pianist who is just pretending not to know how to play? "Not playing the piano" would be information that is quite difficult to verify.

An example of a market with private information is the market for used cars. The purchase of a used car, especially one that is no longer on a manufacturer's warranty, places much risk on the buyer. What if that beautiful car that appears to be in such excellent condition actually suffers from some severe problems, which will only manifest themselves after the car has been driven for a while? One problem is that low-quality cars, often called "lemons," are not always easy to distinguish from high-quality cars until after their purchase. As a result, we are likely to see prices in the used-car market in which the existence of "lemons" forces the owners of high-quality cars to accept a lower price than they would accept in a market where automobile quality was transparent to everyone. In the extreme, the owner of a high-quality used car might decide not to sell the car at all, since the low market price is less than the owner's reservation price for selling the car.

On the other hand, it might be possible to provide some kind of credible signal that a car is not a lemon. For example, the seller of a high-quality car might offer a limited warranty to the buyer, whereas such a warranty would be too costly to offer for the low-quality seller. Or, the owner of the high-quality car might be willing to pay for an inspection by a local independent mechanic. At this stage it is useful to note that it is the high-quality-car owner who must bear the cost of signaling that his car is not a "lemon."

Now consider a related problem in which the car has been inspected and revealed to be high quality. Suppose the car was sold for a high price to someone who lives far away. The original owner offers to drive the car to the buyer's home and hand over the keys in person. Since the sale has already been made, the original owner no longer has an economic incentive to drive the car in a careful manner. Thus, the car might be driven more harshly than if the inspection and sale had not yet taken place. Moreover, the original owner might discover some new problem during the delivery trip. If this new problem is not readily visible, the original owner does not have much incentive to reveal this new problem to the buyer. Or suppose that, instead of the original owner, the new owner hires some university student to deliver the car to his home, with an agreed-upon fee to be paid in advance? What incentive would the university student have to drive carefully?

In this section we analyze the effects of private information on market contracts. In cases like the market for "lemons," we will show how contracts may be designed to illicit truthful revelation of private information. In the case of the driver/deliverer of the new car, we will show how particular contracts might induce desirable behavior.

12.1 Adverse Selection

If there was just one market price for all used cars, that price would be more attractive to the current owners of "lemons" and less attractive to the current owners of high-quality cars. As a result, there would be a disproportionate share of low-quality cars for sale. This is a classic example of a phenomenon known as "adverse selection." Indeed, the first real economic analysis of this problem propelled George Akerlof to a Nobel Prize.

Another classic example is an insurance market, as first examined by Rothschild and Stiglitz (1976). To make the example more concrete, let us consider the auto insurance market. In this market, various laws allow the insurance companies to base their prices on several observable features of the insured, such as past driving history and the type of car she drives. Let us assume that we restrict ourselves to drivers who all fall within the same insurance classification and thus would face the same menu of prices from the insurer. Of course, all drivers within this classification are not identical. To focus on the adverse selection aspects, we assume that individuals are identical except for their probabilities of loss. A loss, if it occurs, is of a fixed size L. There are two types of drivers within this risk classification: "good" drivers and "bad" drivers, with loss probabilities given by p_G and p_B, respectively. We assume that $0 < p_G < p_B < 1$. Each driver is assumed to know his or her own loss probability, whereas the insurer cannot observe an individual's type and only knows the distribution of types within the population.

12.1.1 Full Insurance

As a point of comparison, consider first a market in which p_G and p_B are public information and where the insurer is free to offer a different menu of contracts to each type. Because insurers can diversify the independent individual risks, they are assumed to be risk neutral and seek to maximize their expected profits. The market is assumed to be in a long-run competitive equilibrium, so that the expected profit is zero for each of the insurance companies and for each supplied contract. This means in particular that good drivers pay a premium that is equal to p_G dollar per dollar of indemnity, and that bad drivers pay a larger premium rate p_B. Since this implies actuarially fair pricing, we know from Mossin's Theorem (3.1) that full insurance would be optimal, if offered. To see that full insurance would indeed be offered in such a market, suppose to the contrary that some level of coinsurance $\alpha^* < 1$ was the highest available level of coverage. We know from Chapter 3 that a level of coinsurance $\alpha^* + \varepsilon$ at a fair price would increase the consumer's EU, for any $\varepsilon > 0$ such that $\alpha^* + \varepsilon \leqslant 1$. But in this case, it must be true that offering $\alpha^* + \varepsilon$ at a price slightly higher than an actuarially fair price also would be preferred to α^* at a fair price. As a result, the insurer offering $\alpha^* + \varepsilon$ would earn an expected profit. In a long-run competitive equilibrium, we will assume that competition drives this profit out. The end result is that there must be full insurance at a fair price offered to each type of driver. The good drivers pay a premium of $P_G = p_G L$, while the bad drivers pay a premium of $P_B = p_B L$.

Now let us suppose that the driver type is private information. Each driver knows his or her own type, but this information is not observable nor verifiable by the insurer. If we continue to offer full coverage insurance policies at two separate premium rates, P_G and P_B, it is likely that all consumers would claim to be good drivers in order to pay price P_G, since $P_G < P_B$. This implies that the insurers will all lose money and the market will not be able to survive with these prices. One possibility of the market surviving with full insurance policies is for the insurers to all charge a premium of P_B. In this case, the good risks will either decide that the price P_B is too high and that they are better off with no insurance; or the good risks will decide that full insurance with a premium of P_B is better than no insurance. If the premium P_B is too high, the good drivers will buy no insurance at all. In this case, we have an extreme example of the "lemons" phenomenon, since only bad drivers buy insurance.[1] This is illustrated in Figure 12.1.

In Figure 12.1, we draw a state-claims diagram, as introduced in Chapter 5. Both types of drivers have an initial state claim of $(w, w - L)$. Both also have the same von Neumann–Morgenstern utility function; however, their expected utilities differ

---

[1] The analogous used-car market situation would be a market in which the only used cars that are for sale are "lemons."

due to their differing probabilities of a loss. The preferences of the two agents satisfy the important single-crossing property. It means that at any point in Figure 12.1, as at point A, for example, the indifference curve of the good-risk type is steeper than the indifference curve of the bad-risk agent. This is the graphical expression of the fact that bad-risk agents are willing to pay a larger premium in the good state to get more to consume in the bad state, which is more likely. In other words, bad-risk agents are more reluctant to buy a high deductible insurance. The so-called "fair-price lines" are also drawn for both the bad-risk and the good-risk types. These lines represent all of the possible state claims that arise from paying a fair premium of $p_t \alpha L$ in return for a net payment by the insurer of $(1 - p_t)\alpha L$ in the event of a loss, for $t = $ B, G. The bad-risk price line is flatter due to the higher probability of a loss p_B, which of course entails a higher premium. With full information, both types of drivers will be offered full insurance, with their final contingent wealth claims at the points labeled "B" and "G" for the bad and the good risks, respectively.

12.1.2 Pooling Contracts

The above analysis assumes that only full-coverage insurance is available. Of course, unlike used cars, we can sell partial insurance contracts. To this end let us suppose that an insurance contract consists of a pair, specifying both a premium P and an indemnity level α, where the indemnity itself is understood to be αL. A Rothschild–Stiglitz equilibrium in this market is defined as follows.

Definition 12.1. A set of contracts is an equilibrium set of contracts if

  (i) all contract pairs that are offered earn an expected profit of zero,

  (ii) there is no other contract that could be added[2] to the equilibrium set of contracts that would earn a positive expected profit.

Consider the full insurance contracts described above. For the good risks to demand any contract, their final wealth must be preferred to their wealth with no insurance. That is, we must have the contingent claim $(w - P, w - P - L + \alpha L) \succeq_G (w, w - L)$, where " $\succeq_G$ " denotes the preference relation for good drivers and P denotes the premium offered for insurance. This inequality represents the so-called "individual rationality constraint" for the good drivers. It is simply a constraint for participating in the market.

To analyze insurer profits, we assume that there is public information available on the proportion of bad drivers in the population. Let λ denote this proportion of bad drivers and assume that $0 < \lambda < 1$. Consider a full coverage insurance premium of $P_\lambda \equiv [\lambda p_B + (1 - \lambda)p_G]L$. Such a contract would break even, on average, if both

---

[2]For readers familiar with some game theory, this is a Nash equilibrium among insurers, where each insurer's strategy is its set of insurance contracts offered.

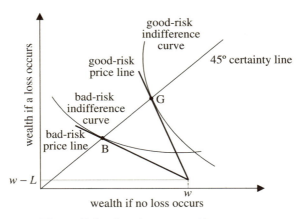

Figure 12.1. Auto insurance with two types.

types of drivers bought this contract. Of course the bad drivers will want to buy it, since the price is even lower than a fair price. But, this contract will, of course, lose money if only the bad drivers buy it. However, if the good drivers find this contract better than no insurance, the contract will earn a positive profit on the good drivers. Given the design of the premium P_λ above, this full coverage insurance contract would earn an expected profit of zero. Such a contract that is purchased by both types of individuals is called "pooling contract." If such a contract is an equilibrium contract, we refer to the equilibrium as a "pooling equilibrium."

The idea for this type of contract was carried to the extreme in the United States in the early 1990s, when then-First-Lady Hillary Clinton was attempting to set up such a pooling contract for health insurance. Indeed, the idea then was even more encompassing; it was to pool everyone, not just those individuals within a particular risk classification. However, there is a problem with pooling those with observable classification differences. We can illustrate this by assuming that type is observable within our automobile-insurance pooling contract above, so that we have in essence two observable classifications. Suppose the government imposed such a pooling contract as the only available contract, with no choice allowed to obtain private insurance from elsewhere. Obviously, the good drivers would be the losers in this setting, since they will not be offered insurance at a price of $P_G = p_G L$. The problem then becomes one of voter disenfranchisement. The good risks are disenfranchised and will resist this government action. But what if we restrict ourselves to pooling within one particular risk classification with two types, where type is not observable? Will we then be able to support such a pooling contract as an equilibrium contract?

The situation in this case turns out to be somewhat similar. The good risks are once again disenfranchised. To see this, consider the situation depicted in Figure 12.2. The full coverage pooling contract leads to the contingent wealth claim C, which

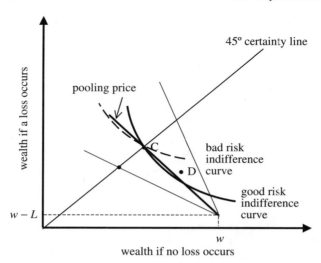

Figure 12.2.   No pooling equilibrium.

offers full insurance to both types at the same premium P_λ. At C, the insurers earn a zero profit. The good risks are seen to prefer C to zero coverage, since the contingent wealth claim C is on a higher indifference curve than $(w, w - L)$. However, full coverage pooling cannot be an equilibrium. Consider a partial insurance contract such as the one leading to contingent wealth D in Figure 12.2. This contract will be preferred by the good drivers to the full-coverage pooling contract, but it will not be preferred to the full-coverage contract by the bad drivers. Since D lies below the fair-price line for the good drivers, this new partial insurance contract will earn a positive expected profit. As a result, an equilibrium cannot contain the full coverage pooling contact.

The problem is essentially the same for any fair-priced pooling contract, not just for full insurance. Since the good-risk indifference curve will always be steeper than the bad-risk indifference curve everywhere along the fair-price line for pooling contracts, we can always find a new contract that will attract only the good drivers and make an expected profit. If your competing insurers only offer a pooling contract, this means that you can offer a new contract with a larger deductible and a smaller premium. Because bad-risk agents are more reluctant towards larger deductible, there exist a reduction in premium that is large enough to attract good-risk agents, but it is not large enough to attract the bad-risk agents. Because the good-risk agents initially paid a premium which is much larger than the actuarial value of their policy, this new contract is profitable. We thus have the following conclusion.

Proposition 12.2. *In a Rothschild–Stiglitz equilibrium under adverse selection, there cannot exist a pooling equilibrium.*

So if there are no pooling contracts in equilibrium, what other type of equilibrium contracts might be possible?

12.1.3 Separating Contracts

Since the EUs of the good drivers and bad drivers are different, we can design a set of contracts in such a way that each type prefers a different contract in equilibrium. Such an equilibrium is called a "separating equilibrium." Since the insurers cannot directly observe or verify an individual's type, these contracts serve as a mechanism by which insurance can segregate the population into the good drivers and the bad drivers. Since each individual is free to select his or her own contract, the mechanism is often referred to as a "self-selection mechanism." It is also an example of what is called a "revelation mechanism," since by self-selecting a contract, the individual reveals his or her type to the insurer.[3]

To see how this type of contract is designed, we need to introduce a new type of constraint, called the "incentive-compatibility constraint." In the Rothschild–Stiglitz model, this constraint is that each type of driver likes its own insurance contract better than the alternative contract. Let (P_t, α_t) denote the contract purchased by type t, $t = \text{B, G}$, and let $\succsim_t$ denote the preference ordering of type t. There are two incentive constraints in our insurance model, one for each risk type:

(i) $(P_B, \alpha_B) \succsim_B (P_G, \alpha_G)$,

(ii) $(P_G, \alpha_G) \succsim_G (P_B, \alpha_B)$.

Since each type of contract offered must earn an expected profit of zero, we first note that the bad drivers must be offered full insurance at a fair price, $\alpha_B = 1$ and $P_B = p_B L$. If this were not the case, if the bad drivers were offered a different amount of insurance, new contract offerings could lead to a profit in the same manner as discussed in Section 12.1.1. The insurers would not be concerned if good drivers also bought this contract, since any contract that breaks even or earns a profit from the bad drivers will also earn a profit, on average, from any good drivers who purchase it. As a result, long-run competition ensures that the bad drivers will be offered full insurance at a fair price, with a contingent-wealth claim of B in Figure 12.1. With the bad-risk contract $(p_B L, 1)$ in place, the good-risk contract must be designed so as to not attract the bad drivers. Competition will force the insurers to offer as much insurance as possible to the good drivers at a fair price for the good drivers. Thus, the incentive compatibility constraint for the bad drivers, (i) above, must be binding. The good drivers are offered the contract that yields contingent-wealth claim G'

---

[3]One might think that once the insurers know the individual's type, they can charge a premium based on that information. However, we assume that type is revealed only by the actual purchase of insurance. If the insurer could renegotiate all contracts, this would cause individuals to behave strategically, so as not to always reveal their true type.

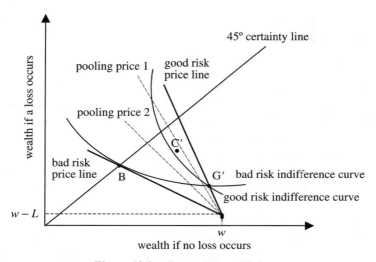

Figure 12.3.   Separating equilibrium.

in Figure 12.3. This contract leaves the bad drivers just indifferent to their full-coverage contract, and we will assume that they opt for the full coverage contract with contingent wealth B. Thus, this pair of contracts causes the two types of drivers to reveal their type via their contract choice.

However, is this pair of separating contracts an equilibrium? As it turns out, there may be a problem. Certainly no other separating contracts could dominate the separating contracts discussed above, but what about a pooling contract? In particular, suppose the fraction of bad drivers λ is relatively small, so that the actuarially fair pooling price line is represented by the line labeled "Pooling price 1" in Figure 12.3. In that case, consider the pooling contract that leads to the contingent-wealth claim C' in the figure. This contract is preferred by both types of individuals to their respective separating contracts. Hence both the bad drivers and good drivers would purchase it, if it were offered as an alternative to their separating contracts. Moreover, since contingent claim C' lies below "Pooling price 1," it would earn an expected profit if both types of drivers purchased it. Thus, part (ii) of Definition 12.1 is not satisfied by our pair of separating contracts. Of course, we have already seen in Proposition 12.2 that a pooling equilibrium cannot exist. Hence, in this situation, a Rothschild–Stiglitz equilibrium fails to exist.

If the proposition of bad drivers λ is relatively large, such as is illustrated by the pooling price line labeled "Pooling price 2" in Figure 12.3, then no fair-priced pooling contract can attract the good drivers. Hence, the separating contracts defined above are indeed an equilibrium. Thus, we obtain the following result, which summarizes what we have discussed here.

Proposition 12.3. *If there are sufficiently many bad drivers in the population, then a Rothschild–Stiglitz equilibrium consists of separating contracts in which the bad drivers receive full insurance at a fair price, while the good drivers receive partial coverage at a fair price. In this context, the number of bad drivers is sufficiently large whenever no fair price pooling contract attracts the good drivers.*

If an equilibrium does exist, it is interesting to note that adverse selection does not affect the welfare of the bad drivers at all. They receive full insurance at a fair price, exactly the same as if there was full information. It is only the good drivers who are affected by accepting less-than-full coverage. In the same way that the owner of a high-quality automobile had to bear any cost of signaling that his car was not a "lemon" in the market for used cars, the good driver here must bear the cost of signaling that he is not a bad driver by purchasing partial insurance.

12.2 Moral Hazard

Moral hazard deals with hidden actions or with the fact that effort is typically not observable. For example, an individual with insurance might not drive as carefully as she would if she had to pay for all of her own losses. Or consider the effect of airbags on driver caution. Knowing that there is state-of-the-art protection in the event of an accident might cause a driver to be less cautious. Consider the incentive effect of an airbag compared to that of a device that was mounted in the steering wheel and was triggered exactly the same as your airbag, except that this alternative device triggered a bomb that was attached beneath the car, so that any front-end impact caused an explosion and immediate death as opposed to a nice inflated pillow that offers protection from injury. In which car would you have the incentive to drive more carefully?

The fact that one's market choices might lead to incentives that alter one's behavior is the general problem of "moral hazard." In particular, we focus on the impact of contracts on one's behavior. Although the settings for moral hazard can be quite complex, much can be gleaned by examining the simplest case possible, namely a case where there are only two levels of effort. Again, to keep the story more concrete, we maintain the setting of an insurance market with only two possible loss states. Either no loss occurs or a loss occurs and is of size L. Rather than two types of individuals, we will consider only one individual, but with two possible effort levels. With no effort the probability of an accident is p_N and with effort the probability is p_E, where we assume that $0 < p_E < p_N < 1$. The setting is not too unlike that of the previous section under adverse selection, except that individual can now choose his or her own type. Of course everyone would choose to take the effort if effort is costless. We thus assume that there is a cost for taking effort that is measured in utility terms for an individual. In particular, taking effort costs the individual c units of utility.

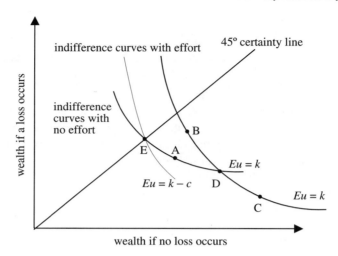

Figure 12.4. Indifference curves and effort.

In order to study how effort is affected by market contracts, let us first take a look at how the decision to take effort is affected by an individual's distribution of random wealth. When there are only two states of nature, we consider two competing probability distributions. Consider the indifference curve through a contingent-wealth claim on the certainty line, such as at E in Figure 12.4. Since wealth at E is the same in both states, the probabilities p_E and p_N play no role in calculating the EU of wealth. Let us suppose that the EU at E with no effort is equal to k. If effort were costless, utility would also be k with effort; but because effort has a utility cost of c, the individual's EU with effort is $k - c$. The single crossing property also holds here: indifference curves when effort is taken are steeper at every contingent wealth claim, since $p_E < p_N$. Since EU of wealth is lower at E when effort is taken, we consider a higher indifference curve, one for which the EU of wealth with effort is also k.[4] In Figure 12.4, this occurs on the indifference curve with effort, passing through contingent claims BDC.

Now consider the individual's choice about whether or not to take effort. At claim B in Figure 12.4, the individual has k units of utility when effort is taken. On the other hand, B lies above the indifference curve for k units of utility when no effort is taken (the indifference curve drawn through points EAD). Consequently, if the individual's contingent-wealth claim is B, the individual will decide not to take effort, and achieve a utility higher than k. Similarly, we can consider the contingent-wealth claim denoted by A, for which k units of utility are obtained when no effort

---

[4]Of course this will require $(1 - p_E)u(y_1) + p_E u(y_2) = k + e$, where y_1 and y_2 are wealth in the no-loss state and loss state, respectively. We assume that such contingent claims exist and that y_1 and y_2 are both strictly positive.

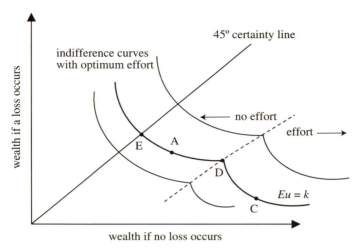

Figure 12.5. Indifference curves with optimal effort

is taken. If the individual with contingent-wealth claim A decides to take effort, she will be on a lower indifference than the one through BDC. Indeed, we can see that, as drawn, making an effort with contingent claim A would lead to a utility somewhere between $k - c$ and k. Thus, if the individual's contingent-wealth claim was A, no effort would be made.

Note that at claim D, the individual is indifferent as to whether or not effort is taken. When effort is endogenized, the reader can easily verify that the state-contingent claims E, A, D and C all have utility k, after optimizing with respect to the effort level. As a result, they can all be considered to lie on the same indifference curve, where we allow the level of effort to be chosen optimally. This indifference curve for k units of utility is depicted in Figure 12.5, together with some indifference curves for other levels of satisfaction. We can see how the "kinks" on each indifference curve divide that level of utility into state claims that induce effort and those that do not induce any effort. Each "kink" is itself a contingent-wealth claim for which the individual is indifferent between taking effort and not taking effort. Thus, by considering these claims for which effort is indifferent, we can naturally divide the space of state-contingent claims into two regions: one region for which effort is optimal, and second region for which no effort is optimal. For the sake of clarity, we will assume that the individual makes an effort if she is indifferent between making an effort and not making an effort.

In general, claims closest to the 45° certainty line will lead to no effort. For these claims, the difference in wealth between the loss state and the no-loss state is literally "not worth the effort." On the other hand, for claims such as C, where there is a fairly substantial difference in wealth between the no-loss state and the

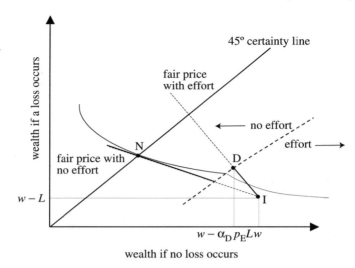

Figure 12.6. Nonlinear insurance pricing.

loss state, the individual finds the cost of effort to be worthwhile. That is to say that the expected monetary reward from decreasing the likelihood of the loss state will increase the individual's EU by more than c, the cost of effort. Thus, even though we cannot observe or verify whether the individual makes an effort, we have information about what the individual's incentive is, based on her contingent wealth. This allows contracts to be written, based on this information.

Let us see how an insurer can use this information in offering insurance contracts. If we maintain the assumption of long-run competition, any profits will be driven away. We thus look at only actuarially fair contracts. Of course individuals would prefer to have full insurance at a fair price, but we know that with full insurance, the individual would take no effort. Consequently, the price for full insurance is the no-effort fair price, $P = p_N L$. Only if the level of insurance is small enough will the individual have an incentive to take any effort. This is illustrated in Figure 12.6. If I denotes the initial contingent-wealth claim with no insurance, then the highest level of insurance that can be sold at the lower with-effort price is that level which takes the individual to wealth D. This level of insurance is labeled as α_D in the diagram. Any additional insurance coverage at this low price would cause the individual to stop taking any effort and, consequently, the insurer would expect to make a loss on the contract. If more coverage than α_D is desired by the individual, the insurer will charge the higher "no-effort" price. This leads to a nonlinear set of insurance prices:

$$P(\alpha) = \begin{cases} \alpha p_E L & \text{for } \alpha \leqslant \alpha_D, \\ \alpha p_N L & \text{for } \alpha > \alpha_D. \end{cases}$$

For any fixed level of effort and assuming that insurance is offered at a fair price, the individual's EU is monotonically increasing in the level of insurance coverage for all levels of coverage below full insurance. Thus α_D is the most preferred level of insurance that is offered at the lower "with-effort" price on the nonlinear pricing schedule. Of course, at the higher "no-effort" price, full coverage would be most preferred, leading to the contingent-wealth claim labeled N in Figure 12.6. As a consequence, we only need to compare two contracts: the ones with $\alpha = 1$ and with $\alpha = \alpha_D$. Whichever of these two levels of insurance coverage leads to a higher EU is the one chosen by the individual. As drawn in Figure 12.6, D lies above the indifference curve through N. Thus, the individual would choose $\alpha = \alpha_D$, leading to the contingent-wealth claim D as well as a decision to take the effort to reduce the probability of a loss. Although not drawn in the diagram, it also would be possible to have preferences for which full coverage is preferred, together with a decision not to take any effort.

It is interesting to compare our moral-hazard solution presented here to the separating equilibrium in the adverse-selection model. In both cases, the consumer has (essentially) a choice between two contracts: one contract in which a limited amount of coverage is offered at a low price, and another contract in which full coverage is offered but at a higher price. In the adverse selection model, the limited-coverage contract at the low price is set in such a way as to segregate the good risks, i.e. those with a lower probability of a loss. In the moral-hazard model, the limited-coverage contract is set in such a way as to segregate good behavior, i.e. behavior that lowers the probability of a loss.

12.3 The Principal–Agent Problem

We now consider a variant of the moral hazard model that has a wide array of applications. Consider an individual or a firm that has two possible final wealth levels, X_1 and X_2 where $X_1 > X_2$. The probability of state s is p_s for $a = 1, 2$. We will refer to this individual or firm as the "principal." In many circumstances, it is possible for the principal to hire someone to increase the likelihood of the good outcome in state 1. For example, consider someone who is being sued and who hires a lawyer to help win the case. Or consider a firm trying to win a construction contract from a city and suppose that the firm hires a consulting company to present its proposal to the city council. The lawyer and consulting company are examples of what is referred to as the "agent." The agent thus works on behalf of the principal to increase the likelihood of state 1 (or, equivalently, to decrease the likelihood of state 2). Suppose we pay the agent a fixed fee for its service. If we ignore long-term considerations, such as reputation effects, what incentive does the agent have to take any effort? Of course if effort is observable, we can write a clause into any contract denying payment in the event that no effort is taken. But in a situation where effort is both unobservable and unverifiable by the principal, we cannot base compensation on the level of effort taken. If the lawyer works extremely hard and increases our probability of winning the case, we might still lose due to plain bad luck. Or if the city council grants our construction contract, it might be that we were awarded the contract in spite of the fact that the consulting firm did not work very hard. In other words, the principal cannot be sure, even *ex post*, whether effort was taken by the agent or not.[5]

12.3.1   Binary Effort with a Risk-Neutral Principal

We will keep the model as simple as possible by assuming that the agent has only two possible choices: effort or no effort, similar to our insured in the moral hazard model above. Once again, effort is assumed to have a direct cost in terms of EU, with effort reducing utility by an amount c. Of course, if the agent makes no effort, which is often referred to as "shirking" in the principal–agent literature, the principal would prefer to pay the agent zero. That is, the principal does not want to pay the agent who shirks. At the same time, the agent needs to find it worthwhile to work for the principal.

We assume for now that the principal is risk neutral, with the agent being risk averse. Since a fixed-fee form of compensation to the agent will not induce the agent to take any effort and since effort itself is unobservable, we need to examine whether it might be possible to induce the agent to take effort by offering compensation in the form of a contingent claim. Let (a_1, a_2) denote the contingent claim that is paid by the principal to the agent, where $a_1, a_2 \geq 0$. The principal thus retains the claim $(X_1 - a_1, X_2 - a_2)$.[6] Although the principal receives less wealth in every state of the world after paying the agent, the principal will have a higher probability of state 1 by hiring the agent, assuming that the agent does not shirk. Of course, if we do not have $a_1 > a_2$, there is not going to be any incentive for the agent to make any effort. On the other hand if we make a_1 so much larger than a_2 that $X_1 - a_1 < X_2 - a_2$, the principal will have no desire to hire the agent.

The method by which we can induce effort is the same as that we analyzed in the previous section. Reinterpreting no-loss-state wealth as a_1 and loss-state wealth as a_2, Figure 12.5 shows the set of contingent-claims contracts for the agent that will induce effort. To operationalize the principal–agent model, we will assume that the agent is offered a contract that yields a level of utility that is identical to the level of

---

[5]In our two-state model, it is easy to define the effect of effort as increasing the probability of the good state. With more than two states, the beneficial effect of effort is a bit trickier. It usually involves a better set of outcomes via first-order stochastic dominance, with some additional restrictions.

[6]We could add a fixed wealth to both the claim of the principal and that of the agent, but that does not affect the model and only adds notation. We will therefore conveniently assume that (a_1, a_2) and $(X_1 - a_1, X_2 - a_2)$ are the final contingent-wealth claims of the agent and of the principal, respectively.

utility obtainable from the agent's next best alternative. Let this level of utility be denoted by k. The level of effort is denoted as e and is assumed here to be either zero or one. The corresponding probability of state s is $p_s(e)$, with $p_2(e) = 1 - p_1(e)$. The cost of effort is denoted c. We assume that $p_1(1) > p_1(0)$.

Our objective then is to find the contract (a_1, a_2) to solve the following program

$$\max_{a_1, a_2, e} p_1(e)(X_1 - a_1) + p_2(e)(X_2 - a_2) \qquad (12.1)$$

subject to

$$p_1(e)u(a_1) + p_2(e)u(a_2) - ce = k, \qquad (12.2)$$

$$p_1(1)u(a_1) + p_2(1)u(a_2) - c \geqslant p_1(0)u(a_1) + p_2(0)u(a_2). \qquad (12.3)$$

Thus, the principal chooses the contingent payment to the agent (a_1, a_2) and, indirectly, the level of agent effort e that maximize its expected payoff. It might seem odd at first that we include a choice of e, since e is unobservable by the principal. In our model with just two levels of effort, this effectively amounts to the principal somehow choosing $e = 1$. How this occurs becomes clear once we examine the two constraints. The constraint (12.2) is the individual-rationality constraint of the agent. The agent needs to be at least as well off as it would be in the next-best alternative. In the principal–agent set-up, this constraint is also referred to as the "participation constraint" for the agent. Constraint (12.3) is the agent's incentive-compatibility constraint. Recall that in the adverse-selection model the incentive-compatibility constraint guaranteed that each type of risk liked its own contract at least as well as it liked the other type's contract. In the current principal–agent setting, the incentive-compatibility constraint guarantees instead that the agent likes working at least as much as shirking, in which case we assume that the agent takes the effort. In effect, the incentive-compatibility constraint (12.3) guarantees that $e = 1$. In other words, although the principal cannot observe effort e directly, it can effect a choice of $e = 1$ by an appropriate choice of a_1 and a_2.

Figure 12.7 illustrates the solution to this problem. Here we show the payment to the agent as a contingent claim. Just as in the moral-hazard case, we can partition the space into contingent payments for which effort is optimal for the agent and payments for which taking no effort is optimal. The incentive-compatibility constraint (12.3) forces our solution for the optimal (a_1, a_2) to lie somewhere within the "with-effort" set of contingent payoffs. The participation constraint (12.2) forces us to be on the agent's indifference curve for which $Eu = k$ in this "with-effort" set of contingent payments. The contracts that satisfy the two constraints lie on curve DE. Given these constraints, the contingent payment to the agent that maximizes the expected payoff to the principal is precisely the one that minimizes the expected payment to the agent. This is illustrated by the principal's indifference curves as

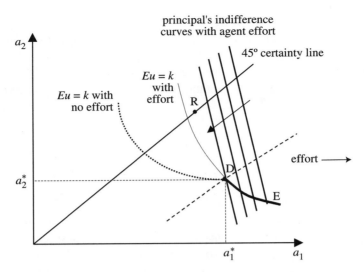

Figure 12.7. Principal–agent model with a risk-neutral principal.

drawn in Figure 12.7. These indifference curves are parallel straight lines with a slope of $-p_1(1)/p_2(1)$. The principal, as well as the agent, would receive the same expected payoff everywhere along such a line so long as effort is taken by the agent. We know from Chapter 5 that risk aversion of the agent implies that the agent's marginal rate of substitution, $p_1(1)u'(a_1)/p_2(1)u'(a_2)$, is less than $p_1(1)/p_2(1)$ for all $a_1 > a_2$. This leads to a corner solution at D in Figure 12.7, with a contingent payment to the agent of (a_1^*, a_2^*). In other words, we pay the agent barely enough to make the effort worthwhile.

Note that the "reserve utility" of the agent, k, might be viewed as arbitrary. That is, we might think about changing k in (12.2). In this sense, we can view the solution to (12.1) as being Pareto efficient: we maximize the principal's "EU" (which is the same its expected payoff under risk neutrality) subject to a given level of EU k for the agent. Since we are only Pareto efficient with respect to a reduced set of possibilities, namely those satisfying both the constraints (12.2) and (12.3), the solution is often referred to as a "second-best" solution. That is, we must qualify the way in which our solution is "Pareto efficient."

To see what this difference entails, consider a world in which effort could be observed. Notice that the solution of paying the agent (a_1^*, a_2^*) is not Pareto efficient in this case. In this full-information world, let us make the agent's contingent payment conditional upon the agent exerting effort. With no effort, the agent gets paid zero. In this case, we can find other contracts, such as at contingent payment R in Figure 12.7, for which both the principal and the agent are better off. The agent will be on a higher indifference curve while at the same time receiving a lower expected payment, meaning that the expected payoff to the principal is higher. In other words, at R, both the principal and the agent are better off. The contingent payment at D is thus Pareto dominated in the sense of efficient risk sharing. However, for the case where effort is fixed at $e = 1$, note that all of the contingent payments to the agent that Pareto dominate D (i.e. all contingent payments that offer more utility with a lower expected payment to the agent) involve contingent payments to the agent for which no effort, $e = 0$, would be optimal. In other words, a contract such as R is not incentive compatible. Thus R does not dominate D in our world with unobservable effort. In a very real sense, compared to the "first-best" case with full information and risk-sharing efficiency, the principal needs to "overpay" the agent in the good state in order to induce the agent to take effort. This is precisely the reason most lawyers for the plaintiff in a liability case are paid on a so-called contingent-fee basis: the lawyer receives an exceptionally high payment if he wins the case, but receives little or nothing if the case is lost.

One might think that this inefficient risk-sharing property of our solution is due to the fact the we have a risk-neutral principal. In the next section we show that this is indeed not the case, while extending our model to a more realistic case with a continuum of effort levels by the agent.

12.3.2 Continuous Effort with a Risk-Averse Principal

Let the risk-averse utility of the principal be given by the function v. We assume that effort can be any level $e \geq 0$, with $p_1(e)$ increasing and concave, that is $p_1'(e) > 0$ and $p_1''(e) < 0$. In other words, there are diminishing marginal returns to the agent's effort. In order to avoid a corner solution, we further assume that $p_1(e) < 1 \; \forall e$, so that it is not possible to guarantee state 1 with certainty, regardless of how much effort is used. The cost of effort is assumed to be c units of utility per unit of effort. We can now write the principal's objective as follows:

$$\max_{a_1, a_2, e} \; p_1(e)v(X_1 - a_1) + p_2(e)v(X_2 - a_2) \tag{12.4}$$

subject to

$$p_1(e)u(a_1) + p_2(e)u(a_2) - ce \geq k \tag{12.5}$$

$$p_1'(e)[u(a_1) - u(a_2)] - c = 0. \tag{12.6}$$

The inequality (12.5) is the individual rationality constraint, the same as before. Since preferences are assumed to be continuous, we will treat this constraint as effectively an equality constraint, fixing the agent's utility at its reservation level. Equation (12.6) is the incentive-compatibility constraint. Since we now allow for continuous effort levels, this equation identifies the optimum level of effort by the agent. Indeed, for a given level of contingent payment to the agent of (a_1, a_2), this equation is simply the agent's own first-order condition to maximize its level of effort e. Once again, although the principal cannot directly observe or verify the agent's level of effort, the principal will bring about the agent's optimal effort, as determined by (12.6), by choosing the contingent payment scheme. Obviously both the principal and the agent have no reason to contract with each other unless both $a_1 > a_2$, and $(X_1 - a_1) > (X_2 - a_2)$. Since we also have $p_1''(e) < 0$, (12.6) implies a unique level of effort e for any relevant (a_1, a_2).

We can write the Lagrangean for (12.4) as

$$L(a_1, a_2, w, \lambda, \mu) = p_1(e)v(X_1 - a_1) + p_2(e)v(X_2 - a_2)$$
$$+ \lambda[p_1(e)u(a_1) + p_2(e)u(a_2) - ce - k]$$
$$+ \mu\{p_1'(e)[u(a_1) - u(a_2)] - c\}.$$

This leads to the following first-order conditions:

$$-p_1(e)v'(X_1 - a_1) + \lambda p_1(e)u'(a_1) + \mu p_1'(e)u'(a_1) = 0, \quad (12.7)$$
$$-p_2(e)v'(X_2 - a_2) + \lambda p_2(e)u'(a_2) + \mu p_2'(e)u'(a_2) = 0, \quad (12.8)$$

and

$$p_1'(e)[v(X_1 - a_1) - v(X_2 - a_2)]$$
$$+\lambda\{p_1'(e)[u(a_1) - u(a_2)] - c\} + \mu p_1''(e)[u(a_1) - u(a_2)] = 0. \quad (12.9)$$

Our constraints, (12.5) and (12.6), are the final two first-order conditions.

To characterize the solution, consider first the condition (12.9). The first term is obviously positive, whereas the second term must be zero by the incentive compatibility constraint. Since $p_1''(e) < 0$ and $a_1 > a_2$, it follows that the optimal value of the Lagrange multiplier μ must be strictly positive. This turns out to be quite important. To see why, rewrite the first two first-order conditions above as follows:

$$v'(X_1 - a_1) = \left[\lambda + \mu\frac{p_1'(e)}{p_1(e)}\right]u'(a_1) \quad (12.10)$$

and

$$v'(X_2 - a_2) = \left[\lambda + \mu\frac{p_2'(e)}{p_2(e)}\right]u'(a_2). \quad (12.11)$$

Recall from Chapter 10 that efficient risk sharing (here in the sense of "first best") requires that there exists some constant, call it γ, such that $v'(X_s - a_s) = \gamma u'(a_s)$ for each state $s = 1, 2$. Clearly that is not the case here, since $p_1'(e) > 0$ while $p_2'(e) < 0$. Further note that, since $\mu > 0$, it follows from (12.11) that our other Lagrange multiplier λ must also be positive. Using (12.10) and (12.11), we obtain

$$\mathrm{MRS}_v \equiv \frac{p_1(e)v'(X_1 - a_1)}{p_2(e)v'(X_2 - a_2)} > \frac{p_1(e)u'(a_1)}{p_2(e)u'(a_2)} \equiv \mathrm{MRS}_u,$$

where MRS_v and MRS_u denote the marginal rates of substitution for the principal and for the agent respectively, both evaluated at the optimal payment for the agent, (a_1^*, a_2^*). This inequality implies that both the principal and the agent would be better off, in terms of efficient risk sharing, if the agent traded some state-1 wealth for some state-2 wealth. However, just as in the case with only two effort levels, reducing the state-1 payment to the agent would reduce the agent's level of effort. Thus we see that, once again, our second-best solution involves in a certain sense "overpaying" the agent in state 1 in order to induce the proper amount of effort.

12.4 Bibliographical References, Extensions and Exercises

The adverse-selection problem was modeled by Akerlof (1970). The analysis of equilibrium in a competitive market is due to Rothschild and Stiglitz (1976). Since the Rothschild–Stiglitz model often has no equilibrium, several authors considered non-Nash types of solutions to extend the results. Wilson (1977), for example, shows how pooling contracts might be an equilibrium if we allow nonprofitable contracts to be removed from the market. Riley (1979) allows for strategic responses to new contracts. His equilibrium was applied explicitly to the Rothschild–Stiglitz insurance setting by Engers and Fernandez (1987). Miyazaki (1977) and Spence (1978) use Wilson's model of equilibrium, but require only that the insurer earns zero profit, allowing for profits from some contracts to subsidize losses from others.

The moral hazard model as presented here is adapted from Stiglitz (1983). The principal–agent problem was introduced by Ross (1973) and our model is adapted from the so-called "first-order approach" of Holmström (1979). A potential problem with the optimization in Holmström's model, essentially that a local maximum might not yield a global maximum, was discovered by Grossman and Hart (1983). However, some reasonable restrictions avoid this potential pitfall, as was pointed out by Rogerson (1985).

Chapter Bibliography

Akerlof, G. 1970 The market for lemons: qualitative uncertainty and the market mechanism. *Quarterly Journal of Economics* 84:488–500.

Engers, M. and L. Fernandez. 1987. Market equilibrium with hidden knowledge and self-selection. *Econometrica* 55:425–439.

Grossman, S. and O. Hart. 1983. An analysis of the principal–agent problem. *Econometrica* 51:7–45.

Holmström, B. 1979. Moral hazard and observability. *Bell Journal of Economics* 10:74–91.

Miyazaki, H. 1977. The rat race and internal labor markets. *Bell Journal of Economics* 8:394–418.

Riley, J. 1979. Informational equilibria. *Econometrica* 47: 331–359.

Rogerson, W. 1985. The first-order approach to principal–agent problems. *Econometrica* 53:1357–1368.

Rothschild, M. and J. Stiglitz. 1976. Equilibrium in competitive insurance markets: an essay on the economics of imperfect information. *Quarterly Journal of Economics* 90:629–650.

Spence, M. 1977. Product differentiation and performance in insurance markets. *Journal of Public Economics* 10:427–447.

Stiglitz, J. 1983. Risk, incentives and insurance: the pure theory of moral hazard. *Geneva Papers on Risk and Insurance* 8:4–33.

Wilson, C. 1977. A model of insurance markets with incomplete information. *Journal of Economic Theory* 16:167–207.

Exercises

(12.1) Consider a competitive insurance market with adverse selection, as proposed by Rothschild and Stiglitz. We know that a pooling equilibrium will not exist. But suppose the government makes full insurance mandatory, at the fair pooling price. Are individuals better off or worse off than they would be under the Rothschild and Stiglitz assumptions? Explain carefully.

(12.2) Consider a Rothschild–Stiglitz adverse-selection economy with three (unobservable) types of consumers. In addition to the good risks and the bad risks, there also exist a medium-risk-type with loss probability p_M, where $p_B > p_M > p_G$.

   (a) Describe the separating Nash equilibrium that might exist in this economy.

   (b) Can other types of equilibria exist in this economy? (Note that in addition to a pooling equilibrium, you need to check the possibility of an equilibrium where there are two different contracts and two of the types of consumers pool to buy one of these contracts.)

(12.3) Consider a risk-averse entrepreneur who owns a project paying x_1 in state 1, with probability p_1, and paying x_2 in state 2, $x_1 > x_2$. The entrepreneur can hire a *risk-neutral manager*. The manager maximizes her expected utility, where utility is separable in wealth and effort. In particular, $u(w) = w$ is a von Neumann–Morgenstern utility of wealth, but effort costs the manager c units of utility for each unit of effort e. The entrepreneur pays the manager a fee of a_s in state s. The probability of state 1 is an increasing, concave function of the level of manager effort.

   (a) Suppose first that effort is *observable*, i.e. there is no moral hazard. Show that the first-best contract involves Pareto-efficient risk sharing. (Hint: show that $\exists k > 0$ such that $a_s^* = x_s - k$. If k is chosen to satisfy the participation constraint, a_s^* is the optimal payment to the manager in state s, so that the agent bears all of the risk.)

   (b) Now suppose that effort is *unobservable* by the entrepreneur. Show that the payment schedule above is still optimal, and the above level of effort, e^*, is still optimal.

Remark. This solution is sometimes described as the entrepreneur "selling" the project to the manager for a fixed price k. Note that, unlike the usual principal–agent model, with a risk-averse agent, we achieve Pareto-efficient risk sharing in this case.

(12.4) Consider a competitive insurance market with adverse selection and two types of individuals, good risks and bad risks, as proposed by Rothschild and Stiglitz (1976). Assume that there are enough bad risks in the population so that an equilibrium exists.

    (a) Carefully explain the Rothschild–Stiglitz *separating* equilibrium.

    (b) Now suppose that *everyone* has the higher bad-risk probability of a loss p_B to start, $p_B > p_G$. The "bad risks" will always have loss probability p_B, but the "good risks" can lower their probability of a loss to p_G, if they make the effort. If they do not make this effort, their loss probability remains at p_B. Making an effort will cost the good-risk individual c units of utility. Explain carefully whether or not a separating equilibrium will still exist, and if so, whether it is the same as the one in part (a).

13

Alternative Decision Criteria

The purpose of this book has been to characterize the properties of optimal decisions in the face of risk, at both the individual and collective levels. As modeled thus far, any decision under uncertainty can be described as essentially selecting a specific lottery L^i from a choice set $C = \{L^1, L^2, \ldots\}$. If there is a finite number S of possible states of nature, together with an objective probability distribution, each lottery can be defined as a vector $L = (x_0, p_0; x_1, p_1; \ldots; x_{S-1}, p_{S-1})$, where x_s is the outcome in state s, and p_s is the corresponding state probability. An essential component of modeling choice under uncertainty is to determine the way by which individuals make their choice in C. As in the general theory of consumer choice, it is quite innocuous to claim that, at the individual level, the individual chooses a strategy in order to maximize welfare. This statement leaves open the problem of how to evaluate welfare under uncertainty.

At the highest level of generality, welfare must be a function of the set of possible state-dependent outcomes and of the corresponding probabilities; that is, it must be a function of L. Let $V(L)$ denote the welfare of the decision maker who would select lottery L. Many possibilities exist for the form of V, each of them capturing a different type of economic behavior. For example, $V(L) = \sum_{s=0}^{S-1} p_s x_s$ would model risk-neutral preferences. Or consider the case of $V(L) = \min\{x_s\}$, which captures "infinite risk aversion." An individual with such preferences would be the extreme pessimist, who always assumes that the worst outcome will happen.

Throughout this book, we have followed the assumption first made by Daniel Bernoulli in 1738, that individual welfare can be measured by computing the EU of the outcome of the lottery. That is, we assumed that each agent has a utility function u such that his welfare, conditional on selecting any lottery $L = (x_0, p_0; x_1, p_1; \ldots; x_{S-1}, p_{S-1})$, takes the following specific form[1]:

$$V(x_0, p_0; x_1, p_1; \ldots; x_{S-1}, p_{S-1}) = \sum_{s=0}^{S-1} p_s u(x_s). \tag{13.1}$$

---

[1] We pointed out in Chapter 1 that the utility function u was unique only up to a so-called affine transformation. In this sense, the utility is cardinal. However, the preference functional V is equivalent to any increasing transformation of itself. In other words, welfare V is ordinal.

It is interesting to note that our example of risk-neutral preferences is a special case of EU, with $u(x) = x$. The preferences of the person who is infinitely risk averse ($V(L) = \min\{x_s\}$) can be modeled via EU using, for example, function $u(x) = -\mathrm{e}^{-Ax}/A$, with A tending to infinity.

Although it is widely used, the expected utility (EU) preference functional (13.1) is very restrictive. In particular, it is additive with respect to the states of nature, and it is linear with respect to the probabilities. The property of additivity with respect to the states of nature implies that the marginal value of the outcome in state s is independent of the outcome in any other state $s' \neq s$:

$$\frac{\partial^2 V}{\partial x_s \partial x_{s'}} = 0.$$

This additivity/independence property is an essential aspect of the EU model—one that we analyze in more detail in the next section. This property greatly simplifies the analysis of choices compared to a more general consumption theory, although it does so at a cost. For example, the EU model (13.1) makes the assumption that the marginal value of consumption in one state is independent of the contingent amount consumed in other states.

Notice that the case of uncertainty is not the only environment in which economists restrict the decision criterion to be additive. As we have seen in Chapter 6, the classical consumption/saving model assumes that consumers select their lifetime consumption profile in order to maximize the discounted value of their flow of felicity over their lifetime. This welfare functional is also additive with respect to time. It implies, for example, that, seen from the age of 20, the marginal lifetime utility of consumption at age 25 is independent of the level of consumption at the age of 24.

An overwhelming majority of researchers still uses additive choice functionals to model optimal behavior with respect to risk and time. However, this does not necessarily imply that the additive models are best in describing human behavior or in making policy recommendations. For example, consider a world in which we define $y_s = x_s - w$. If x_s and w describe, respectively, current and past wealth levels, y can be interpreted as the increase in wealth. Suppose we define the incremental-wealth lottery $\hat{L} = (y_0, p_0; y_1, p_1; \ldots; y_{S-1}, p_{S-1})$. We can define a welfare functional of the form $\hat{V}(w; \hat{L})$. In this setting, we can think of w as a "reference point." Unless the welfare functional $\hat{V}(w; \hat{L}) = \hat{V}(0; L)$ for each initial wealth w, as is the case in the EU model, then welfare is obviously dependent on more than just the distribution of final wealth. This shows how preferences themselves might be subject to a particular arbitrary choice of the reference point w, which depends upon the framing of the choice problem—a point made well by Kahneman and Tversky (1979) in their Prospect Theory.

Or suppose that we know the lottery outcomes x_s, but we do not know the precise probability for each state. This situation is often referred to as "ambiguity" or as "parameter uncertainty." If a preference functional is linear in the probabilities, we can simply use a mean probability for each state of nature. However, some research has shown that such ambiguity is disliked by the decision maker and affects behavior, a concept known as "ambiguity aversion."

The number of alternative models is growing fast in the literature. Most of them generalize the EU model presented in this book. This suggests that the EU model will remain a cornerstone of the economic theory of risk. The EU theory is simple, parsimonious and quite successful in explaining a wide set of empirical facts. Moreover, many of the types of behavior that we are trying predict are the same in these alternative models as they are in the EU model. Our objective in this chapter is to provide an introduction to a few of these alternative models. Admittedly, our coverage is only a small sampling of the vast literature on this topic. We start with a description of a few of the main attacks on EU theory.[2]

A final remark is in order here. Note that x_s describes the outcome relevant to the agent's well-being in state s. It can be multidimensional, to include, in addition to consumption, parameters describing the health status, the environment, and so on. When those parameters are uncertain, this raises the question of the interaction between these different sources of risk. Moreover, the aversion to risk on consumption can be substantially different from the aversion to risk on health. The risk management problem becomes even more complex when a lower health usually goes with a smaller labor income stream. Finally, the outcome in some specific states can be a lottery. For example, a risky situation described by $\hat{L} = (L, p; a, 1 - p)$ is a situation where you get lottery L with probability p, or you get a. We say that $\hat{L}$ is a compound lottery.

13.1 The Independence Axiom and the Allais Paradox

Consider a game consisting of choosing between two lotteries L^1 and L^2. If you can choose between them, which one would you prefer? Suppose that you prefer L^1. This means that $V(L^1)$ is larger than $V(L^2)$, otherwise you would have preferred L^2. Let us now modify the rules of the game. We consider now lotteries $\hat{L}^1$ and $\hat{L}^2$, where $\hat{L}^i$ is a compounded lottery in which you get lottery L^i with probability p and another outcome a with probability $1 - p$. If you are asked to choose between $\hat{L}^1$ and $\hat{L}^2$, which of the two would you select? If you are an EU maximizer, which implies that V is linear in p, it must be true that

$$V(\hat{L}^i) = V(L^i, p; a, 1 - p) = pV(L^i) + (1 - p)u(a).$$

---

[2]These attacks are quite numerous. A good survey of the classic theoretical arguments is in Machina (1987).

Table 13.1.   Outcome as a function of the number of the ball.

lottery	0	1–10	11–99
M^1	50	50	50
M^2	0	250	50
$\hat{M}^1$	50	50	0
$\hat{M}^2$	0	250	0

Therefore, if you prefer L^1 to L^2, it also must be true that you prefer $\hat{L}^1$ to $\hat{L}^2$. The choice between these two compounded lotteries is independent of the irrelevant common outcome a. This property is often referred to as the "independence axiom." This axiom, introduced by von Neumann and Morgenstern (1944), is a cornerstone of EU theory. When combined with a few other technical axioms, it *implies* that preferences must be linear in probabilities. This is the EU theorem.

The independence axiom is appealing on normative grounds. It is also a quite natural assumption. To illustrate, suppose you are contemplating going to dine downtown, either at restaurant A or at restaurant B. You decide that, all things considered, you prefer restaurant A. Now you learn that your car has developed a fault which means that, with some probability, it will break down after a few miles and prevent you from reaching either destination. Is your preference between restaurants A and B affected by the fact that your choice is no longer a definite one, but only a choice conditional on your not having to spend a few hours repairing the car? If you believe that there is no reason to switch your choice, your preferences satisfy the independence axiom.

When dealing with choices involving only wealth, the oldest and most famous challenge to the independence axiom has been proposed by Allais (1953). The paradox that he raised has generated thousands of papers. Allais proposed the following experiment. An urn contains 100 balls that are numbered from 0 to 99. There are four lotteries whose monetary outcomes depend in different ways on the number that is written on the ball that is taken out of the urn. The outcomes expressed, say, in thousands of euros, are described in Table 13.1.

As in our presentation of the independence axiom, decision makers are subjected to two games. In the first game, they are asked to choose between M^1 and M^2, whereas in the second game, they must choose between $\hat{M}^1$ and $\hat{M}^2$. Many people report that they prefer M^1 to M^2 in the first game, but they prefer $\hat{M}^2$ to $\hat{M}^1$ in the second. Notice that, since M^1 and M^2 have the same outcome when the number of the ball is larger than 10, the independence axiom tells us that these people prefer L^1 with a sure outcome of 50 to L^2 which takes value 0 with probability $1/11$ and value 250 with probability $10/11$. The paradox is that the same argument can be used with the opposite result when considering the preference of $\hat{M}^2$ over $\hat{M}^1$! Thus, many of the people in Allais's experiment do not behave in a way compatible with the independence axiom.

There is another simple way to verify that the pair of choices $M^1 \succ M^2$ and $\hat{M}^2 \succ \hat{M}^1$ is incompatible with EU preferences. This can be done by contradiction. Suppose that the decision maker is an EU maximizer with utility function u. The first choice implies that

$$u(50) > 0.01u(0) + 0.1u(250) + 0.89u(50),$$

or equivalently,

$$u(50) > \tfrac{1}{11}u(0) + \tfrac{10}{11}u(250). \tag{13.2}$$

That is, L^1 is preferred to L^2. Similarly, the preference of $\hat{M}^2$ over $\hat{M}^1$ implies that

$$0.11u(50) + 0.89u(0) < 0.9u(0) + 0.1u(250),$$

or equivalently,

$$u(50) < \tfrac{1}{11}u(0) + \tfrac{10}{11}u(250). \tag{13.3}$$

That is, L^2 is preferred to L^1. Obviously, there is no utility function u that can satisfy both conditions (13.2) and (13.3).

13.2 Rank-Dependent EU

One generalization of the EU model that can solve Allais's paradox has been proposed by Quiggin (1982), who weakened the independence axiom. This generalized criterion is now called the Rank-Dependent Expected Utility (RDEU) model. Consider the lottery $L = (x_0, p_0; x_1, p_1; \ldots; x_{S-1}, p_{S-1})$, and assume without loss of generality that $x_0 \leqslant x_1 \leqslant \cdots \leqslant x_{S-1}$. The index i of the outcome x_i can be interpreted as its rank in the size of the outcomes.

Consider the earlier example of our infinitely risk-averse agent, with $V(L) = \min\{x_s\}$. Since V is ordinal, if $0 < p_0 \leqslant 1$ we can easily write

$$V(x_0, p_0; x_1, p_1; \ldots; x_{S-1}, p_{S-1}) = u(\min_s x_s) = u(x_0), \tag{13.4}$$

where u is any increasing function. Such preferences satisfy the so-called maximin criterion, but they are outrageously extreme, as the decision maker is completely blind to the potential gains $x_1, \ldots, x_{S-1}$ above the minimum potential outcome. For example the lottery $L^1 = (1.01, \tfrac{1}{2}; 1.02, \tfrac{1}{2})$ would be preferred to the lottery $L^2 = (1\,000\,000, 0.99; 1, 0.01)$.

A less extreme decision maker would consider the possibility that, with probability $1 - p_0$, the outcome will be at least equal to x_1. This can be done, for example, by considering the following welfare valuation:

$$V(x_0, p_0; x_1, p_1; \ldots; x_{S-1}, p_{S-1}) = u(x_0) + f(1 - p_0)[u(x_1) - u(x_0)]. \tag{13.5}$$

In addition to the utility of the sure outcome, the decision maker takes into account the minimum additional utility $u(x_1) - u(x_0)$ that will be generated if state 0 does not occur. This case occurs with probability $1 - p_0$. It is natural to assume that the welfare generated by this prospect is increasing in this probability, i.e. that f is an increasing function. Of course, we also need to assume that $f(0) = 0$: when the worst outcome x_0 is certain, outcome x_1 does not matter for evaluating the welfare of the risk bearer. Similarly, if state 0 is a zero-probability event, outcome x_0 should not matter for welfare. This requires that $f(1) = 1$. For $0 < p < 1$, we might wish to assume that $f(p) < p$, which implies that the agent places a lower weight on the probability of the good news that x_0 did not occur, which is a characteristic of pessimism. In the limiting case where $f(p) = 0$ for all $p < 1$, specification (13.5) is equivalent to (13.4).

We can go one step further by also taking account of the other possible minimal increment to utility $u(x_2) - u(x_1)$ that would be obtained when states 0 and 1 do not occur. The probability of such event is $1 - p_0 - p_1$. This aspect is captured using the following specification:

$$V(x_0, p_0; x_1, p_1; \ldots; x_{S-1}, p_{S-1})$$
$$= u(x_0) + f(1 - p_0)[u(x_1) - u(x_0)] + f(1 - p_0 - p_1)[u(x_2) - u(x_1)].$$
$$(13.6)$$

Extending this idea to the $S - 2$ remaining possible increments in utility, we obtain

$$V(L) = u(x_0) + \sum_{s=1}^{S-1} f\left(\sum_{t=s}^{S-1} p_t\right)[u(x_s) - u(x_{s-1})]. \qquad (13.7)$$

This welfare functional defines the rank-dependent EU model. Preferences are referred to as "rank dependent" because a change in the ranking of the outcomes $(x_0, \ldots, x_{S-1})$ on the real line would affect the functional. The only case in which there is no effect of a change in the ranking is when f is the identity function. In this particular case, equation (13.7) can be rewritten as

$$V(L) = \sum_{s=0}^{S-1} p_s u(x_s),$$

which of course is the EU criterion. Thus, EU is the special case of RDEU with a linear transformation function of decumulative probabilities. We can now examine the effect of a nonlinear probability transformation function f on choices made under uncertainty.

First, observe that the RDEU criterion does not satisfy the independence axiom. Therefore, it does not fall prey to the criticism of Allais's paradox. To see this, observe that a RDEU decision maker prefers M_1 over M_2 if and only if

$$u(50) > u(0) + f(0.99)[u(50) - u(0)] + f(0.1)[u(250) - u(50)],$$

or equivalently,

$$u(50) > (1 - \pi_1)u(0) + \pi_1 u(250), \tag{13.8}$$

with $\pi_1 = f(0.1)/(1 + f(0.1) - f(0.99))$. On the other hand, under RDEU, preferring $\hat{M}_2$ over $\hat{M}_1$ implies that

$$u(0) + f(0.11)[u(50) - u(0)] < u(0) + f(0.1)[u(250) - u(0)],$$

or, equivalently,

$$u(50) < (1 - \pi_2)u(0) + \pi_2 u(250), \tag{13.9}$$

with $\pi_2 = f(0.1)/f(0.11)$. Contrary to the case were f is the identity function (EU), conditions (13.8) and (13.9) are not incompatible.

These two conditions, (13.8) and (13.9), can be reinterpreted within an EU framework to be saying that an EU-maximizer with utility u has a certainty equivalent for lottery $N_1 \sim (0, 1 - \pi_1; 250, \pi_1)$ that is smaller than 50, whereas he has a certainty equivalent for lottery $N_2 \sim (0, 1 - \pi_2; 250, \pi_2)$ that is larger than 50. Of course, a necessary condition for this to be possible is that π_2 is larger than π_1. Since $f(1) = 1$, it follows that

$$\tfrac{1}{2}f(0.1) + \tfrac{1}{2}f(1) > \tfrac{1}{2}f(0.11) + \tfrac{1}{2}f(0.99).$$

Because $(0.1, \tfrac{1}{2}; 1, \tfrac{1}{2})$ is a mean-preserving spread of $(0.11, \tfrac{1}{2}; 0.99, \tfrac{1}{2})$, this suggests that f must be convex.

We also can examine the conditions under which a RDEU-maximizer behaves in a risk-averse manner. We will do this first for a special case which is dual to EU theory, where u is the identity function. In this "dual theory", first examined by Yaari (1987), the agent is risk-neutral when f is also linear. Remember that an agent is risk-averse if the certainty equivalent of any risk is smaller than its mean. Consider the binary risk $(x_0, p_0; x_1, 1 - p_0)$ with $x_0 < x_1$. In this case, we can use condition (13.5) to say that the agent is risk averse if and only if the following condition holds:

$$x_0 + f(1 - p_0)[x_1 - x_0] \leqslant x_0 + (1 - p_0)[x_1 - x_0]. \tag{13.10}$$

Of course, this is true if and only if $f(1 - p_0) \leqslant 1 - p_0$. Since p_0 is arbitrary, we conclude that risk aversion holds in the dual theory if $f(p) \leqslant p$ for all $p \in [0, 1]$. It is easy to check that this is also the necessary and sufficient condition when we relax the condition that the lottery is binary. The intuition is that, by lowering the probability transformation function, one reduces the welfare effect of the potential increments in utility above $u(x_0)$. Notice that there is a clear link between the convexity of f and this condition of risk aversion. Indeed, $f(p) < p$ is necessary (but not sufficient) for the convexity of f, taking into account the conditions that $f(0) = 0$ and $f(1) = 1$.

Two important remarks must be made here. First, in the RDEU model, concavity of u does not imply that the agent dislikes all mean-preserving spreads of outcomes. As shown by Chew, Karni, and Safra (1987) in the general RDEU model, this more demanding concept of risk aversion also requires that f be convex. That is, in the general RDEU model, the agent is averse to any mean-preserving spread if and only if u is concave and f is convex. Under this condition, any result presented in this book whose proof relied exclusively on aversion to mean-preserving spreads remains true in the RDEU framework. This is the case, for example, for the optimality of a straight deductible contract in insurance, as proven in Proposition 3.5. It can be shown that this is also the case for the efficiency of the mutuality principle in the allocation of risk. Indeed, the mutuality principle guarantees that there exists no reallocation of risk which generates a mean-preserving contraction of all individual consumption plans in the economy.

Second, it is important to note that, whenever f is nonlinear, risk aversion will yield a first-order effect. Consider an agent with initial wealth w_0 who must bear a zero-mean risk $(-k, \frac{1}{2}; k, \frac{1}{2})$, where $k > 0$ can be interpreted as the size of the risk. In the dual theory, welfare can be measured as

$$w_0 - k + f(\tfrac{1}{2})2k = w_0 - k(1 - 2f(\tfrac{1}{2})). \tag{13.11}$$

This is the certainty equivalent of the risky wealth of the agent. Under the condition of risk aversion, $f(\frac{1}{2}) < \frac{1}{2}$ and the certainty equivalent is smaller than the expected wealth w_0. But the interesting point here is to observe that the risk premium $(1 - 2f(\frac{1}{2}))k$ is increasing proportionally to the size of the risk. This is typical of first-order risk aversion. This is quite different from the EU model, where the risk premium is approximately proportional to the square of the size of the risk (second-order risk aversion). This has several implications. For example, risk-averse RDEU investors may prefer to stay 100% invested in bonds in spite of a positive equity premium. Or a risk-averse RDEU consumer may prefer to purchase full insurance in spite of a positive loading factor on the insurance premium.

When there are only two states of nature with outcomes x_0 and x_1, the RDEU welfare functional can be written as

$$V = \begin{cases} (1 - f(1 - p_0))u(x_0) + f(1 - p_0)u(x_1) & \text{if } x_0 < x_1, \\ f(p_0)u(x_0) + (1 - f(p_0))u(x_1) & \text{if } x_0 \geqslant x_1. \end{cases} \tag{13.12}$$

In Figure 13.1, we depict the indifference curves associated to these preferences. The main difference with EU curves is that there is a kink at the 45° line that illustrates first-order risk aversion. As shown in this figure, this kink allows for the optimality of full insurance even when the insurance premium is actuarially unfair.

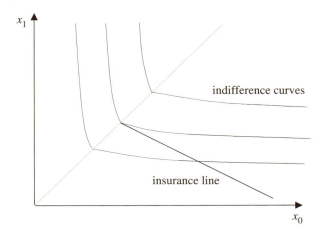

Figure 13.1. Indifference curves with the RDEU preference functional.

Recent experimental studies have shown, however, that f is neither globally concave nor convex. Rather, it is concave for small probabilities, and convex for large probabilities. This suggests that individuals transform probabilities consistently with the psychological principle of diminishing sensitivity, with the two end points of the probability interval serving as reference points. Consider three individuals endowed respectively with a zero chance of winning 100, a 0.50 chance of winning 100, and a 0.99 chance of winning 100. How might these agents measure a 0.01 improvement in the chance of winning? A reversed S-shaped function f implies that agents with the 0 or 0.99 probability of winning value this improvement the most. They view the change much more favorably than the person with a fifty–fifty chance of winning. This illustrates the so-called "possibility effect" and "certainty effect."

13.3 Ambiguity Aversion

The linearity of the EU functional with respect to probabilities implies that EU-maximizers are neutral with respect to any uncertainty about the state probabilities. To illustrate this feature, let us reconsider the framework presented in Section 8.1.2. To simplify the analysis, since we are only concerned with probability changes, we fix the set of possible outcomes $(x_0, \ldots, x_{S-1})$ so that a (simple) lottery can be represented by the vector of probabilities $P = (p_0, \ldots, p_{S-1})$ associated with these outcomes. We now introduce some uncertainty that affects this vector of probabilities. Suppose that there is some hidden information that would affect our beliefs about the distribution of outcomes. If this information were to become known, the agent could revise his beliefs of the distribution of outcomes. This can be formalized by assuming that there are M possible signals $m = 1, \ldots, M$. If signal m is observed, the revised probability distribution of outcomes would be $P^m = (p_0^m, p_1^m, \ldots, p_{S-1}^m)$.

Table 13.2.   Prize as a function of the color of the ball.

lottery	red	black	white
L^a	50	0	0
L^b	0	50	0
M^a	50	0	50
M^b	0	50	50

If q^m denotes the probability of receiving signal m, a (compound) lottery would be described by the vector $(P^1, q^1; \ldots; P^M, q^M)$. This is a situation where there is some uncertainty about the true distribution of outcomes, which we describe as a type of "ambiguity" about the risk.

The agent must choose between different compounded lotteries. Contrary to what was assumed in Section 8.1, we assume here that the agent must select his preferred lottery *before* observing the signal. To illustrate, this is the kind of decision problem that we face when determining whether to reduce greenhouse gas emissions in spite of our limited knowledge about the effect of these gases. The cases of genetically modified food and new drugs are similar. An EU-maximizer would evaluate his welfare as follows:

$$V(P^1, q^1; \ldots; P^M, q^M) = \sum_{m=1}^{M} q^m \sum_{s=0}^{S-1} p_s^m u(x_s) = \sum_{s=0}^{S-1} p_s^0 u(x_s),$$

where $p_s^0 = \sum_m q^m p_s^m$ is the prior probability of state s. This means that agents should make their choices as if they would face no uncertainty about the distribution $P^0 = (p_0^0, p_1^0, \ldots, p_{S-1}^0)$ of outcomes. This implies that EU agents should be indifferent between two compounded lotteries with the same prior distribution. Because of the linearity of the EU functional with respect to probabilities, the uncertainty about probabilities has no effect on welfare.

This can be illustrated by the following example, adapted from Ellsberg (1961). Consider an urn containing 90 balls. Thirty of them are red balls. The remaining 60 balls can be either black or white. The proportion of black and white balls is not announced. It is common knowledge that the number $m \in \{0, \ldots, 60\}$ of black balls is taken at random from a uniform distribution ($q^m = 1/61$). A ball is taken out from the urn, and the player gets a prize that depends upon the color of that ball, as described in Table 13.2. The player is confronted with a choice between the lotteries L^a and L^b prior to getting any information about the composition m of the urn. Ellsberg observed in laboratory experiments that many players prefer L^a over L^b. This is not compatible with the EU model since the two lotteries L^a and L^b have the same prior probability distribution $(0, \frac{2}{3}; 50, \frac{1}{3})$. It suggests that the player penalizes lottery L^b because of the ambiguity about the probability of success.

This can be confirmed by considering the choice between lotteries M^a and M^b using the same urn. We observe that many players who preferred L^a over L^b also prefer M^b over M^a. This is in spite of the fact that M^a and M^b have the same prior distribution $(0, \frac{1}{3}; 50, \frac{2}{3})$. This also suggests some form of aversion to ambiguous probabilities, since the choice of M^a yields an ambiguous probability of success, whereas M^b has unambiguous probabilities. Only their expected probabilities are the same.

Under Expected Utility Theory, the first choice can be explained only by assuming that the probability of a black ball with L^b is less than $\frac{1}{3}$. Thus, a proponent of the EU-model could claim that players prefer L^a over L^b because they do not trust the experimenter about the composition of the urn. This absence of confidence could induce players to believe that the experimenter biased the probability of the wining black balls below $\frac{1}{3}$. However, such beliefs are incompatible with the preference $M^b \succ M^a$, which requires that the probability of a black ball be larger than $\frac{1}{3}$.

Gilboa and Schmeidler (1989) proposed a decision criterion that can explain this paradox. The decision maker computes his EU for each possible posterior probability distribution P^m. His welfare is measured as the minimum of these various EU valuations:

$$V(P^1, q^1; \ldots; P^M, q^M) = \min_{m=1}^{M} \sum_{s=0}^{S-1} p_s^m u(x_s). \tag{13.13}$$

In a sense, players believe that they play against nature which always reacts to their choices by selecting the worst possible probability distribution. This is an extreme form of pessimism. It does have the advantage that the players do not need to know the distribution $(q^1, \ldots, q^M)$ of the hidden information. When there are only two states with outcomes x_0 and x_1, the welfare function can be written as

$$V = \begin{cases} p_0^{\max} u(x_0) + (1 - p_0^{\max}) u(x_1) & \text{if } x_0 < x_1, \\ p_0^{\min} u(x_0) + (1 - p_0^{\min}) u(x_1) & \text{if } x_0 \geqslant x_1, \end{cases} \tag{13.14}$$

where $p_0^{\max} = \max_m p_0^m$ and $p_0^{\min} = \min_m p_0^m$. Observe that this function is equivalent to the RDEU function (13.12) if we set $1 - f(1 - p_0) = p_0^{\max}$ and $f(p_0) = p_0^{\min}$. It follows that the behavioral properties of ambiguity aversion are much the same as those generated by rank-dependent EU. For example, ambiguity aversion implies that full insurance may be optimal even if the insurance premium is actuarially unfair based on the prior distribution of loss.

Ambiguity aversion can explain choices $L^a \succ L^b$ and $M^b \succ M^a$. Indeed, from (13.13), the welfare generated by lottery L^b equals $u(0)$, whereas the welfare generated by lottery L^a equals $(\frac{1}{3})u(50) + (\frac{2}{3})u(0) > u(0)$. Similarly, M^b is preferred to M^a because

$$\tfrac{2}{3}u(50) + \tfrac{1}{3}u(0) > \tfrac{1}{3}u(50) + \tfrac{2}{3}u(0).$$

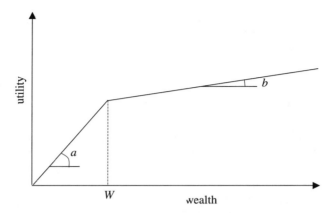

Figure 13.2. A piecewise linear utility function.

This illustrates how the decision criterion of Gilboa and Schmeidler (13.13) exhibits aversion to ambiguity.

13.4 Prospect Theory and Loss Aversion

Some authors, such as Kahneman and Tversky (1979), have suggested that there is a discontinuity of the marginal utility at some wealth level W. This is the case, for example, with the following utility function:

$$u(w) = \begin{cases} aw & \text{if } w \leqslant W, \\ aW + b(w - W) & \text{if } w > W. \end{cases} \tag{13.15}$$

If $a > b$, as in Figure 13.2, this function is globally concave in wealth. Using laboratory experiments, Kahneman and Tversky claimed that a is approximately twice as large as b. This means that a one euro loss has approximately the same effect on welfare as a gain of two euros, in absolute value. We say that the agent is loss-averse in this case.

Note that the Arrow–Pratt approximation cannot be used here since it requires that the utility function be differentiable. In fact, loss aversion is a case of first-order risk aversion at W. This can be checked by evaluating the risk premium for an agent with utility function (13.15) and initial wealth $w_0 = W$, who faces risk $\tilde{x} \sim (-k, \frac{1}{2}; +k, \frac{1}{2})$. When $a > b$, it can be checked that

$$Eu(w_0 + \tilde{x}) = u\left(w_0 - \frac{k}{2}\left(1 - \frac{b}{a}\right)\right),$$

which implies a positive risk premium $\Pi = \frac{1}{2}(1 - (b/a))k$. This is linear with the size of risk k. When initial wealth is at a point of non-differentiability of a piecewise

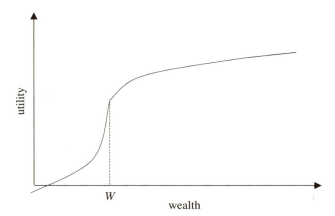

Figure 13.3. A utility function yielding loss aversion, risk loving in the domain of losses, and risk aversion in the domain of gains.

utility function, the risk premium is proportional to the size of risk. Small risks matter.

Absolute risk aversion is zero everywhere except at W, where it is not defined. However, utility function (13.15) can be approximated by a smooth function that exhibits zero risk aversion everywhere except in a small neighborhood of W where absolute risk aversion tends to infinity. In this sense, this function exhibits increasing absolute risk aversion below W, and decreasing absolute risk aversion above it. In their Prospect Theory, Kahneman and Tversky (1979) proposed an S-shaped utility function with a kink at perceived initial wealth at W, a convex branch below W and a concave branch above W. This is illustrated in Figure 13.3. The kink at the current wealth level, yielding first-order risk aversion, also means that the agent has a prospective behavior: what matters for welfare is not how much wealth he has but rather how wealth changed compared to his "reference wealth" W. The convexity of u in the loss region means that an uncertain loss is preferred to a sure loss. The concavity of u in the gain region means that the agent prefers a sure gain to an uncertain gain.

The key departure of note in Prospect Theory is that utility u as defined above is conditional on the reference wealth level W. Their hypothesis is that decision makers frame each decision with reference to some status quo or some initial wealth level W. Thus, the framing of the problem at hand becomes crucial. Another economic decision, or even the same problem with a different framing, will lead to a different objective and, hence, a different optimal solution. For example, suppose you just found out that you have won 10 000 euros, which is on its way to you as cash in the mail, but with a 50% chance that it will never arrive. Whether you frame the problem as having an initial wealth of 10 000 with a 50% chance of losing it all or as having an initial wealth of zero with a 50% chance of gaining 10 000 will make a difference in your decision choices under prospect theory.

In this static framework, once the reference point is fixed, the theory of loss aversion is nothing more than a particular case of the EU model. Prospect theory is enriched in a dynamic framework when the reference point W changes over time. For example, W might be the wealth level attained in the previous period. Under this specification, the hypothesis is that consumers and investors extract direct utility from changes in wealth over time. We also can enrich the model by combining this assumption with rank-dependent transformations of cumulative probabilities, yielding the so-called Cumulative Prospect Theory of Tversky and Kahneman (1992).

13.5   Some Concluding Thoughts

Although the EU model has received much criticism in the literature, it remains a cornerstone for modern research. Part of the reason for this might be that competing theories to date each suffer some flaws of their own. A current trend in economics and in finance is to take more of a "behavioral" view of decision making. However, it seems that modeling human behavior with any precision will remain an impossible task.

Consider, for example, that in May 2000 seven states in the USA jointly sponsored the "Big Game Lottery," which had the largest payout ever for a lottery, at $363 million. The lottery brought in a total revenue of $565 million. Thus, the mean expected payout on every dollar invested in this lottery was less than 65 cents. Theory thus implies that millions of people, everyone who purchased lottery tickets, must have been risk loving. Now consider that, for this particular lottery, the main prize was split equally between two winners, who were two of the many participants who exhibited this risk-loving behavior. Suppose that these two winners were offered a chance to flip a fair coin one time, to award the entire $363 million to only one of the winners. Would either of these winners prefer the coin toss to simply taking their one-half share of $181.5 million?

Of course buying lottery tickets provides some satisfaction in and of itself. In particular, as stressed by Caplin and Leahy (2001), buyers may savor the anticipatory feeling of winning the big prize, before the name of the winner is announced. Who would not like to daydream about winning $363 million? We doubt that purchasing a lottery ticket by itself is an indication of risk-loving behavior, although this example shows how any model, with EU theory being no exception, must be used with caution.[3] One approach to this dilemma is to model decision methodology as being

---

[3]Rabin (2000), for example, makes a strong case against using EU for small gambles. Based only upon the concavity of utility u, he shows how even mild risk aversion for small slightly unfavorable gambles leads to implausible rejections of large highly favorable gambles.

unique to the individual situation at hand, which unfortunately does not allow one to make any positive predictions or normative assessments.

In presenting EU modeling throughout this text, the authors make no claim that it gives an accurate description in every situation. However, does the theory give us any usable information as to how market decisions are made and how financial assets are priced? We believe it does. Moreover, economic and financial decisions are typically modeled in isolation, whereas many complicated decisions in the real world are often intertwined. Using EU theory as a starting point and adapting the theory by including such modifications as acknowledging background risks or applying hyperbolic discounting can hopefully improve the explanatory power of decision models.

13.6 Bibliographical References, Extensions and Exercises

This chapter presents a perspective on the development of non-EU models. Much of the relevant literature has already been reviewed in the text. An excellent and easily readable critique on the EU model can be found in the paper by Machina (1987). In a recent counting, the number of decision-criteria alternatives to the EU model is larger than 40. Our presentation here obviously covers only a small part of this large and growing literature. However, the RDEU model is often considered as the most promising alternative to EU theory, together with variations on Prospect Theory as developed by Kahneman and Tversky (1979). These two models have been combined by Tversky and Kahneman (1992) in a model known as Cumulative Prospect Theory. An abundance of the behavioral arguments against EU theory and against many other decision models is presented in Kahneman (2003). Tversky and Kahneman (1992), Wu and Gonzales (1996, 1999) and Abdellaoui (2000) have estimated the probability transformation function. A very lucid set of arguments as to why these behavioral objections really only call for the modification, rather than the destruction, of existing theories is presented in Glaeser (2003).

Chapter Bibliography

Abdellaoui, M. 2000. Parameter free elicitation of utility and probability weighting functions. *Management Science* 46:1497–1512.

Allais, M. 1953. Le comportement de l'homme rationnel devant le risque. Critique des postulats et axiomes de l'école américaine. *Econometrica* 21:503–546.

Caplin, A. J. and J. Leahy. 2001. Psychological expected utility theory and anticipatory feelings. *Quarterly Journal of Economics* 106:55–80.

Chew, S., E. Karni, and Z. Safra. 1987. Risk aversion in the theory of expected utility with rank dependent preferences. *Journal of Economic Theory* 42:370–381.

Ellsberg, D. 1961. Risk, ambiguity, and the Savage axioms. *Quarterly Journal of Economics* 75:643–669.

Gilboa, I. and D. Schmeidler. 1989. Maximin expected utility with non-unique prior. *Journal of Mathematical Economics* 18:141–153.

Glaeser, E. 2003. Psychology and the market. NBER Working Paper 10 203.

Kahneman, D. 2003. Maps of bounded rationality: psychology for behavioral economists. *American Economic Review* 93:1449–1475.

Kahneman, D. and Tversky, A. 1979. Prospect theory: an analysis of decision under risk. *Econometrica* 47:263–291.

Machina, M. 1987. Choice under uncertainty: problems solved and unsolved. *Journal of Economic Perspectives* 1:121–154.

Quiggin, J. 1982. A theory of anticipated utility. *Journal of Economic Behavior and Organization* 3:323–343.

Rabin, M. 2000. Risk aversion and expected-utility theory: a calibration theorem. *Econometrica* 68:1281–1292.

Tversky, A. and D. Kahneman. 1992. Advances in prospect theory: cumulative representation of uncertainty. *Journal of Risk and Uncertainty* 5:297–323.

von Neumann, J. and O. Morgenstern. 1944. *Theory of games and economic behavior*. Princeton, NJ: Princeton University Press.

Wu, G. and R. Gonzales. 1996. Curvature of the probability weighting function. *Management Science* 42:1676–1690.

———. 1999. Nonlinear decision weights in choice under uncertainty. *Management Science* 45:74–85.

Yaari, M. E. 1987. The dual theory of choice under risk. *Econometrica* 55, 95–115.

Exercises

(13.1) Sempronius has to choose between two lotteries $\tilde{X}$ and $\tilde{Y}$. Lottery $\tilde{X}$ is distributed as $(4, \frac{1}{4}; 16, \frac{1}{2}; 36, \frac{1}{4})$, whereas $\tilde{Y}$ is distributed as $(1, \frac{1}{2}; 49, \frac{1}{2})$. Which lottery will Sempronius prefer in each case below?

(a) If he is an expected utility maximizer with $u = \sqrt{R}$, where R is the result of the lottery as in the good old times of Bernoulli and Cramer.

(b) If he is infinitely risk averse (or infinitely pessimistic).

(c) If he is an RDEU decision maker with $u = \sqrt{R}$ and a function $f(p)$ such that:
$$f(p) = \begin{cases} 0 & \text{for } 0 \leqslant p \leqslant \frac{1}{2}, \\ 2p - 1 & \text{for } \frac{1}{2} \leqslant p \leqslant 1. \end{cases}$$

Explain why your conclusion goes in the same direction for the RDEU decision maker as for an infinitely risk averse one.

(d) Represent the lotteries $\tilde{X}'$ and $\tilde{Y}'$ which correspond to $\tilde{X}$ and $\tilde{Y}$, respectively, after the probability transformation induced by $f(p)$.

(e) Comparing $\tilde{X}$ with $\tilde{X}'$ and $\tilde{Y}$ with $\tilde{Y}'$ show that the probability transformation induced by $f(p)$ leads to an FSD deterioration of $\tilde{X}$ and of $\tilde{Y}$.

(13.2) In this chapter, we have put the emphasis on the axioms underlying the alternative models, so that it can be seen as complementary to Chapter 1. However, individual or collective decisions can also be analyzed with the help of the alternative models, which may produce interesting results and predictions. The main purpose of this exercise is to illustrate this claim.

A decision maker has a wealth W_0 subjected to a potential loss $\tilde{x}$ described by a binary random variable $(-x, p; 0, 1 - p)$, where $x < W_0$. This decision maker has the opportunity to buy proportional insurance (denoted by β as in Chapter 3) for a premium defined by:
$$P = (1 + \lambda) p \beta x$$

(a) What is the distribution of final wealth?

(b) Express the agent's welfare if the adopts the axioms of Yaari's dual theory with the function $f(p) = p^2$.

(c) Show that his optimal decision will be either $\beta^* = 0$ or $\beta^* = 1$ depending upon the values of p and λ. In fact you must obtain that $\beta^* = 1$ if λ is "not too high" for a given p.

(d) Convince yourself that $\beta^* = 1$ may be optimal even if the loading is strictly positive. Contrast this result with the one obtained under EU.

Index